Letters From Brenda

Emma Kennedy is a prolific author, screenwriter, actress and presenter. She wrote the BBC1 series *The Kennedys*, which was an adaptation of her bestselling book *The Tent, the Bucket and Me* and was a Radio Times Comedy Champion Award winner. She has won *Celebrity Masterchef* and is a Guinness World Record Holder.

First published in Great Britain in 2022 by Hodder Studio
An imprint of Hodder & Stoughton
An Hachette UK company

This paperback edition published in 2023

1

A CIP catalogue record for this title is available from the British Library

Paperback ISBN 9781529372007
eBook ISBN 9781529371987

Typeset in Plantin Light by Palimpsest Book Production Limited,
Falkirk, Stirlingshire

Printed and bound in Great Britain by Clays Ltd, Elcograf S.p.A.

Hodder & Stoughton policy is to use papers that are natural, renewable
and recyclable products and made from wood grown in sustainable forests.
The logging and manufacturing processes are expected to conform to the
environmental regulations of the country of origin.

Hodder & Stoughton Ltd
Carmelite House
50 Victoria Embankment
London EC4Y 0DZ

www.hodder.co.uk

EMMA KENNEDY

Letters From Brenda

My Mother's Lifetime of Secrets

CORONET

For everyone who ever loved her

I want to tell you the story of my mother.

When she died, I was a mess, caught in a riptide of grief I had no chance of escaping, but by small degrees, I found myself floating out of it. I wasn't quite sure what to do next. Grief does funny things to you. It makes you wary and desperate as if you've found yourself in an unwanted friendship with someone who is overly needy. It demands things of you – forcing you to lay bare a life, cradle to grave. It requires you to stare at a person under an unflinching light. Grief is a terrible burden.

It has taken me seven years to be able to write this book. It is a story of a girl, a teenager, a woman, a wife, a lover, a mother. It's a story that involves betrayal, bigamy, disappointment, a suicide attempt, affairs, love, passion and fury.

My mother and I had a complicated relationship: she was difficult and volatile, but I knew that wasn't the whole story. In fact, I realised, I didn't really know her story at all.

I had no idea what I would find when I lifted the rocks of her life. I hadn't intended to do it, but a sudden, unexpected call from my father changed all that.

This book is the story of Brenda.

One

My mother died on a warm spring day.

Two weeks previously, she had been sitting on a low chair, looking up at my cousins, Ben and Tom, waxing lyrical about a pair of tight white trousers she used to wear as a young teacher. 'They were marvellous,' she told us, 'but they were hideously embarrassing when I had a sexual ooze. You could see everything.'

My cousins had screamed, my dad had put his head in his hands and I had rolled my eyes. My mother, as she always did, rocked backwards cackling, absolutely delighted she'd been outrageous.

'Sexual ooze!' she said again, with a determined wickedness. 'Oh, for a sexual ooze!'

I didn't know it, but it was to be the last time I saw my mother laugh.

I was called home, summoned by a telephone message picked up during a lunchbreak. I was in a writers' room for a children's animation series and, as everyone tucked into their sandwiches, laughing and exchanging light gossip, I took myself outside and stood on the pavement in London's Portland Place, staring up at a clear blue sky.

'You have to come home,' my dad said. 'As soon as you can.'

I felt a dull dread. Brenda's cancer had returned eighteen months previously: another lump in her breast. We had sat in a small consultant's room at The Royal Marsden, lined up on plastic chairs, backs to the wall, as if we were about to be given detentions. A man with salt-and-pepper hair and his sleeves rolled up came in and told us the cancer was back. This time, there was no fixing it. I reached for my mother's hand and neither of us said anything.

The following months were no fun for my mother: she lost her hair, developed debilitating lymphedema, a build-up of fluid in the soft body tissue of her left arm, and lost all interest in living. It was a terrible, sad withering of the most vital person I have ever known. Brenda was not the dying kind.

I wasn't quite sure what to do. I was contracted to work for the rest of the day and I was with people I didn't know well. I was shell-shocked, anxious and heavy, unable to tell anyone what had just happened, so I sat in that writers' room and tried to contribute but my heart was sinking. I had to go home, and I had to do it now. But you don't stand up in a room of relative strangers and say, 'Sorry, my mother is dying, I have to go,' so I lied and said I was leaving for a voiceover I'd forgotten about. Everyone, I'm sure, thought I was awful.

When I arrived home, I was greeted by my father who burst into tears. He ushered me into the sitting room, where we stood in front of a large mirror as he told me to expect the worst. She was upstairs, he told me, had deteriorated, this was it. We held each other. I caught a glimpse of our reflection, broken, holding each other up. It was one thing to feel it; I didn't need to see it.

Before I went upstairs to see her, Brenda had asked my father to show me something. It was a DVD from one of my uncles: he'd found some footage of my parents' wedding day and had sent it off to a place that converts old film reels. Now it was in my father's hand, a silver disc with the past on it. He put it on.

It was 1966. England was about to win the World Cup and my mother was in a minidress run up the day before by my dad's sister. She looked like Julie Christie. My dad looked like he couldn't believe his luck: his sleeves shoved up beyond his elbows, ready for business, and a grin so wide it could have torn his face in two. They were in the back garden of a miner's terraced cottage in Wales. A string of washing flapped behind them. They were laughing and dancing and smiling at the camera, their whole lives ahead of them – and here we were, watching it with leaden hearts. I cried, then pulled myself together. I had to go upstairs.

There is a weight like no other, treading towards the dying. There's a turn in the stairs of my family home and I stopped there for a moment, holding on to the banister for dear life. It was like being at the top of a steep drop – that moment when you know you have to commit to the jump.

She was in my childhood bedroom, in the double bed they had only got for me after I had my own flat and lived half an hour away. It had been a running joke: I had no need to ever stay over again. My mother had presented it to me with a loud, '*Ta-a-da-ah!*' before adding, 'It's got drawers underneath the mattress,' as if that were an unimaginable magic. She pulled them all out to prove it. Every single one was stuffed with old pillows.

'So many pillows,' I had offered.

'You can never have enough pillows,' she replied.

For the best part of forty years, every time I returned home, I had slept in an ancient single bed, slammed into the corner of the room. It had an old metal frame that rattled every time I moved. The mattress was like a coffin; the springs furious. Every time I shifted, pulled at the covers or breathed, it was like listening to someone clattering about on a pogo stick. I'd hear my mother laughing from the room next door. She never stopped finding it funny. But that bed was now gone and instead there was this new bed, with all the pillows hidden inside it.

I pushed open the door. She was lying on her side, cheek pressed into the sheet. She couldn't sit up.

'Hello, you.' I kept my tone light, as if this was just another little set back. She reached her hand out and I knelt down to take it and, in that moment, I collapsed.

I hadn't expected sadness to take my legs away, but it did. This was suddenly very real. My mother, the inimitable Brenda, the woman to whom I owed everything, the woman who had made my life exciting, complicated and hard, the woman who had made me laugh the most, cry the most, the woman who had been the cloud, the light, the joy, the terror, the burden, was leaving. I didn't know what to do.

As I wept, she looked at me. Her voice was shallow and thin. 'At least I know you love me.' It might strike you as an odd thing for her to say, but we'll get on to that.

A month before, a doctor had rung my father to tell him that yes, the X-rays they had taken of my mother's chest had revealed the cancer had spread to her lungs. We had decided not to tell her. Instead, we told her she had a chest infection, something that might clear up. She knew that wasn't true, of course, but for a while, it helped us all to pretend it was.

There's a settling in when someone is dying, where the purpose of any given day is simply to get through it. My mother was in a terrible state in those final weeks: her left arm so swollen her wrist looked dislocated, her skin red and leathery. She had bloody lesions across her chest and neck. She stank of death: I could smell her rotting.

Still, I was in a state of denial. I knew my mother wasn't going to get better, but I refused to absorb or accept it and so those last days were spent in a state of suspended shock.

In the mornings, volunteers from the local hospice would come and change her dressings and wash her. Every time they came, I would stand at the bottom of the stairs and cry. Kindness is such a small, simple thing but it's so rarely given: I am always astonished by it. In the afternoon, we would be visited by the district nurse and Dad and I would heave a sigh of relief. My mother loved all the nurses who looked after her: she was nothing but sunshine and light for strangers, putting on the dazzle for people she would never see again. She was a master of the brief encounter. Longer friendships were harder for her.

She slipped into a cycle of trying to sleep and sitting up when she felt unwell. Occasionally, I would try and feed her a few mouthfuls of salmon and avocado – her favourite – but she was having difficulty swallowing. When she slept, I lay in the bed next to her and worked. I had an animation script to finish, was working on a novel and was also finalising the pilot script for *The Kennedys*, the show in which my mother was the lead character. I had a call from Katherine Parkinson who had been cast to play Brenda. She asked if she could meet her, but we'd left it too late. I had to say no. It's still one of my greatest regrets.

The slow grind towards death was relentless and yet, through the thick of sadness, there were moments where the old Brenda peeped through. She had asked me to read her the script of *The Kennedys* and, as I was relaying a dinner scene, she placed a hand on my arm to stop me. I'd just read out a speech of my father's, one where he names someone I'd known as a child. 'You'll have to take that out,' she whispered. 'He still sees her in Sainsbury's.'

The days dragged on. My cousin, Adrian, arrived with his wife and children. They stood at the end of the bed and said their goodbyes. 'Have a nice life,' my mother said to them as they left, and I had to slip into another room and cry. I asked her if there was anyone else she wanted to see, whether she wanted to be given the last rites or be buried in a Catholic Church. She said no to everything except her sister, Phyllis, and her nephews Ben and Tom. She tried to tell me the name of a Gerard Manley Hopkins poem she'd like read at her graveside but couldn't recall the name of it. I ran a few by her to see if it might help but she was so weak, I had to give up.

Sunday came. It was beautiful and warm. Phyllis arrived with my cousins. It was such a relief to see them. Dad was exhausted. I don't think he'd slept properly in weeks. We took it in turns to sit with her, sometimes holding her up, other times sitting beside her cradling her hand. She had quiet conversations with her sister, with whom she'd had a tumultuous and difficult relationship; apologies were offered. Brenda was saying goodbye.

The district nurse popped in. I'd had difficult, serious discussions in the days before as to when would be the right time to put my mother on to the syringe feed that meant we wouldn't see her awake again. I had been concerned my mother was suffering but as long as she could eat a little and speak a little there was a reluctance to do this.

'I've been trying to feed her but she's having trouble swallowing.'

We were talking over my mother who was propped up on one pillow – one pillow, when she was lying on a bed rammed with the things. Why we didn't think to get out four or five and make her more comfortable, I will never know. She looked like an abandoned sack.

'I tried giving her some chopped up apple earlier,' I added.

The district nurse looked at me as if I was quite mad. 'Why are you trying to give her apple? Give her something that's easy to swallow like yoghurt or ice cream.'

'Ooh. Ice cream.' My mother's eyes suddenly lit up.

'Do you want some ice cream?' She nodded. I didn't need asking twice.

I ran down the stairs with a jump in my step. She was rallying, I thought. Perhaps this was a little set back, after all. I put two scoops of vanilla ice cream into a bowl and took them up to her.

'Do you want me to feed you?' She shook her head and took the spoon.

I walked the district nurse out, thanking her, as I did every day. She told me to call her if there were any problems. I told her I would.

Phyllis and the boys had brought some picnic-style food with them and had started to lay out plates in a small sun-filled room off the sitting room that looked out over the garden. It was Mum's favourite place to sit. I pulled out some serving spoons for them and went back upstairs.

Mum had finished the bowl of ice cream. I stared down into it, eyes wide. 'Have you eaten all that?'

She looked up at me and nodded. 'It was lovely.' Her voice was barely more than a whisper but it was music to my ears.

Ecstatic, I ran downstairs to tell Dad. 'She might be on the mend.' Dad looked at me and said nothing.

My cousin Ben took over sitting upstairs with her and I returned to the lunch things, helping to lay them out. The mood was light; there was laughter. Phyllis was her usual entertaining self, reeling out stories about old family members and complaining about her wrinkles. I had just scooped some food onto my plate when Ben appeared in the doorway, his face ashen.

'Brenda's vomited. It's a lot.'

Everyone jumped up – Dad, Phyllis, Tom and my fiancée, Georgie, who had arrived that morning with bags of clothes for the long haul. I stood, plate in hand, frozen, watching them all run out of the room. The moment I had dreaded had arrived. I could do many things for my mother but looking after her when she was vomiting was not one of them.

When I was seven, my father had arrived, unexpected, at my school. I remember sitting at my desk, watching him drive in, wondering why he was there. Moments later, I was taken out of class and delivered to him. My mother had been admitted to hospital – she had renal colic – and Dad had come to get me. I had never been in a hospital before, and as I walked through the corridors that smelled of disinfectant a previously unknown fear snaked through me. Brenda was sitting up in bed, a thin blue blanket pulled over her knees. I stood and stared at her and, suddenly, she threw up over herself. I thought she was going to die.

A month later, the BBC showed their first ever fly-on-the-wall documentary series set in a hospital. The first episode featured a young woman having her stomach pumped. Watching it, I was dragged back to the moment that I thought Brenda was dying. I ran from the room and sat on the stairs, hands over my ears as I listened to the sounds of the woman being sick. I have suffered from emetophobia ever since. It's a morbid fear of vomit and now, standing still as everyone else ran to her, that fear was back, like ice hardening over my feet. This time, Brenda really was dying.

Upstairs, I could hear my father calling for something, anything, for my mother to be sick into. She was sick again and again and again. Tom came down and sat on the stairs I'd sat on all those years ago, his hands covering his cheeks. There are moments of intense shame that visit us through our lives: nobody can get everything right, but standing there, listening to what was unfolding and not being able to go to my mother will haunt me till I die.

I rang the district nurse. 'She can't stop being sick.' She told me she would come as soon as possible.

The vomiting stopped and I trod slowly up the stairs. My aunt was on her knees helping Brenda out of her pyjama bottoms. I found a clean pair and held Mum up as we got her changed.

'Here you are,' my mother said pointedly at me. I knew what she meant. It was the short but targeted criticism I deserved. Sadly, it was to be the last thing she said to me.

The district nurse, good to her word, arrived and I slipped away, terrified Brenda would be sick again. Phyllis and the boys drifted back to finish their lunch.

I felt useless.

I don't think I fully appreciated what was happening. Upstairs, I thought my mother was getting an anti-sickness injection, but she wasn't. She was being put on the syringe feed that would carry her to her final moment. This was going to be the last time we saw her awake and I wasn't with her. Before the district nurse did what she needed to do, Dad told me, Brenda looked at him and said, 'Thank you for looking after me.' When the District Nurse asked her if she'd like to sleep, she replied, 'Yes, I'd like to sleep.' Those would be her final words.

When it was done, Dad came to get me. He wanted to reassure me that Brenda was resting. He took me up to see her. She was sleeping and peaceful. It was all right, I thought. She'd have a rest and then she'd wake up, but before the District Nurse could leave, she came in to have another look at Mum. Something had changed. My mother's breathing had become heavy and ugly. The nurse shook her by the arm and called her name. There was no response. She turned to me. 'You need to prepare. It's going to be today.'

I clutched at my lips and stared at the ceiling. This was a nightmare and I had mucked everything up. I had given her the ice cream that made her sick. I had not been able to help her when she was vomiting. I had not been with her when she was put under. I hadn't heard her final words. This was going to be etched into my heart forever. I had been a coward and now I had to live with it.

There wasn't much chat as we gathered round, just the odd weepy sniffle underpinned by the steady, heavy rasps of my mother's breathing. About an hour in, my aunt told us to go and sit in the sunshine for a bit, get some fresh air. So, with things not looking imminent, Ben, Tom, Georgie and I went out into the garden. Dad would call down to us if anything changed. The four of us sat and drank Pimm's, as if we suddenly found ourselves at a garden party. We managed to laugh about something, but I can't remember what. It felt like any other Sunday, but it wasn't. We finished our drinks, made comments about the flowers and went back to be with Brenda.

A blue line had started to snake its way up the inside of her wrist. 'Look at that,' said Dad, watching her carefully.

I put my hand on her arm. 'We're all here, Mum.'

At that moment, my beagle, Poppy, who was devoted to my mother, appeared in the doorway. In all the days we had been there, she hadn't come to Brenda once, but now she padded her way towards my mother's hand, touched it with the end of her nose, then moved back to the doorway and sat. Five minutes later, Brenda stopped breathing. As Brenda took her last breath, Poppy got up and returned downstairs.

'Has she gone?' asked my aunt.

Dad nodded and everyone began to weep thick, heavy tears.

I reached for my mother's wrist and pressed my fingers into her pale skin but I could still feel a weak pulse.

'Wait.' I waved a hand into the air. 'Wait. I don't think she's dead.'

It's the end my mother would have loved. Was she dead, or wasn't she? She was hooked up to oxygen so I couldn't be sure. It was like one last joke she'd pulled at the final moment. But she was dead. Brenda was gone. A terrible noise filled the room. I was horrified to discover it was coming from me.

My father hadn't had a drink in seven years, not because he was an alcoholic, but because my mother had gallstones. She'd given up alcohol and so had he. That evening, he sat in a chair at the end of my mother's bed with a beer in his hand. I sat next to her, stroking her forehead and Poppy returned, jumped up onto the bed and lay herself against Brenda's body. We didn't want her to be on her own. Georgie let in the doctor who declared Mum officially dead and he handed my father a little green book. We were given a number of an undertaker.

An hour later, a man in a three-piece suit arrived at the house. He was tall, built like the *Carry On* actor Bernard Bresslaw, his hair slicked back. He was softly spoken and respectful and he'd come to carry Brenda down the stairs and take her away.

Georgie ushered me and my father into the sitting room and shut the door. She insisted on it. She took the undertaker upstairs, put some slippers Brenda loved on her feet and waited as they zipped her into a bag. She followed her down the stairs, mopping up the drops of urine that fell onto the carpet, and saw the undertaker out, thanking them, then came to tell us it was done. There are moments in life when love sets itself into stone. Neither I nor my father will ever forget that act of kindness. Thank you, Georgie, it made a world of difference.

That night, we all went to bed heavy and stunned with grief. It was over. Brenda, the towering force in our lives, was gone. She had been the person who controlled us, who set the mood, the one everyone was scared of. She had loomed over every aspect of our lives, like the crow that terrifies Tweedledum and Tweedledee. She had been, at times, a monster, yet here we all were, utterly bereft, grieving a woman who had often made our lives an utter misery. So, why be sad? Why grieve the loss of that burden? Because my mother, it seemed to me, had been entirely mad. She wasn't awful. She was ill.

The next day, the three of us sat in the garden. The sobbing over, there was now a steady, undramatic drip of tears, as if my body was wringing out the sadness slowly by hand.

It was here, toes pressed down into the grass, that I finally had the conversation with my father I'd been waiting to have for forty years. 'Do you think Mum had an undiagnosed mental illness?'

It was a thought that had hung heavy for as long as I could remember. We'd sat in a consultant's room, ten years previously when Mum was sixty-one, listening to her telling an unsuspecting doctor she'd been given cancer by a CIA operative in a bookshop in Cambridge. She thought her phones were bugged. She refused treatment because she thought it was a plot between Dad and the doctors to have her killed. She thought her neighbours had secretly bought her garden. She thought Freemasons and secret government forces were behind every entirely normal setback any of us faced. My mother was paranoid, occasionally violent, sometimes completely out of control. To anyone with half a scrap of sense, none of this was normal, yet to us it was, and so nobody, not once during her lifetime, tried to address it or find her a scrap of help.

'Yes,' he said quietly. 'I think she probably did.'

There are so many things to feel guilty about when someone dies: your relief at their passing, the fact you sat and watched them suffer, the never-ending doubts that perhaps you could have been nicer, kinder, more tolerant but the one thing I felt most ashamed of was this. My mother, I was positive, had had a serious mental illness and I did absolutely nothing about it. What had been wrong with her? Was it genetic? Caused by trauma? Was it hormonal? Did anyone else in her family have a history of mental illness?

I didn't have a clue.

It's difficult, being around someone who is unpredictable. Brenda could be the greatest person in any room: she had immense presence and charisma. She was so funny she could leave you breathless and begging for her to stop. She could entertain a crowd, she could hold anyone rapt; she could be generous to a fault, but she could also turn on a sixpence, as fast and as furious as a lightning strike – and it was that Brenda, the dark, mean, vicious Brenda that we all wanted to avoid. So, we didn't ask, we didn't discuss, we didn't question. We all had a form of Stockholm syndrome and nothing ever got better.

A day, for my mother, was not fulfilled without complaining about something: politicians, the monarchy (although she always watched the Queen's Speech and secretly loved her), neighbours, the state of the drains, anyone who disagreed with her, her father, my father, not doing what she wanted when she wanted, driving (she didn't drive), lorries on motorways, credit card bills, Tory voters, men (all of them), the ripeness of a pear, it didn't matter what it was. My mother loved complaining but when it came to herself and actual bona fide suffering, she complained not a jot and it struck me, suddenly, that she may have spent her entire life suffering and if she had complained, she might still be alive.

The days and weeks and months after my mother's death took their toll. Not a day passed when I didn't think about her. Six months after she died, she came to me in a dream. She was crawling on the floor, wearing the heavy cardigan she wore on the day she passed. She looked weak and tired. 'Well,' she said. 'That was quite the journey.' Then she reached for a bowl to be sick in. I've dreamed of her a handful of times since. Each time she has been a little younger, more well. I felt haunted and empty and the only memories I felt left with were of the difficult Brenda, the sick Brenda, the woman I wasn't sure I'd got on with. Life drifted on, I found myself out of the riptide but, for me, there was no calm. All I was left with were questions that had never been answered.

Then three years later, we found the letters.

* * *

My dad, finally, had decided that Dallington, my childhood home, was going to be sold. I was glad, in a way. It was a house where I had many happy memories, but it was also a place of anxiety, tension and the ultimate sadness. On the day Dad moved out, I was left behind on my own to lock up after the cleaning. I thought I would feel devastated, but I found myself relieved. We were finally leaving the house to Brenda for whom Dallington had been the totem of her life's achievements. She'd been so obsessed with it, I have absolutely no doubt she'll haunt it.

A few weeks later, Dad rang me. The new owner had found two old leather suitcases in the loft. They were filled with letters addressed to me. I had completely forgotten about them. Did I want them? A week later, the suitcases arrived. They were rammed with letters from Brenda, a treasure trove of light and love and pride. They are letters from a great storyteller, a bold exaggerator, a mischief maker, an absolute devil and suddenly, I remembered the Brenda I had loved so fiercely; the woman I adored. In that moment, I made a promise: that I would endeavour to discover who she really was and provide the answers I craved. I was going to, finally, try and work out what was wrong with Brenda and why.

My mother's mother, Elizabeth, had died two months before I was born, but to understand my mother, I had to go back to the beginning. I had to understand where she had come from and what her formative years had done to her and to do that, it all starts with Elizabeth.

* * *

My mother's letters are reproduced here unedited apart from the bits that are so libellous, no sensible editor would allow them. None of them are dated and they are not presented in chronological order. Brenda wrote most of her letters when she was away, travelling with Tony, my dad. She loved an escapade but most of all, Mum always liked to butt in. I didn't want this book to be any different.

Dear Emmy

Have enclosed bottle of Holland & B. Hope they are the right thing. We have just had two swelteringly hot days; we couldn't do anything, but temperature is down to the 70's today, thank goodness. We had a good journey home, but I am starting to become overly neurotic about driving.[1] We had a nervous hour or so as we came through Northumberland, a motorcycle rally was obviously taking place north of our position, and about 500 motorcyclists drove AT us in a disconcertingly speedy way. I don't like being on the roads anymore.

We have been looking for reviews, saw Ben's[2] – the Guardian *gave him 4 stars must see. That's lovely! We are waiting for yours now. Tony has started the new additions for the scrapbook.*

My gullet is nutritiously awash with organic home-grown vegetables. It's beetroot this week. Tony picked some of the Mirabelle plums and made a Sabayon tart – it was 'tart' but delicious. Pity we can't send one up to you. Hopefully there will still be plenty of veg, apples etc when you come back to London.

---

1 My mother could not drive. She tried once, when I was eleven, attempted to pick me up from school during a driving lesson and reversed into a tree. On the day of her test, she chastised the examiner. When he slapped his hand on the dashboard for her to do an emergency stop, she turned to him and complained, 'Don't be ridiculous. I can't stop here. I'm on a hill.' She failed. I don't think a day went by when Tony and I didn't thank our lucky stars she never tried again.

2 The writer and actor Ben Moor. My mother loved him. I had been in the Oxford Revue with him and he was forging a career writing and performing wonderfully inventive one-man shows.

For some crazy reason I started to cut my toenails when I got back to the hotel in a very dim light.[3] I cut part of one toe above the nail and then while I was cutting my big toe and trying to cut that tricky corner bit, I sliced that as well. Staunching the blood of both toes and whimpering with the pain I then started to pick my nose for a bit of comfort[4] and promptly had a heavy nosebleed. Tried to reach sink with blood smeared across hand, stumbling with two toes wedged with tissue. Tony, naked at the time,[5] had to put his pants on, dash outside to the bathroom to get wads of toilet paper for the nosebleed. Couldn't get into bed for thirty minutes as blood was cascading from three different wounds. Felt very sorry for myself. Big toe gets infected, swells up menacingly and can't walk for two days.

LESSON   HAVE EYE TEST
SEAL NOSE
TAKE MORE MENTAL EXERCISE

Am reading Foucault's Madness and Civilisation.[6] *I am sure it is doing me good. Tony is fixing garage shed roof and*

3 And now we get to why she wrote the letter in the first place. Nothing gave Brenda more pleasure than a small, dramatic tale of disaster. She's preambled us into this gore-filled incident, but be under no illusions: this is a champ at the top of her game.

4 One of the very rare occasions my mother made explicit reference to her self-harming. She didn't think of it as self-harm. She thought it was funny.

5 Get used to my father always seeming to be naked at moments of high crisis. I have no idea why this appears to be the norm.

6 I'm fascinated, in hindsight, to find my mother reading a seminal study on the meaning of madness through the ages. Foucault was fixated on the evolution of madness within society and culture, from the Renaissance, where the mad were revered as truth tellers, revealing what men *are* as opposed to what they *present* themselves as, through to the modern era, where madness has become an illness that must be cured or confined. Foucault was criticised at the time for cherry picking to suit his argument. Natch.

I am going to walk to town to post this. Write if you have time.

Hope everything continues to go well. Keep eating properly and have plenty of rest. Don't offer to be in anyone else's plays etc. Two's enough.

We think you are wonderful.
All our love
Mum and Dad
Will write soon.
XXXXX

PS Thought you and girls might like some Naughty Bits.[7]

Love.

★ ★ ★

---

7 I am devastated to have to tell you that I have no recollection of what these Naughty Bits might have been.

Dear Em[1]

How are you? Hope you are keeping well and not getting too wet in Edinburgh – the weather forecasts always seem to offer the worst in eastern Scotland.

We had a good drive home. Left Edinburgh at 9.00am and arrived in Hitchin at 4.15pm – including three short breaks. The garden wasn't too bad although the tomatoes have suffered a bit from lack of regular watering. We haven't done a great deal since we've been back – enjoying the sunshine really. We've had a few nice long walks and a trip to Saffron Walden[2] etc. I shall be starting my job[3] in a few weeks and I am looking forward to that although it seems I have to have a medical before everything is confirmed. There haven't been any mention of your shows in the Guardian.[4] *I check every day – perhaps we missed something while we were in Edinburgh. Do let us know if anything comes out in the nationals. I expect you will keep cuttings but it's nice to see things in context so to speak.*

There should be some veg for you when you get back. I've

1 Highly unusual. The beginning of this letter is written by Tony, hence the preponderance on timings for journeys, vegetable updates and newspaper clippings. He was the Keeper of the Scrapbook, of course.

2 Every single time my mother would make Tony drive her to Saffron Walden (it's a ninety-minute drive via the A505 there and back again), he'd pull a face and go, 'Not bloody Saffron Walden again,' as if he was in Gallipoli and had been asked to run ten miles through trenches. I have no idea what her obsession with Saffron Walden was, but she considered it quite the treat.

3 My father was starting a new job in further education, teaching life drawing to art foundation students.

4 The chances of our shows being reviewed in the *Guardian* were nil. Bless them for looking.

*got loads of onions in storage and next week I will be taking
up the potatoes – I think there will be lots. The broccoli is
continuing but in smaller amounts and the beans are more or
less over. There will be plenty of beetroot, cabbage and later
on sprouts and parsnips if you would like some. We have
lettuce coming out of our ears. I have started preparing some
ground for next year so we must keep everything on the go. If
you have any supplies of manure knocking around do let me
know.[5]*

Here's Mum.

*I've decided to call Tony cornucopia. Hasn't he done well? He
should start a market garden. I haven't done anything so
productive but I'm not apologising. I bought a little book of
essays by JB Priestly the other day and one was written in
praise of idleness – the essential need to gaze at the sky, dream
and contemplate. So that's me. You never know, I might get a
book out of it.*

*We hired some computer games and a Playstation[6] –
Resident Evil 2 and Circuit Breakers. Tony is addicted. He
wasn't coming to bed until 12.30. I quite like playing for about
fifteen minutes but I can't control left and right movements very
well so I end up being killed quite frequently. I also find that
playing these games makes me very irritable and aggressive.[7]
Not for me.*

Now make sure you are eating properly and take the

---

5 I have absolutely no idea why my father thinks I might have a surfeit of
manure. I am in Edinburgh in a show.

6 I don't have to tell you how great a surprise this came as, do I? From
nowhere, my father became obsessed with shooting zombies. He even drew his
own game map so that he knew every room inside out and where the zombies
were coming from. I cite my mother's realisation that violent shooter games
were not the best use of her downtime as one of her greater decisions.

7 No shit, Sherlock.

tablets.[8] *Write if you have time. We'll try to phone again – if you're not in, I'll leave a message.*

Take care. All our love.
Mum and dad.

PS If you need anything, let us know.

★ ★ ★

8 My mother often made reference to tablets I'm supposed to be taking. There's only one problem with this: I didn't have any and never had.

Two

My grandmother, Elizabeth, was the youngest of seven children, born in 1909 to Henry Kynes and his wife, Bridget, in a small terrace house in Dublin South Dock. My great-grandfather was a carpenter by trade, good with his hands. He would die at the age of seventy-four, from a combination of heart failure and hemiplegia, a paralysis on one side of the body caused by brain damage or spinal cord injury. Bridget would die ten years before him from a heart attack. She was just sixty. They were Catholics and had experienced tragedy twice. In 1911, at the time of the census, only six children were still living. I don't know who their seventh child was, so must presume he or she died in childbirth or shortly after. It's entirely possible Bridget lost more children in childbirth, as Brenda always used to tell me her mother had been one of thirteen. Death, then, hung heavy over the Kynes. Their son, Arthur, died at the age of fifteen, the cause registered as 'pneumonia for nine days and meningitis for five'. He was away from his family, in St Kevin's, Glencree, an inmate of the Reformatory School where he had been for the three years before, most likely because he had committed a crime.

Elizabeth had one other brother, William, who went to England in 1941, leaving his wife, Alice, and children in Ireland. By 1945, however, he'd got himself into a bit of bother and on 11 September, he was front page news in the *Evening Herald*.

FOR BIGAMY

Father of six children, William Kynes, 40-year-old Dublin Joiner, was at the Old Bailey London today sent to prison for four months for bigamy. Kynes came to England in 1941 to work on bomb damage repairs, said Mr H. J. Hamblan prosecuting. In London he married Miss Mary Thompson, 39-year-old house-keeper, at whose home he had obtained lodgings. Kynes declared that although he told Miss Thompson he was married and had six children, she persuaded him to go through a form of marriage at Poplar register office in 1941. Miss Thompson, who also pleaded guilty to aiding and abetting Kynes, was also sent to prison for four months.

Her eldest sister, Jane Ileen, may have suffered a worse fate. She had married a man called Michael Wine, the son of a Jewish art dealer. This would have been a good marriage, especially for a girl from a poor family, but within months, they had both disappeared. Two years later, Michael Wine reappeared, named in a notorious court case in Scotland. He had married a woman called Mrs Bamberger, a fresh-faced beauty who had fallen for his film-star looks. She was the daughter of a navvy and had left her parents aged sixteen to join a theatrical chorus. The details of the case aren't entirely clear but the marriage at Gretna Green to Michael Wine was her third, presumably without being divorced. She was sent to jail not for bigamy but for perjury. After the trial, Michael bought a ticket to New York and set sail on the SS *Nieuw Amsterdam*, departing from Plymouth on 3 October 1920. There is no sign of poor Jane though and her death was not recorded in Ireland or England. It's entirely possible Michael Wine murdered her, but we will never know. My aunt Phyllis didn't even know she existed: my grandmother, Elizabeth, never spoke of her.

Elizabeth's other sisters, May and Gerty, were, like many Irish men and women before the war, experiencing privation.

There wasn't enough work or food, and many were emigrating in the hope they could make a better life for themselves. May was thinking of going to Canada but Gerty had already left for England. She'd married an able seaman, Leslie Taylor, in 1926. She didn't know it yet, but he was homosexual.

Gerty and Leslie had set up home running a guest house in Southend-on-Sea and it was here that my grandmother, Elizabeth, arrived, suitcase in hand, to help out and find her feet. She had dark hair and green eyes, a prominent jaw and an expression of seriousness. She lacked the sociableness of her sister, Gerty, preferring to be quiet and go unnoticed. At the same time, a rather shy young man with a shock of strawberry-blond hair was running away from his father in Battersea. Bob was nineteen and yet to discover that the man he thought was his father wasn't at all, but here he was, by the sea, a world away from the grime of the Battersea terrace he lived in. As he walked the streets, he chanced upon my great-aunt's guest house. It was at this moment that my grandparents met. They were two quiet people who had left home to find something different, something better. They fell in love and were married in Portsmouth in June, 1939. My grandmother told Robert she was twenty-one. She wasn't. She was ten years older.

It was a difficult time to be an Irish Catholic on mainland Britain. The Irish Republican Army (IRA) had bombed two London Underground stations that February and, in August, they would plant a bomb in Coventry that killed five and injured seventy. Irish migrants were treated with suspicion, not least because the negative stereotypes of the Irish as innately criminal or the carriers of disease still lingered. My grandmother, looking for cleaning work, would have been turned away by signs on doors that read:

'No Blacks, No Dogs, No Irish.'

It was a prejudice that created a sense of shame and wariness, one that engendered a suspicion of strangers and deterred the making of friends. It would set a course of behaviour that would have profound consequences.

There was quite a wait for their first child: four years after taking their vows, my mother was born on Friday, 5 February 1943 at home, 42 Lower Brook Street in Basingstoke, a small, terraced house that looked out over a patch of grass and a few trees. It was an eventful time: General Friedrich Paulus, the leader of the German Sixth Army, the man who had led 250,000 German troops in the siege of Stalingrad, had been defeated, surrendering days before my mother was born and in defiance of Hitler's orders to 'fight to the death'. It was to be a significant turning point of the war and the beginning of Hitler's fall. Hope was in the air.

My grandparents had moved to Basingstoke for work. My grandfather, deaf in one ear, had been refused conscription and was sent, instead, to work at Thornycroft, a factory building motor vehicles for the war effort. He's described on my mother's birth certificate as a 'Jig borer, motor works', in other words, he punched holes into metal. It was here that my grandfather discovered his two great passions: politics and women. Stirred by the Herculean efforts of the Soviets on the Eastern front, my grandfather became a communist and was duly appointed shop steward on the shop floor. My grandmother was a strict Catholic who voted Conservative for the entirety of her life. One can only imagine the conversations that were taking place over the dinner table, but my grandfather had started to see other women and trouble was brewing.

It's not possible to pinpoint precisely when my grandparents' marriage began to irretrievably break down. It was the war and women were well used to turning a blind eye, but Elizabeth was Catholic and come what may that meant one thing: she could not divorce. In any event, there was a natural separation. At the end of the war, my grandfather was sent to Germany to help with the clear up. He would be away for a year. My mother liked to tell me this was when he became a spy, but we'll get to that later.

On his return, the family moved to Ashley Lodge cottage, a small boxy council house on the edge of the Frescade

Crescent estate in Basingstoke. It was a house that looked and felt different from the rest: there was a sign on the front bearing its name and it was off a long rural-looking lane. It's striking, looking at it now, that the lane bears an uncanny resemblance to where Brenda ended up in Dallington. Flanked by trees and stretching off, it was a lane that suggested adventures and secrets.

Directly opposite Ashley Lodge was a house that must have looked to my mother's young eyes rather 'posh'. It was detached, with a wooden porch, and had more than two rooms upstairs. It all felt rather exclusive. It's not clear why the semi-detached council house bore the name Ashley Lodge, but it may have been an estate office, somewhere the developer sat, waiting to show new tenants into their newly built homes.

This was the house where my mother told me she was happiest: she was with her mum and dad and she had a lane to play in. She put on plays and bossed about the other children, she was outside and free. At the top of the lane were the large green fields of the Basingstoke Sports and Social Club. It must have felt idyllic. Brenda was in her element. Whether this is misty-eyed remembrance is another matter. Her parents were clearly miserable but despite that, on 24 June 1949, a little sister, Phyllis, six years Brenda's younger, arrived and was brought home to Ashley Lodge.

It's difficult to surmise what my mother may have been like as a child before Phyllis came along, but she was about to experience a double trauma. With another child in the house, the decision was made to move to a slightly larger council house at 47 Lefroy Avenue. Brenda was taken from the home she loved: there was no more rural lane and she now lived in a house you wouldn't be able to pick out in a police line-up, but worse was yet to come. Two years later, after an endless stream of affairs, Bob had met a woman and run off with her, a rather exciting communist called Kathleen. Elizabeth, in accordance with her religious beliefs, refused to grant him a divorce.

It was at this point that the shutting down began. All of Elizabeth's feelings of inferiority crowded in: she was Irish, she was a Catholic and now she was an abandoned woman. Not only that, but Gerty's husband, Leslie, had taken to indulging in acts of indecency with other men. Embarrassment was overwhelming her on all fronts. 'Don't let people know our business,' she would tell the girls. Shame, she was teaching them, was to be kept hidden from other people, but there was another, more complicated facet to Elizabeth's character. For all her feelings of inadequacy, she was a bit of a snob.

To make ends meet, my grandmother worked as a cleaning lady: in the mornings she would clean the local bank, in the afternoons she would clean professional people's houses. She would tiptoe through large rooms filled with lovely things and, when on her own, she could imagine herself the mistress of all she surveyed. If her life had only been a little bit different, all these things might have been hers. Elizabeth, getting used to being around middle-class people, began to develop notions. She had a chip on her shoulder about being Irish and not having a husband so, in order to circumvent her sense of inadequacy, she elevated herself to an odd status: they were far too good to be living on this council estate, she decided, and her daughters, Brenda and Phyllis, were to know their worth. Brenda, in particular, took this all to heart.

My aunt's memories of my mother during their Lefroy Avenue years are clear cut: Brenda was 'the mad sister' who would think nothing of opening her bedroom window to shout at Phyllis's friends and tell them to be quiet. Given the six-year age gap with Brenda coming into her mid-teens, I think we can forgive her ignoring her mother's constant pleas to 'take your sister with you' but one incident stands out – when my mother was twelve, just after Bob had left, Brenda tried to kill herself.

Phyllis recalls the moment well. She was out in the street, on her haunches, playing marbles. Behind her, from the house, she could hear Brenda shouting at their mother. It was another row, of which there seemed to be more and more. Brenda would have what Phyllis described as 'temper tantrums', where she lost all control. She would, during one blind fury, run her hand across the top of the mantelpiece, sending every single one of her mother's precious ornaments scattering, breaking them all. She threw her dinner against the wall and, on one occasion, threw a book at a child who had dared to answer her back, eliciting a complaint from a furious parent. Phyllis, entirely used to her big sister screaming, ignored it all and on that day was concentrating on her marbles but behind her, the shouting stopped and moments later, there was a thud.

'Your sister's just jumped from the upstairs window,' a play-mate commented. Phyllis turned to see Brenda lying face down on the floor.

I remember my mother telling me she had done this as a child, but it was treated, as difficult things often were, as a bit of a joke. She'd tried to kill herself by jumping from an upstairs window, she'd laugh. She wasn't complaining.

'Were you sent to see a psychiatrist?' I think I asked her once. (Questions about mental health were tolerated in the context of her thinking what she'd done was hilarious.)

'No,' she replied. 'Nobody did anything. I think I was sent to Aunty Gerty for a bit of cake.'

Miraculously, she was unhurt. 'I was carried by a guardian angel,' she would tell me in all seriousness. It was a funny thing to say: she hated the Catholic Church, bitterly so, but once a Catholic, always a Catholic, and she could never pass a Catholic Church without going in and lighting candles.

I never managed to find out why she had thrown herself from that window. It strikes me now that a child of twelve only does that if they're disturbed or traumatised, but which was it? The bottom line here was, Brenda loved telling this story. It thrilled her. She'd tried to kill herself. How dramatic.

Drama was something my mother loved. It recharged her batteries, of that there was no doubt. I can recall an incident, later on, when I was living in London and Mum was with me as I pulled into a garage. A perfectly pleasant woman, in a large-brimmed hat, had inadvertently driven onto the forecourt the wrong way around and taken the pump we'd been waiting for. I had grumbled something under my breath but thought no more of it. The woman, realising her mistake, came over to my open window to apologise. My mother tore into her with a viciousness you'd normally reserve for child killers. I remember sitting, my forehead in my hands, listening to my mother hurl insult after personal insult at this poor woman who just stood, bent down, staring into my car with a look of absolute astonishment. As she finally walked away, my mother was punch drunk with glee. She'd loved it but then, this was far from an isolated incident. Fights, for Brenda, were to be run into, head first, fists pumping. They produced in her a visceral thrill.

Conflict presented no fear to my mother and Phyllis recalls only seeing Brenda cry twice. She was a yeller, not a crier. The first was when Brenda discovered the actor James Dean had died; the second, at the death of her mother Elizabeth. Other than that, she was steel itself. Thinking about this, I was stunned to find myself struggling to remember my mother crying at all. It was like a sucker punch. This was the woman who left me in tears on hundreds, if not thousands of occasions. She would start rows, yell and howl, make accusations, say unforgivable things, but she never cried. She was like a pressure valve that needed to blow. She felt relief at her outbursts, while the rest of us lay about, broken.

After Bob left, Elizabeth did everything she could to keep the girls warm and fed and safe. To help pay the rent, they had a lodger, Miss Callaghan, a librarian in her forties. Phyllis remembers she lived with them for years, yet she only saw her once, which seems impossible yet is true. Occasionally, Elizabeth would come home with gifts from her rich employers. She was given an Axminster rug and a writing desk, both of which had to be hidden away when the Assistance Man came to check they were as poor as they said they were – he would be sent by the council to spy on families claiming financial help – but there were to be no doubts on that score – they really did have nothing.

Phyllis remembers her mother living on a diet of bread and jam. 'We'd have pies, stews. Mummy was a very good cook. But she never ate a meal with us.' All the food she could afford, Elizabeth gave to her girls.

A bitterness had set in though. Elizabeth's life had not turned out how she had hoped. Miss Callaghan had moved on and, unable to cope with the rent, the family moved again, to a smaller house on the same estate. It must have been hard for Elizabeth, scraping to make ends meet, having to endure repeated humiliations. Yet through it all, she instilled in her daughters the hope that they could make a better life. But if they wanted to pull themselves out from this, they had to work to do it.

Occasionally, Bob would turn up to visit. Elizabeth loathed seeing him, and Brenda, full of resentment, would disappear every time he came over. Phyllis hated him coming too, not least because she'd find herself the only one willing to entertain him. He'd changed. No longer was he the quiet, retiring boy on the pushbike. He was now a bearded womaniser who thought nothing of shouting across the street in his thick cockney accent, 'Fancy coming to see me in London, darlin'?', at any woman who took his fancy. It was mortifying and Phyllis took to hiding in the coal shed to avoid him. Brenda hated him so much, she told people her father was dead. She concocted a story that he'd been a war hero, who'd come home, only to die of malaria. Of course, she did.

It's not difficult to draw some conclusions about my mother from this time. Here was a teenage girl who hadn't felt happy since the moment her sister was born. Wrenched from the house she had convinced herself was the keeper of all her happiness, she had to endure the shame of being abandoned by a profligate father and the stigmatism of being Catholic and having an Irish mother. You can see it, can't you? The quiet accumulation of shame and embarrassment, having it drummed into you that you must never tell anyone anything.

Phyllis was more than aware her sister wanted very little to do with them. She was rarely in, but when she was, Brenda would lock herself in her bedroom 'writing letters to James Dean', fantasising about the life she might be leading. She made friends with the daughter of a wealthy man who ran a local garage and started hanging out with people who were higher up the social pecking order. It was also around this time she started telling strangers her name was Becky.

It was another detail Brenda used to mention lightly. My mother didn't want to be Brenda, the poor kid who lived on an estate with her Irish mother. She wanted to be Becky Sharp from Thackeray's novel, *Vanity Fair*. It's an interesting choice. There are two schools of thought on Becky: she's the repellent social climber, craven with ambition, an amoral schemer, utterly ruthless, a near-the-knuckle sociopath, or she's the poor kid who has, quite rightly, understood precisely what is required to pull herself out of her impoverished circumstances. I can understand how this might have resonated with my mother. She had ambitions. She wanted to be better than she was. She was driven. She was also rather beautiful: dark chestnut-coloured hair, green eyes and cheekbones you could cut yourself on. A cross between Julie Christie and Audrey Hepburn. And if Brenda struggled, it wasn't with attracting men.

Whatever else she was doing in that locked room, she was also working hard and proving herself to be clever as well as beautiful. She managed to get herself into The Shrubbery Secondary Modern School for Girls. It was a source of great pride for Elizabeth, a proper achievement. More than that, for Brenda, it was the opening of a door into a more well-to-do world. There were tennis teams and trips to Paris (my mother could never afford to go), plays, speech days and prize-givings. There was a teacher who would arrive each day in an open-topped Bentley, driven by her husband. This was where Brenda wanted to be; this was the place where possibilities could become realities. Brenda was on the up.

At home, Phyllis remembered there was no laughter. The house was a miserable one to be in, only enlivened when Elizabeth's sister, Gerty, came round to play cards. Gerty ran a Shoe Club and would visit the estate each week, collecting the money for people who wanted to save for a pair of shoes. She enjoyed the job and it got her away from Leslie, whom she could not divorce. She was sociable and funny – everything Elizabeth was not.

I'm in awe, really, of what Phyllis endured. She shared a bed with her mother, was lumped with a father she didn't much care for, had a sister who was cold towards her and disinterested. She had next to nothing and was being raised in an atmosphere of secrecy and exclusion. When I think about my aunt, how young she was and what a weight must have been on her shoulders, I am astonished by it. Her resilience is extraordinary.

But then, there was her father, Bob, to deal with. He was the thorn in everyone's side.

Dearest Emma
Friday, Paziols, southern France

Well. What a week.[1] The house has an old narrow, wooden staircase out of 'Hansel and Gretel'. It was probably built by the Grimm brothers. My knee is now playing up with the agony of constantly turning on an angle around twisting bends. There are 30 of these evil little steps.

The house is, quite frankly, a disaster on a par with Bourrigues.[2] The bath needs industrial cleaner and the enamel has worn away leaving black scum-like marks along its length. It cannot be used. The shower is in another rank outer shed, the breeding place of scorpions and crawlies. We have not had a bath or shower since we arrived! We rang the local English[3] caretaker, not the owner, and she came round and tried to make pathetic excuses about the place.

I had to have a filthy rug removed from our bedroom which she hastily replaced with a posh one – so – there was no excuse for this. I did my usual I'll have you in court act[4] and within 30 minutes the owner in England offered all our money back plus £100–£450 in all. I

1 Look at her, thrilled from the off.

2 Bourrigues, merrily cited in our family as the worst holiday we ever had.

3 Woe betide anyone English encountered by my mother on the continent. She would treat them with nothing but suspicion despite the fact she dreamed of living there herself.

4 I'm sure, by now, you've got a fulsome grip on a Brenda 'court act' but if not, it mostly involved her pushing herself up onto her tiptoes and pointing a lot while booming like a bittern until she got what she wanted. I'll give her credit here – it always worked.

refused this as we had nowhere else to go – no hotels or
self-catering and I will contact her when I get home.[5]

Lone and Finn[6] *came to stay for 2 nights, bless them. I told*
them the place was a shambles, but they still came – no
showers for them either! Lone had never seen a staircase like it.
Apart from the house, the area of Cathar castles[7] *and moun-*
tains has a grandeur we've not seen elsewhere. We've been up
the mountains to the Cathar castles twice and we had to climb
on foot. It was the most thrilling and terrifying thing I've ever
done.

We climbed with a party of Danish pensioners and we
congratulated each other on how wonderful we were for our
age. The wind buffeted around us and we screamed and
laughed and hung on to each other as we climbed to the top
and the spectacular views of the mountains and a limestone
escarpment that went as far as the horizon. It was a climb
of nearly 3000 feet! At one point, we were all caught in a
wind tunnel and the force was so great our clothes flew
off our backs.[8] *I'm sure it was too dangerous to climb in*
those conditions, but we all helped each other gasping for
breath to the top. It was wonderful. I hadn't felt so alive
for years. We've also been to Rennes le chateau of Da Vinci
fame, another glorious view of Limestone escarpments,

---

5 I love this casual aside. She'd gone to all the trouble of threatening them with nothing short of biblical destruction and then, having been offered very reasonable financial compensation, she's suddenly realised she'd have to leave and that would be a faff, so she stays to be a brave soldier instead. Be careful what you wish for, Brenda!

6 Finn and Lone lived in the house at the end of the lane for a short time. They were from Denmark.

7 The Cathar castles are in the Languedoc region of France and are medieval citadels.

8 *narrows eyes*

gorges and the Pic de Canegu[9] – the big mountain.

The church in Renne le Chateau[10] is dedicated to the wife of Jesus, Mary Magdalene. In the café there was a bizarre event occurring. An elderly gentleman was playing mournful melodies on a piano, and young women were invited to sit close to him and meditate, pray or sob. Most of them did the sobbing or the eyes closed in deep prayer performance. Of course, they were all young and beautiful – the old craggy ladies weren't invited. Wouldn't have missed it.

Finn and Lone thought the area was magical – and it is. The Cathar castles give the landscape an air of mystery and romance.

We are off to Spain to Figueres – Salvador Dali's museum in northern Spain. Will be there until Tuesday. Paris on Wednesday. Home on Thursday.

Hope your arm is OK and that Phyllis didn't leave my doors open.[11] Love and cuddles for you and Poppy.

★ ★ ★

9 I'm not clear which mountain she's referring to here, as there is no Canegu I can find. There's a Canigó in the Pyrenees and it might be safe to assume this is the one she means, but the Pyrenees are almost 300 km away from the region my parents were staying in. Nobody's got that good eyesight.

10 You'll be delighted to know that Renne-le Château is quite the bullseye for enthusiastic conspiracy theorists searching for a treasure that may or may not exist. It's also wrapped in the mysterious cloak of the Knights Templar, another subject Brenda was drawn to. She was an avid devourer of anything churned out by Dan Brown and considered him not so much an author of popular commercial fiction, but more a visionary akin to an ancient prophet and a High Priest of Mischief to the Catholic Church.

11 I had, for want of a technical medical term, a 'bad arm'. I had fractured my elbow catching my Vespa as it fell. I must have a high pain threshold because I didn't get it X-rayed for five weeks. By then, of course, there was no point in having anything put in plaster. The doctor stared at me in disbelief. I must have retired to Dallington while the pezzers were on holiday, something I liked to do, and Phyllis must have come to see me, no doubt thrilled at the thought she wouldn't have to see Brenda. Still, it's clear to see here that Brenda is still treating her younger sister as the naughty one who leaves doors open. *rolls eyes*

Three

Bob's ninetieth birthday was celebrated in a wood-panelled conference room at the National Liberal Club in Whitehall. It's a private members' club, established by British statesman William Gladstone in 1882. It came as something of a surprise to me that my grandfather, the committed communist, seemed to be a member of a rather posh London club but there were so many swirling contradictions about Bob I'd long given up trying to make sense of them.

We had reached the highlight of the party: there was to be a screening of a short film some students had made about my grandfather. It was called *Bob*. The lights had gone down and here we were, in a room of around fifty people. We'd had a decent enough lunch and a few glasses of wine. There had been some speeches and my grandfather had given his usual rabble rouser about how much he hated Margaret Thatcher. She hadn't been prime minister for over a decade but it didn't matter – he hated her for life. My cousins, Ben and Tom, were standing with me at the back, trying not to be noticed. The lights went down, and the film began.

'Oh my God,' muttered Ben, his hand covering his mouth.

Oh my God, indeed!

There was a ripple of polite coughs.

My aunt gave a short scream.

Every single one of us was staring up at my grandfather's cock and balls. In the opening shot, he lay naked on a single bed and then, without warning, he raised his legs up to his ears and there it all was, arsehole, leathery old testicles and cock. Everyone was stunned into silence. I glanced over at where he sat. He was grinning like a loon. He'd done it again. And Brenda, next to him, was leaning back, crying with laughter. They were more alike than she cared to admit.

Rumours and mysteries swirl around my grandfather. Nineteen years before he met my grandmother, in Gerty's boarding house, Bob had been born in a small, terraced house in Clapham, south London. The address given by his mother, Violet, at the time, was 12 Robertson Street. There was only one problem with that: the man named as his father, Albert Mitchell, didn't live there. Albert was an optician's assistant and had married my great-grandmother five years earlier. His address was 24 Brassey Square, Battersea. It's the house he lived in till he died, and the house Bob continued to live in until he died too.

So, why is that a problem, you may ask? Here begins the mystery. What was Violet doing in a house in Clapham? Well, she was in love with another man, William Payne, and in the February of 1919, they were embroiled in an affair. My mother always told me William Payne was Bob's real dad and that Violet had moved out to be with him. After a quarrel with William, she moved back to Brassey Square but left again when my grandfather was two, abandoning him in a cardboard box with nothing but two OXO cubes to keep him going. He was discovered by two Polish sisters, Mitzi and Poldi, who took him in. At some point, Bob ended up back at Brassey Square and – here's the kicker – Violet eventually married William Payne, in February 1950. The problem: Violet was still married to Albert Mitchell. She was a bigamist. Until 1904, according to the Judicial Statistics of England and Wales, there was an average of ninety-five cases of bigamy a year, so to discover that I've got two, possibly three cases in my family is quite the eye-opener. It may well be that during World War I and World War II, when marriages were rushed into or abandonments were commonplace, many acts of bigamy simply went unnoticed. Now though, with the glaring light of the internet bearing down on my ancestors, it can't be ignored.

When I was a child, I was rather fascinated with my grand-father. He introduced me to liquorice, specifically Pontefract cakes; the sitting room of his house was upstairs, which felt exotic; he had an outdoor toilet, which made me feel I might be in a museum, and he was a vegetarian, naturist communist. I didn't know anyone else who was a vegetarian or a naturist or a communist and here he was, all three at once. Every time we went to see him there would be a pot of cabbage and bean soup bubbling on his stove. He ate muesli he made himself and was totally committed to the smashing of capitalism. There were posters on his wall of revolutions he may or may not have been part of and he had a small black book into which he wrote appointments to play bridge or tennis or cricket or golf and scribbled about meetings with mysterious women. He thought nothing of cycling a hundred miles. I'd never met anyone like him and nobody, not one of us, quite knew what he did for a living.

'I'm a telephone engineer,' he'd tell me, on yet another day when he didn't seem to need to go to work.

'He's a spy,' my mother would say, every time we left after seeing him.

'But who for?' Dad would ask.

Brenda would stare out the window and narrow her eyes. She'd purse her lips. 'I don't know . . . Probably everyone.'

The hunch that Bob wasn't quite what he said he was received a substantial boost at the end of the seventies. We were on our way to see Tommy Steele in a panto (my mother was thrilled), and we'd decided to pop in and see Bob on the way. Mum had a key to my grandfather's house. As we walked in, she called out his name. Nothing. So, deciding to wait, we made our way up the stairs to the sitting room. As we walked in, we saw a man in a heavy overcoat, done up to the neck, sitting on the sofa. He had an enormous black handlebar moustache and was wearing a furry Russian hat. In front of him, on the coffee table, were photographs of missiles. We stood staring at him. It was like something out of a dream when you've eaten too much cheese. Without saying a word, he gathered up the photos, nodded to my mother and left.

Not one of us has ever been able to explain this. Ever.

That to one side, it was difficult to know what was real and what wasn't. My mother used to tell quite the tall tales about her father, most of which would stretch all credulity, but he didn't help matters. Whenever asked at point blank range what he might be up to he'd just laugh and tell my mother she was mad. He seemed to disappear for periods at a time. I have a vague recollection of being told he'd been arrested in China or may have gone to jail, but there is nothing to substantiate any of it. Bob's line was forever the same: he fitted telephones in people's homes and that was the end of it. Only problem was, he never seemed to actually do it.

As I was writing this, in the midst of the pandemic, my cousin, Ben, arrived with his new partner, Philip. It was a rather grey Sunday and neither of them were allowed into the house so we all stood, masked up, as Ben handed over bundles of photo albums and boxes of documents he'd cleared from Bob's house, after his death, a few years ago.

'Do you know about Kathleen?' he asked.

I shook my head. 'No. Was she a girlfriend?'

Ben's eyes widened. 'More than that. I think Grandad might have married her.'

'He can't have. Granny never gave him a divorce.'

'There's a photo album with pictures of him and Kathleen. The word "HONEYMOON" is written above them.'

'Oh.'

'Yes. Oh,' he said.

I went inside and wrote myself a note:

Find out if Grandad married a woman called Kathleen.

My grandfather was, I suppose, a handsome man, but there was something of the rake about him – a firm jaw set to mischief and an air of doing what the damn he pleased. He had the loucheness of a man untethered, the fox in the hen house. The stream of women in his life was endless. When I was three, we went to London for the day and met the woman with him: she was extraordinarily beautiful and wore a long, white fur coat. She looked like a film star. I can remember my mother side-eyeing her and wondering later how in the name of hell Bob had managed this. We went to Selfridges on Oxford Street, where a poster was pointed out to me. It was the woman. She was a famous model. Later, I sat on her lap, wrapped up in that white fur coat as we watched the Russian Circus. It felt magical, like meeting the Snow Queen herself. We never saw her again, of course, but for a lowly telephone engineer from Battersea, my grandfather seemed to cross the social divide with ease.

My grandfather's photo albums are filled with pictures of him with his arms around women, sometimes two, often more. He has the same expression in all of them, not unlike a dog seeing the treat bag being pulled from a pocket. My grandfather loved women: he loved being around them, he loved looking at them, he loved having sex. What he didn't love was the monogamous, steady, boring love that went hand in hand with long term partnerships. He couldn't do it. Fidelity was not for him.

He wasn't great at relationships. Thinking back, this doesn't surprise me. He had a brashness that bled into unpleasantness. He was a pest who would think nothing of sexualising everything. As a young teen, he would grab me and my friends (much to my horror), and hug us tight while shouting, 'Oooh lovely, I can feel your tits!' He was, in every sense, a dirty old man and yet, to my astonishment, women flocked to him.

What he did have was a magnetic energy. Bob just never stopped. Politically engaged, if there was a demo to be organising or marching in, he was there. His photos are a kaleidoscope of righteous protest: there's Bob at the Aldermaston march in 1958, Ban the H-Bomb, Yankee Go Home, CND, Stop McCarthyism, Anti-Vietnam, Greenham Common, No to the Common Market, Miners' Strike, March for Jobs, Free Nelson Mandela, Stop the War, A Demo for Nurses and – my personal favourite – Return the Photocopier Rights to the Wandsworth Ramblers. If there was a cause that promoted peace or equality or workers' rights or denounced racism, fascism and all the -isms that are frowned upon, he was there, tabard on, holding a banner, shouting. It's admirable, really, to be so bothered on other people's behalf and yet I wonder, when he was so politically committed, why he never ran for public office. Perhaps something else was going on.

In his papers, I found a small, battered, beige book. It has writing in small capitals on the front. *BOB MITCHELL 1976. WORKERS TOUR no. 7*, followed by a handy list of how to say Good morning, Thank you, Goodbye, Comrade and China in Chinese. My grandfather, for some reason, had been sent to China. The days are meticulously recorded. He writes:

> Workers and peasants organise and manage their work . . . They have political and practical studies where they exercise social responsibility through neighbourhood committees where no workers are redundant and the old and ill are cared for with no inflation or foreign speculations and no pay problems. They have no cars or tv but are happy. No wonder they are smiling.

He visits textile factories, pig farms; he bears witness to a tonsillectomy performed under acupuncture; he carefully notes banana trees, the use of chop sticks, swivel chairs. He goes to an agricultural machine factory and jots down how many people are employed, the annual output and makes reference to the fact that every other day, time is set aside to study Marx. He goes to a workers' parade, a middle school, a steel foundry, a theatre. He goes to meetings about the Chinese economy where he discovers, very precisely, the efficacy of the Yangtze River, its irrigation canals, the percentage of crops it feeds, the aqueducts, tunnels and pumping stations. He goes to a power station, sees a dam, observes an embroidery factory. He goes to a school for the deaf and dumb and, despite my finding photos of him standing on the Great Wall of China, he mentions not a single thing about sight-seeing or travel companions. His notebook is peppered with odd lists and pronouncements:

SPITOONS NOT NEEDED AT MEETINGS

ALL MALE OR FEMALE TOURS. NO NUT CASES

And one that stuck out: *Work hard and study hard (no sex)*

In the middle, Bob scrawls *Summary of Tour*, presented with a lazily executed underline. He then lists:

NO SPECULATORS
NO RUN ON CURRENCY
NO INFLATION
NO UNEMPLOYMENT
NO INCREASE ON PRICES
NO CARS
NO TVS
NO HUNGRY
NO ILL CLOTHED
NO ILL SHOD
NO THUGS
NO MUGGING
NO TIPPING
NO PRESENTS
NO BAL OF PAYMENT PROBLEMS
NO LITTER
NO PROSTITUTES
NO DRUGS

It's clear this trip to China is not a holiday and he's being given access to places from Peking to Canton that must have been beyond the reach of a casual visitor. Yet, what he was doing there is unclear. So, too, is why he was required to note specifics of economic capacity wherever he went. There are photos of great crowds gathered to meet him, cheering him on as if he's a visiting dignitary. Children sing to him. Dinners were held in his honour. What was going on?

You can excuse me, I think, for pausing here. Bob was a telephone engineer from a housing association slum in Battersea that had no central heating and an outside toilet. He was, by any standard, a very ordinary man and yet, somehow, he wasn't. The seed of madness he accused my mother of whenever she questioned what he was up to actually seemed bedded in something tangible – and it doesn't require a leap of mental gymnastics to be able to see that the story of Robert Ernest Mitchell, as presented, stank like a rat. Something was off.

This all created, I suppose, an air of mistrust. My mother would always declare, with genuine vehemence, that she hated her father – as a child she would avoid him like the plague. She refused to have him at her wedding and didn't even see fit to tell him that Elizabeth had died. Bob was, as far as Mum was concerned, the man who had abandoned them and, in so doing, had reduced their circumstances and social standing. He had left Brenda shrouded in a cloud of shame. Their relationship was prickly and so difficult that, on one occasion, he pulled a knife on her and threatened to kill her. They could go for years without speaking, so it was something of a surprise to discover this letter from Mum to him, written when I was three:

Dear Daddy, it begins, *I knew I'd forget! Well, better late than never! I'll have to get you a jumper at the end of the month as we will just get through the month without being overdrawn and if we don't spend any money on anything other than food.*

She goes on to discuss the mini budget and how dreadful it is, asks him to organise a protest, then makes enquiries of Susan, the glamorous fur-clad model we'd just met. A small detail I had forgotten about our day at the circus – Brenda had somehow wangled a trip back to her flat (I imagine she'd offered her a lift home in order to have a good snoop). Mum writes: *When we went back to Susan's flat, we met her hubby.*

He's very dishy so I don't know what your chances will be like. Are you still seeing her?

The casualness of it strikes me as significant. Brenda clearly knows precisely what is going on and it's treated as if it's neither scandalous nor shocking but then, the seventies were a very odd time. The sexual revolution of the sixties had settled into something a little more pernicious. With Germaine Greer rabble rousing for the emergence of female sexuality, there was now a grubby expectation that pervaded everything: everyone was supposed to be having sex, and not necessarily with the person you might be married to. Men expected women to have sex with them, whatever the circumstances, and vice versa. Neighbours threw their car keys into bowls at parties. People were having affairs left, right and centre and if you didn't like it, there was something wrong with you. I mention this because my mother was to have her own affairs years later, but we'll get to that in due course. The point being though, it had become a new kind of normal.

There's a small twist to this story: my aunt, Phyllis, also met Susan who, it turned out, had asked Bob to bug her telephone (she thought her husband was having an affair) and in so doing, began an affair herself. Phyllis recalls Susan telling her, with some delight, that Bob 'was the only man who ever kissed her with a mouth full of nuts and raisins'.

The letter from Brenda ends with a rather vivid report of a bout of gastroenteritis and a hope she'll see him before Christmas . . . '*lots of love, buy yourself a couple of whiskies*' is followed by a line of nine kisses. This doesn't strike me as the letter you might write to someone you're determined to hate. It's a bright, breezy piece of correspondence, light and affectionate. And she's clearly included some money so he can go off and get himself a few drinks.

We long for people to be the person we want them to be, don't we? Brenda was ten when her father left them. Phyllis would have been two and has no memory of living with him. Brenda, of course, did and was left with a humiliated mother, old enough to see it and feel it but not old enough to do anything about it. She resented what he had done to them, despised his inability to remain loyal to her mother and was left devastated that he didn't love her enough to stay. It hardened her edges, put steel in her veins and left her with the knowledge that love, whatever that was, was fleeting and cursory. Love, her father taught Mum, was about doing what you wanted, with whomever you wanted and damn the consequences.

It was a lesson she would take to heart.

Tuesday

Darling Emmy

Well, we have had a very enjoyable time so far, but with a few disasters.[1]

The first was Venice. We had a wonderful journey by boat from the airport to San Marco at sunset, passing all the small islands of the Murano and the Lido with a glorious red sunset and excellent weather. It was something akin to the opening of A Death in Venice *as the boat approaches Venice from the sea.*[2]

Great start, we thought and hurried off to find our hotel. What a disappointment! We had to carry the luggage up three flights of stairs, two elderly people – how Tony managed to carry the suitcase up those stairs I'll never know. But your dad's a strong kid yet. The room was about 5 by 7 room for a bed, chest of drawers. There was nowhere to put the case. We were in the garret with one small window and already it was suffocating. £70 a night – no breakfast!

The great advantage at that moment was that the hotel was behind San Marco so we were promenading around a virtually empty square at 9 in the evening. The air was balmy and warm after freezing cold England and we were very happy.

That night a battalion of mosquitoes entered the 5 by 7

1 *rubs thighs*

2 I've only been to Venice once and Georgie, because she is the greatest human being on the planet (I will accept no arguments on this), had arranged for us to do just this: travel to Venice from the airport via speedboat. It was incredible. It was expensive but a proper once in a lifetime moment and I can't recommend it enough.

bedroom and lay about a bloody massacre on two old bodies. In the morning Tony had two large disfiguring red lumps, one behind the other, on the end of his nose. I had a HUGE red lump on my cheek another in the middle of my forehead and another – guess where – on the very end of my chin! My chin![3] As if it wasn't pointed enough – now I had a large red marker, making it worse.

Tony found a few of the bastards and set about revenge. As he splattered one in his hands, OUR blood hit the wall. Terrible. So we slunk around Venice like two pock marked lepers. And I'd bought a lovely new jacket to swank about in and now I had to keep ducking my head. But Italians are so strange – my jacket and my new bag from a Conran shop were a great success. Heads turned and the girls in the Peggy Guggenheim gallery shop wanted to know where I'd got it. While I told them, they stared fixedly at the spot on my chin. We had a lovely time, met a family from the Bronx in New York with Rod Steiger accents and a 40's film ambience. Have you noticed that about Americans? They seem to project a 40's/50's Doris Day meets Al Capone image of themselves without even trying.

Our nearest town is Verona. Verona is wonderful. We weren't really expecting that much. The pavements are marble, smooth and luxurious, like the shops. I have never seen such exquisite clothes. Since I have never been into

---

3 It was a long-standing family joke that my mother had a witch's chin not unlike the Wicked Witch in *The Wizard of Oz*. She would stroke it, like a proper villain, then say, 'I'll get you and your little dog too,' followed by a loud cackle. She took great pride in her Old Lady Chinny Whisks that sprouted up like weeds the nano-second she became menopausal, and thought nothing of asking complete strangers to excuse her 'beard'. She'd also flatly refuse to kiss anyone she was introduced to, explaining she was doing it to save them the horror of 'feeling my moustache'. Nobody tells you about the Old Lady Chinny Whisks. They're coming.

fashion,[4] I have never really aspired to posh clothes[5] but
here, well nothing would fit ME but I have been very
tempted to get you something. Tony, however, reminds me of
the innumerable times my attempts to buy you clothes have
been failures.[6] Oh, but I so wanted to buy you[7] something
– they are so lovely.

The funniest thing in Verona is Juliet's house. It is covered in
graffiti – Silvio loves Franky stuff. It is on every surface.
Bought you a great present there. Wonderful shops, wonderful
palaces and churches. All we need is the weather.

So far it has been very warm and we've had one dramatic
storm. We had a heat wave while we were in Venice but we are
higher now and it's cooler but still sunny.

Yesterday we drove round Lake Garda, lovely drive but
we didn't want to stay there for any length of time. Lake
Garda is great if you've got a boat or like wind surfing
apart from that there is little of interest except the view of
the mountains, so we drove on into the Dolomites which are
spectacular.

Found an amazing comic shop in Trento and bought a batch
of old American, Italian and Japanese comics for less than

---

4 Total lie. My mother was mad for fashion. If she could have spent every
penny she earned on clothes, she would have. She was an early devotee of the
epic Biba and I have fond childhood memories of trips to the store on the
King's Road.

5 This, from the woman who bought me corduroy culottes from Harrods.
Please. You fool no one, Brenda.

6 We went through a sustained phase where Brenda came up with the cunning
wheeze that she would hoodwink Tony into agreeing to her buying some
clothes on the pretext they were a present for me. They bloody weren't. They
were for her. I would be presented with things that were clearly not in my size
or not my style and we would then have to endure the Oscar-winning performance in which her bottom lip would droop, she'd say, 'Oh, what a shame,'
pause, pick it up, look at the label and say, 'I wonder if it'll fit me? Shall I try
it on?' Every. Single. Time. The woman was an evil genius.

7 *herself

£10. The Europeans regard comics as ART and treat them accordingly with respect.[8] *Will spend the rest of the week around Verona and the Veneto.*

Take care of yourself on that Vespa. Italy is full of them and watching the antics of the traffic makes me very nervous for you. Be careful. Love you very, very much. I know you think I'm an annoying old bat.[9] *Mum xxxxxxxx*

★ ★ ★

8 Brenda absolutely loved comics and graphic novels. I can credit her with introducing me to them, and if you've never given graphic novels a go – do! They're wonderful.

9 Another small moment of self-assessment that fills me with sadness. My mother and I, really, got on like a house on fire and it's hard, sometimes, to remember that. Truth is, she WAS an annoying old bat but she didn't want to be. The sadness was she couldn't do anything about it. My entire adult life with her was a constant juggling act, depending on which version of Brenda was turning up on any given day.

Four

My mother would have liked, I think, to be famous. She had aspirations to act. She was certainly beautiful enough and would often tell me, with great pride, of the time she played Ophelia when she was at Nottingham. 'Judi Dench and Ian McKellen came to see us,' she would tell me, misty eyed, as if that, in and of itself, was a passport straight to the Oscars.

Whether or not she would have been any good is another matter. I only saw my mother perform as the shining star in her own dramas. She was a lone wolf in everything she ever did. Acting is a process of collaboration, patience and taking instructions. I'm struggling to think of a single occasion where my mother either listened to advice or acted on it – Brenda was the Queen of her own Kingdom and woe betide anyone who took a shot at the crown. She'd have been a bloody nightmare on set and I'm saying that with nothing but love.

Of course, she did achieve a fame, of sorts, when my second book, *The Tent, the Bucket and Me*, the story of our disastrous attempts to go on holiday, became a surprise bestseller. She would go and stand next to it in the local Waterstones and wait for someone to pick it up.

'I'm Brenda, from *The Tent, the Bucket and Me*,' she would tell strangers, pointing at it with a gentile beam. 'Would you like me to sign it?'

In many ways, Brenda was built to be famous. She should have been, she had the grandeur for it, once met, never forgotten, but she also would have been the household name embroiled in every hoohah going. She'd have offended everyone, behaved disgracefully, shocked the shires to their core. I thank God she was never on Twitter. Part of me wonders if she would have loved all that, but, for all her bravado, Brenda cared deeply about how she was perceived.

She was a strange contradiction: outwardly, she had the confidence of giants but inwardly, she had small, painful hang ups that lingered round her core like barnacles. She could have been an actress. She could have been a writer. She could have been a film director. All these things she could have been, would *liked* to have been, but was born in the wrong place, at the wrong time, to the wrong parents. She wasn't rich enough, didn't quite mix in the right circles. Like so many women of her generation, her hopes and dreams would be scaled back to more realistic expectations. All there was to look forward to, if you were a young girl in the fifties, was the hope that you might marry well. Serious careers were a pipe dream and even if you did manage to find yourself on a path to success, you'd be expected to pack it all in the moment you had children. Women's lives were not their own. They were vessels for their husbands, the carers of children. Women were not to be taken seriously. They didn't matter.

Brenda was from a broken home and lived on a council estate with her Irish mother and sister. Her future, then, was never set to be extraordinary. All Brenda knew, at this point, was that she yearned for something more. Something better. So, what was she going to do with her life?

In the summer of 1961, my mother stood staring down at her A level results. They were not as good as she had hoped, and all dreams she might have had of going to university were dashed there and then. There were tears, shouting and the slamming of doors. Brenda was crushed but, summoning up every scrap of the Becky Sharp within, she pulled herself up and got into a teaching training college in Nottingham instead. If she couldn't get herself into university, she decided, she would become a teacher.

In many ways, for the girl who liked bossing other children about and being in charge, it was the perfect career choice.

She would get to be the star of the show in each and every lesson; she would be looked up to, respected, adored, but beyond that, she would ensure that kids from backgrounds like hers would be instilled with a belief of their own worth. Brenda had a mission.

Meanwhile, back at home, with Brenda shipped off to college, Elizabeth and Phyllis were heaving a sigh of relief. Oh, things were calmer, nicer, more convivial with the 'mad sister' off and away. They began to go on modest holidays down to Hastings and Eastbourne. They'd sit on the beach, stand in the sea, eat fish and chips and Elizabeth would go to the bingo, a small indulgence. The weight was off.

It's a feeling I recognise. There was a burning intensity to Brenda, a danger to her, as if she could go off at any moment. When she died, the first thing I felt was relief. It was over: the endless anxiety of what mood she might be in on any given day, the worry that the wrong word here or there would be the match that lit the fuse, not doing something precisely how she wanted it, not being quick enough for her liking, simply not doing as we were told. She controlled every minute of her own and our days, so much so that I look back at those years and wonder why we, and especially my father, put up with it.

These are questions I keep returning to: why was she worth it? Why were we so in thrall to her? The answer to both, I suppose, is the Good Brenda, the woman who could make you laugh like no other, who had the capacity to be generous and kind, who was engaging and fun, witty, brilliant and bright, was intoxicating. She was one of the most charismatic individuals I've ever met – but there was also a sense she had no control over her bad behaviour. That was a realisation that would take me the best part of thirty years to get to.

People didn't discuss mental health openly until very recently. Anyone who was sent to a psychiatrist was treated with suspicion: it was something to be ashamed of. Here was my mother with a chance to finally make something of her life: a proper career was now within reach, unimaginable for the little girl who had sat in her bedroom writing letters to James Dean. Being held back by the stigma of mental health was clearly a choice she was never going to make, especially given the attitude towards women who presented as remotely mad or sad. Women suffering from nervous breakdowns were sent to institutions where they could expect to be drugged, force fed or lobotomised. Women, until very recently, were expected to be compliant, to observe feminine norms. In Sylvia Plath's *The Bell Jar* (one of Brenda's favourite books), educated women were sexless and abnormal. If you were a clever and creative girl and sexually motivated, society would treat you with nothing but suspicion.

It's a tragedy, really.

I have lost count of all the times I watched Mum spiral out of control. It was like a switch being flicked, nought to a hundred in seconds, her face etched with hatred, the cold, calculating cruelties, throwing a wooden ship my father had made her into the fire, ruining special days, enjoying embarrassments heaped upon me, the dark look in her eye hell-bent on some sort of revenge nobody else could possibly understand, the lack of reason, the inability to simply stop. My diary of 1982 is sprinkled with the listing of bad days: on one occasion, she has torn my English homework from my book and burned it, on another someone has gifted me a book on confidence, I've looked at it, come home and told her something that sent her into a rage. I don't know what. My fifteen-year-old self decided it was too dangerous to be left in a diary and the words are blackened out. Sometimes, Mum would take a carving knife and lock herself in the bathroom. I would stand at the door, quietly asking her to come out, begging her not to hurt herself. A child shouldn't have to provide mental health crisis support but that's what I did, constantly.

It seems inconceivable now that someone suffering to this extent would not be offered help, but she received none. For Brenda, this was her normal. When you don't know anything different, it's astonishing what you will accept. Missed opportunity was heaped upon missed opportunity. Neither my father nor I dared to suggest she was seriously mentally unwell: there was no point when she was in the thick of it and when she was out of it, you didn't want to risk repercussions. The endless cycle of whether Brenda was in a good mood today rumbled on, like a slow-moving tank creaking over a minefield.

I don't know much about her time in Nottingham. She batted questions about it away, but this was because she had lied about it. For years, she told people she had been to Nottingham University. She would carefully refer to 'Nottingham', add nothing else, and allow assumptions to settle in. She would confess to me, when I was in my mid-twenties, that she hadn't been to university at all. It was one of the very few occasions I can recall her expressing a sense of embarrassment or admitting to something she found shameful.

That to one side, it was still a source of great family pride that Brenda got into teaching training college. She was the first in her family to go into further education. It was here that she met Michael, a man of whom I know very little other than he asked my mother to marry him, and she said yes. She kept a photo of him throughout her life and we would take great delight in pointing at his terrible teeth and specs and teasing her that she could have married him instead of the phenomenal physical specimen that was my father. She'd always look a little sad when we pulled her leg about him and would tell us to stop and that he was lovely. I think she kept a small corner of remorse for Michael, not because she called off their engagement, but because of how she did it.

Which brings us to Tony.

PRAGUE[1]

Dear Emmy

Here we are in Prague and it's wonderful. Only one word for our apartment – magnificent! It is on the third floor of a 5 storey turn of the C19 block with decorative original features and highly polished parquet floors throughout. It's huge, a bit of a palace – you enter the large hall and double doors open up to more double doors and on it goes. It's my ideal apartment – I might stay here. The furniture is Czech art nouveau – beds, lamps, wardrobes, cupboards etc. We love it!

The flight wasn't too good.[2] We had too many incidents. Delayed for the best part of an hour – we were stuck on the runway with other planes passing us constantly – very close and very loud. I felt like ordering two gin and tonics straight away. There was a problem with traffic control somewhere in Germany and the pilot did not want to take us back to the terminal – we would have lost our flight slot!

We got our usual seats by the Emergency Exit[3] and our steward, sitting facing us, had a lovely little chat with me about my flying phobia. My neighbour in the aisle seat was a pharmacist on the way to a convention and we had such an

1 This letter already feels like a gritty epic starring Kate Winslet that will surely win her another Oscar.

2 My mother had an inbuilt fear of flying. I think this was only the second time she'd been on a plane, hence her nervousness and astonishment that other planes might be a bit close and loud . . .

3 But of course. If that plane's going down, Brenda has every intention of being the first person leaping off it.

interesting discussion for much of the flight that the steward
thought he was my husband.[4] Tony, as usual, just stared out
the window.[5]

Everything went okay until we came to land. The steward
had returned to sit on her seat and then we felt the first
bounce followed by a second bounce, a bump on the left
followed by an uncomfortable heavy bump to the right. I
looked at the steward – she was scared. The bumps were
followed by a prolonged rocking movement. Tony and I looked
at each other. We didn't speak. The steward's face held a fixed
stare. God, I thought, will she be calm enough to open the
Emergency Exit? Tony might have to do it.[6] The rocking
continued.

I just started talking maniacally about nothing in particu-
lar.[7] No point screaming. Suddenly there was a thump and
the steward's face relaxed.

'We're down' she said. 'He landed on one wheel' She couldn't
hide her relief and she turned to me and said 'You were
marvellous. Wait there.'

After that landing I wasn't intending on spending any
unnecessary time in the plane, but the steward quickly

---

4 My mother's superpower was to be able to find out every last thing about
any stranger within ten feet of her.

5 Two things: one – Tony did not share my mother's obsession with strangers
and would mostly sit, stare and smile whenever dragged into any conversation
with one, and two, he was flat out, eye boggled astonished by anything you
could see from a plane window. He'd sit down, press himself as close to the
window as was physically possible and not move for however many hours the
flight was. No wonder Brenda had to talk to people she'd never met before.
She was bored stiff. Woe betide you, if you bored Brenda. That was as
dangerous a caper as sticking rattlesnakes down your pants.

6 I give Brenda credit here for not insisting Tony do precisely that, there and
then.

7 Yes. This absolutely would have happened. She probably launched into a
fulsome treatise on the lot of supressed women worldwide. That or a good
moan about Margaret Thatcher.

returned with two BA carrier bags. Inside were six bottles of champagne!

'Why?' I gasped.

'For being so brave!' she said. And she gave me a hug.[8]

This was a real adventure. It was our first visit to Eastern Europe, to a previously Communist country – the Velvet Revolution having brought the end of a repressive regime.

As we were travelling independently, – we only had each other to rely on – so Tony's innate talent for learning languages had been put to use five months earlier when he started to learn Czech. He had made his own vocabulary book and without the help of tapes had carefully studied pronunciation notes. He first learned how to say 'Two beers please. One large and one small'[9] *As ever he had at least 20 phrases to cover all emergencies . . .*

'Nerozumin' – I don't understand!

'Mluvite Anglicky' Do you speak English?

'Kolik to stovi' How much is it?

'Jenom se divam' I am just looking . . .

And

'Pochazim z Wales' I am from Wales.[10] *Etc etc*

Can't fail.

Do try it for yourself! I think Emmy, you'd agree Czech is bloody difficult. Your Dad's a clever one.

We gave all the bottles of champagne to the owner, Marie, who let us into the apartment. Her husband was a paediatric

---

8 This doesn't surprise me in the slightest. Wherever she went, whoever she met, she could, if she wanted to, charm the pants off anyone she'd never met before.

9 Always make sure you have the essentials covered first . . .

10 My mother, convinced that everyone hates the English, would always nudge my father in the ribs while urging him to 'tell them you're Welsh', as if that was the passport to any number of red carpets. SHE WAS CORRECT.

consultant earning the equivalent of £200 a month.[11] *By renting out their home and staying with neighbours, they turned a profit.*

Marie had organised a few provisions for us, bread, milk and eggs and we paid her over the true cost which was unexpectedly low. A few extra Krowns made little difference. We had to make sure we spent all our Czech currency, we couldn't take it home. She didn't want to take the money saying that the champagne was payment enough, but we insisted. We hoped that she'd sell the champagne – it might have been worth six months of her husband's pay.

Marie showed us where the local food shop was in our street – Rybna – and we decided to make this our first adventure.[12] *Tony had his phrases and we only needed water and cheese for now. We'd eat out later.*

Everything about the supermarket was unexpected. It was like Harrods food hall! Counters were filled with quality foods – hams, sausages, about 30 types of bread and the cheese section was better than anything that Waitrose could offer. We were so surprised to see French and Italian products. The alcohol section had so many different kinds of beers and wines including French wines that we wondered

11 This reminds me of the time I went to Moscow and Leningrad on a school trip in 1984. We'd asked our history teacher to take us somewhere and he refused, then added, 'The only place I'll take you is Russia and that's never going to happen.' Challenge accepted. It did happen, and he was forced to take us. His wife, the school librarian, warned us to bring torches because 'there is no electricity in Russia'. She also told me not to wear anything 'weird, like thigh boots'. There was electricity. His wife broke her arm clattering down a grand staircase in Leningrad, and we stood watching our guide (we weren't allowed anywhere without her) weeping because we'd given her a packet of ten tights as a thank you. It turned out one pair of tights would have cost her more than a month's wages.

12 My parents have been dogged throughout their lives by episodes in foreign countries where they want the food but cannot persuade the native shopkeeper to part with it.

how the poor Czechs could afford the luxury of it all. That was before we saw the prices. For us, the prices were very cheap for the Czechs on £200 a month, everything was still cheap.

This was Tony's big moment – would they understand his Czech? He started off well. He said, 'Good afternoon, I would like that cheese.' And he pointed to two cheeses. The assistant, a woman in her fifties, wearing a short-sleeved tunic which revealed forearms like a night club bouncer, started shouting at Tony in Czech. Tony responded graciously.

'Nemluvin Cesky' (I do not speak Czech)

The woman continued to shout – forearms raised ominously in a gesture difficult to translate.

'Nemluvin Cesky' Tony repeated and frantically pointed to the cheeses we wanted, one at a time, slowly, first this one and then that one shouting 'CYR' – cheese in Czech but politely followed by 'Prosim' (Please)[13] More shouting from forearms now. She was also showing a substantial fist and swinging her arm. Oh dear. Poor Tony. He had spent five months working on this difficult language.

'Nerozumin' (I don't understand), he tried.

The forearms were now thrashing the air and the assistant shifted her weight towards Tony intimidatingly. Should I intervene?[14] I couldn't. I hadn't learned the bloody language!

But I decided to try English.[15]

'He'd like those two cheeses please. I mean Prosim. Prosim.

13 And we're off . . .

14 Oh, I do hope so.

15 Of course she did. My mother, for all her embracing of continental life-styles and cultures, was still more than capable of being the English woman abroad, shouting loudly in English in the hope that the louder she was, the greater the chance of being understood.

Those two cheeses there, that's right there and there.' I was leaning over the counter now and pointing. 'Prosim, Prosim'

In desperation now, Tony suddenly exclaimed loudly –

'Pochazim z Wales'[16] (I am from Wales) and 'Mluvite Anglicky' (Do you speak English?) Highly unlikely.

The woman was flummoxed. Did she understand anything that Tony said in Czech?[17] If she did, she almost certainly hadn't heard of Wales.[18] What was to be done? I knew he should have got the Czech tapes. His pronunciation must be crap.[19]

While the situation worsened, a number of people had formed a queue. No one uttered a word. They were expressionless and waited patiently. Something Communism had done no doubt. No one complained.

We looked at each other and made one last stand.

'What's the bloody word for cheese?' I yelled.

'. . . Cyr'

Together now . . . 'CYR. PROSIM' Both of us pointing.

The forearms dropped and she shook her head.

We were about to walk away when a small voice spoke in English from the back of the queue.

'She wants to know if you want white or blue cheese?'

We couldn't stop laughing. Turning and calling to the back of the queue, Tony said, 'Could you tell her we do not want blue cheese. Thank you.'

The message in Czech was passed to Forearms. Instant transformation. Forearms now smiling broadly and laughing now. Everyone was laughing.

'Prosim' said Tony smiling.

---

16 I rather like that this was their moment of last resort. If the woman knew he was Welsh, she would surely give him the cheese?

17 Clearly not, no.

18 The ultimate outrage . . . How very dare she.

19 Brenda's Golden Rule For Life: if in doubt, blame Tony.

'Prosim' *I said, as she handed me the two cheeses.*

'Nashledanov!' *(Goodbye) said Tony, preening slightly and waving at the queue.*

'Nashledanov!' *they called back, all smiling broadly.*

Laughing all the way to the street we went back to the apartment with the cheeses and then hurried out to experience Prague's stunning sights.

So – we were in a fabulous city and had a magnificent apartment but one day as we walked along our street, Rybna, we noticed water gushing into the road.[20] We hardly glanced at it, our attention taken by the violin shop and its beautiful musical instruments.[21]

The next morning, we couldn't flush the toilet. Nothing after about 12 attempts. We had to leave it and came back to the apartment about 4pm – the stench was dreadful.[22] We tried flushing again – there wasn't any water. We rang Marie, the owner. She rang back. There was no water in Rybna – a water tank would be there soon. We would find two buckets in the kitchen cupboard. Two buckets!

I looked out of the window as I'd heard a loud grating noise. It was the water tank being put into position. It was nearly the length of the street. People were already crowding round it and were filling buckets and assorted containers with water.

'Quick Tony, get the buckets! There won't be any water left!'
'What?' *He didn't understand.*

'Look!' *I pointed down the street. By now about 20 people were queuing for water. It was a scene from WW2!*

---

20 Here we go. If you've been thinking 'Where are the disasters?' LOOK NO MORE. BUCKLE UP.

21 For the avoidance of doubt, neither of my parents can play the violin. My father once pretended he could play a balalaika. He couldn't.

22 I expect you're all now thinking about my parents' poos and I can't apologise enough.

'Oh, bloody hell,' he said, taking in the drama.

We[23] fetched the buckets. Then it hit us. We were on the 3rd floor. There was no lift. Tony was going to have to carry two heavy buckets of water up four flights of stairs. I've got a bad back and couldn't carry anything.[24] Aaagh. Disaster!

I watched from the window as Tony queued to get his share of water. The scene looked like something out of Germany Year Zero – blitzed Berlin. Were they going to let a Welsh guy have any water? I was ready to go down and do battle – but wait – Tony is speaking to them. Probably saying I come from Wales.[25] Would that make it okay?

No-one was offering to carry his buckets.

Up he came, slowly, struggling. I was out on the landing now shouting instructions.

'Okay. Rest now. Put the buckets down. Take a breath.'[26] He was having to rest at the top of each flight of stairs. This would kill him. I couldn't allow it.[27]

We had enough water from the two buckets to flush an increasingly unpleasant toilet.[28]

'Get two more' I said, 'and that's it.[29] I'm going across to the hotel to find out what's happening.'[30]

---

23 *Tony

24 Total lie. Absolutely zero wrong with her back.

25 We can only hope.

26 Pausing for a moment to imagine quite how annoying that must have been. *Fist bumps Tony*

27 Well, no, because Brenda isn't Welsh and who knows what she'd have to endure without that ticket to the Fast Lane.

28 Too. Much. Information.

29 Please note: she's just stood at the top of the stairs, yelling at him to rest and, without a spit into the wind, she's dispatched him back to the hell-mouth from whence he came.

30 Brenda is on manoeuvres. Brace. Brace. Brace.

The hotel opposite had staff who spoke English and we'd already been over there for some advice. I asked them when the water supply would be re-connected. No idea.

Tomorrow? They shook their heads. Thursday? Still shaking heads. Who could I contact? The police? Stunned silence.

'Don't go to the police' I was told in a very firm manner.

'Why not? They'd know what to do'[31] I was starting to pick up their vibes. Fear.

'It wouldn't be a good idea'

'But why not?' I was getting a bit impatient.

'Because they speak Russian.' The receptionist's face was very serious.

'Russian?' I said incredulously. But the Russians had been kicked out. What did that mean?[32]

I went back to the apartment. Tony had placed the two buckets of water in the kitchen.

They had to be kept for the next morning's ablutions.[33]

'Right. No luck with the hotel. We've got to find an American restaurant.' I said.

'Why American?' said Tony.

'Because the Americans always know what to do. Come on.'[34] And I grabbed my bag.

Prague was inundated with Americans now. The FBI, CIA,

---

31 Really? I'd have thought a plumber or a man who works on drains might be a better bet but OK, Brenda. Police it is.

32 The mystery is afoot. You can only imagine how happy this will have made her.

33 I DON'T WANT TO READ A SINGLE OTHER THING ABOUT MY PARENTS DOING POOS.

34 Again, REALLY? She now thinks a waiter/chef working in an American restaurant is going to know how to deal with a burst main?

Special agents this and that. They had poured in after the Velvet Revolution.[35]

We knew there was a likely place a few streets away as we had only passed it yesterday. I thought I could find it. Within five minutes we had a table and I had my first Manhattan of the night in my hand. I was going to need a few more.

We were halfway through our dessert when I noticed two American women heading for the Ladies.

'Right,' I said getting up and following them. 'I'll be back soon,' I shouted to Tony.[36]

The two women were adjusting their make up in front of mirrors as I came in.

'Could you help me?' I asked, smiling. They turned round. 'Do you live in Prague?' They nodded. 'We have a problem in Rybna. We don't have any water and I'm sure you can appreciate the problems we're having with personal hygiene.[37] *You don't happen to know any officials – or the Mayor of Prague – who could get the job fixed quickly?'*

The women were both tall and paper thin in their 50s, well-groomed and well-dressed. They obviously had tea with the Mayor every now and then.

They were a bit taken aback.[38]

'We've got problems with our faucet tap. It happens.' One said, disinterested.[39]

In my old schoolmarm firm voice, I replied. 'No, this isn't a

---

35 Do I need to say a word? No, I don't.

36 I really, really, really, really hope she was drunk.

37 I'm amazed she didn't draw a picture of her poo and show it to them at this point.

38 You do surprise me.

39 SHE'S BEEN CORNERED BY A WOMAN IN A TOILET TALKING ABOUT HER DIRTY HYGIENE. SHE CLEARLY THINKS YOU ARE MAD.

faucet. It's a whole street without water to wash in and no one can flush their toilets. We've got a water tank but we can't put up with it for longer than 24 hours.'

'Where did you say?' The other woman was more attentive.

'Rybna. I've been over to one of the hotels but the staff didn't want to complain – something about the police being Russian.'

The first woman looked interested now.

'As you can tell, I'm English and my husband and I don't speak Czech[40] and we're on holiday so it's a bit hard for us to deal with a problem like this when you can't get hold of the Public Health Inspector.'

They smiled.

Taking that as a good sign, I continued. 'If you could pass this on so that we could get it fixed in 24 hours or if you could tell me where the British embassy is, I could go there.'

They hadn't moved. I could tell they were gob smacked.[41] Who did she think she was trying to get a mains water supply reconnected when they had a water tank. They looked at each other but they didn't offer any help.

'In Prague in a situation like this the water tank might be supplied for a month.' Said one with a small snarl of satisfaction.

'Oh well,' I said, 'I think I'll have to ring the Guardian *newspaper get them to send over a journalist because there's going to be a cholera outbreak in Prague,' I smiled.[42]*

They gave me a hard look. Neither of them moved.

---

40 If anything, I am bitterly disappointed she didn't tell them Tony was Welsh.

41 And probably trying to work out if you were about to stab them.

42 Amazing scenes. Can you imagine? 'Hello, *Guardian* news desk.' 'Send your finest reporter, preferably Polly Toynbee, I like her.' 'Sorry? What's happened.' 'There is going to be a cholera outbreak in Prague. I need a poo and my husband is Welsh.' SCENE ENDS.

After a few seconds. 'Rybna, OK, we've got it.' Said one.[43]

'Thanks for your help. Bye.' And I left.

Seated at the table again with Tony I told him all.

'I think they got the message,' I said.

'Who were they?' he asked.

'Embassy staff, I hope!'

We walked back home – the water was still gushing into the road from the water pipe.

I went over to the hotel again and made a final plea for action.

'It would be great if it was fixed tomorrow' was my parting shot.

At about 6am a loud, grinding noise could be heard in the street. Not another water tank? More grinding. I got up. A JCB was tearing up the road.

'They're fixing it!' I was delighted. Who did it? The hotel? The Americans?

I went over to the hotel after breakfast.

'I'd just like to thank you for sorting out the water.' I said.

'Oh, just a minute Madam,' said the receptionist. 'Wait there.'

I stood by the desk. Three people came out. One stepped forward, the manager, I presumed.

'We have to thank YOU Madam. The water will be okay by 4pm today.' He shook my hand and the other two smiled broadly.

Now we knew that we had a flushing loo, we were fine.[44]

We were really in love with Prague – it is an artist's dream city. Seeing Mucha's[45] *sublime Cathedral windows was a high point but at every turn you are experiencing some of the very*

---

43 The classic Play Along With the KooKoo Lady and Maybe She'll Go Away move. We've all done it.

44 'Let's have a poo to celebrate, Tony!'

45 Alphonse Mucha – Czech painter best known for his portraits of Sarah Bernhardt and his gorgeous commercial art posters. His stained-glass windows in the Saint Vitus Cathedral are exceptional.

best Art Nouveau, Cubist and Modernist architecture, houses with beautifully illustrated and sculpted facades and for me the magical fairy tale towers. Another real treat for me was the number of second-hand bookshops where I bought many treasures for your inheritance.[46]

One of the funniest things we saw in Prague was a banner advertising a second hand book sale but the English read 'Sale of Dusted off Books'

Hope the flight home is better. Oh! Oh! Oh!
Love and kisses
Mum and dad[47]

★ ★ ★

46 All worthless and in Czech.

47 I think this may be the greatest letter she ever wrote. Bravo, Brenda. Bravo.

Five

I have written elsewhere about the moment my father met my mother but you're going to have to bear with me. It needs to be repeated.

Tony had been working as an art teacher in a comprehensive in Shefford, in Central Bedfordshire. It was the morning break, and he was sitting, coffee in hand, chatting to his good mate Mike, the PE teacher. My father was a very good rugby player, looked fit and was possessed with a pair of twinkling blue eyes and a smile that could melt mountains. He had a mop of curly brown hair and an expression that was nothing but mischief. He'd just taken a bite of a biscuit, a no-nonsense digestive, when in walked Brenda.

'Everything stopped,' he told me. 'It was all hello, hello, hello. Who's this?'

My mother, we have established, was drop dead gorgeous. 'She looked a bit Spanish,' said Tony, but he wasn't going to muck about. This was serious. 'I turned to Mike and said, she's mine.'

In fact, they had an arrangement. They took it in turns to have a crack at any new female teacher who walked through the door. They were mates and enjoying quite the high old time in a house share in the village of Broom. As luck would have it, it was Dad's turn, and the charm offensive began.

'I found out she was engaged,' Tony told me.

'Didn't it put you off?'

'No.'

Brenda had met her fiancé, Michael, in Nottingham, as I've already said. Phyllis recalls him precisely: 'He was tall and had dark hair and glasses and every time he opened his mouth, his gums were bleeding.'

Michael did nothing to enamour himself to his fiancée's family. Whenever he came to visit, he would say very little except sit and stare. 'He was creepy. I have no idea what she saw in him,' Phyllis adds. But see something in him, she did. They were together for the best part of five years. He was clever, which Brenda always adored, but perhaps the most important attribute Michael possessed was that she was able to boss him about.

'I mean, he would say nothing. Absolutely nothing. You'd stand there, waiting for a conversation to dribble out of him but no. It was just standing and staring and waiting to be told what to do by Brenda.'

The horror for thirteen-year-old Phyllis was about to intensify. With Elizabeth recovering from a mastectomy (she had been diagnosed with breast cancer), Brenda was ordered by their mother to take her little sister away on the holiday to Cornwall she had planned with Michael. There were protests, naturally, but with Elizabeth in desperate need of a rest, Brenda did the honourable thing.

'She didn't want me there,' recalls Phyllis. 'But then, who would? Off for a romantic week and, "by the way, we're sharing the tent with my little sister".'

Michael had a car, a battered old Ford Anglia. 'If you looked down at the floor,' remembers Phyllis, 'you could see the road. I'm not even sure he'd passed his driving test.'

They headed to Bude and pitched their tent on the beach for no other reason than they couldn't afford the fees at the nearby campsite. Phyllis recalls: 'It was so small you had to get on your knees to get into it. I was in one sleeping bag and they were in the other. It was horrendous. I'd have to put up with all the huffing and puffing and was regularly dispatched on errands which were clearly thinly veiled attempts to get me out of the way so they could have sex. Every morning, at dawn, we'd have to take the tent down because it wasn't allowed and every night, I'd lie awake terrified about the tide coming in. We had no toilet. "Just use the beach!" Brenda yelled at me as if it was totally normal to do a poo in front of a promenade. And we had no money for food. I'd spend the days searching hedgerows for berries. "Go and find berries!" Brenda told me like I was an extra in *Tess of the D'Urbervilles*. At one point I was so hungry, I took to scavenging through bins. I did quite well. I found a bag of crisps. I was constipated for a fortnight. I never went camping again.'

Curiously, Brenda didn't tell her mother or sister she was engaged. Instead, she brought home another man, Tony, to meet them. Tony made an instant impression. He was open and affable and made Elizabeth laugh. He brought her a sack of coal and another of onions. She also liked the fact he was Welsh. For years, when asked if she was Irish, she'd reply, 'No, I'm Welsh,' in her Irish accent, as if that would serve as a convenient and cunning disguise as to her true origins.

My father held no fear of the man to whom Brenda was engaged. When I asked him whether he was remotely mindful of the fact the exotic-looking creature who had walked into the staff room had an engagement ring on her finger, he looked at me as if I was mad for even thinking it.

My father had, of course, already been engaged himself, to a girl called Ursula from the Rhondda valley. That had come to a grinding halt when Ursula took it upon herself to start an affair with a man on the back seat of a coach to Cardiff. 'I think she was fed up I wasn't having sex with her,' said Dad, rather wistfully.

No such worries of that not happening with Brenda.

Brenda, it turned out, was sex mad.

It didn't take long for my parents to get cracking. Tony had asked Brenda to go to the pub with him for a few drinks and the few drinks had led to a snog which led to Dad driving his Ford Consul Mark 1 down a dirt track into a field. There they were, banging away like billy-o, when the farmer casually strolled up, had a good look and strolled off again. Unbeknown to my father, he dragged a large log across the entrance to the field which, when Tony reversed out, took his exhaust box off.

'Was there . . .' I wondered, idly, 'any resistance from Brenda? I mean, she was engaged.'

'Don't be ridiculous.'

Their affair settled in and Monday to Thursday, Brenda was all his, but come Friday, Michael would appear in his knackered Ford Anglia and pick her up at the end of school and drive her off to wherever he was living in Cambridgeshire for the weekend. He would deliver her back on a Monday morning. Occasionally, the two suitors would exchange sharp glances in the car park. 'I could have had him in a fight,' Tony recalls, with some confidence. 'He had terrible teeth.'

This isn't the first time my mother would be juggling two lovers throughout her illustrious career so I suppose we could consider this as the moment she realised it was perfectly acceptable to be committed to one person and have it away with another. By Christmas of that first term, though, Dad had decided it was probably time for her to make a choice, and choose she did. She sacked off Michael and sent a note to my father in Wales telling him to come and see her in Basingstoke.

'Did she want to tell you she'd called off her engagement?' I asked, wondering if my parents were a bit like an episode of *Bridgerton*.

'No,' he replied. 'She just wanted sex.'

And there it is.

They decided to get married when Tony got a new job in Uppingham, outside Corby. He told Brenda he was leaving whereupon she mustered a wistful gaze and decided she might try and get a job nearby. So, she did, and that August, before they upped sticks to Northamptonshire, they travelled to Treorchy in Wales to exchange vows. Of course, there was a small Brenda-shaped hitch when my mother, the modern woman all for freedom and female emancipation (despite being engaged twice in short succession), decided that perhaps, having seen the vicar, she didn't want to get married at all. She waited until they were in the car driving back to my grandmother's house to tell Tony this. A friend of his, Margaret, was sitting in the back.

'Oh good,' Margaret said. 'If you don't marry Tony, I will.'

My mother narrowed her eyes and the next day, just to make sure she got one over on Margaret, turned up. All the same, she refused to cut the wedding cake.

'My family all thought she was bonkers,' recalled Tony, shaking his head. Well. Yes.

They spent their wedding night in a hotel opposite Cardiff Castle where their attempts at marital bliss were accompanied, for hours on end, by the dulcet honks of a brass band. With no money between them, there was to be no honeymoon holiday. Instead, they set off for Corby, with a tent, where they lived in a field until they got a council house. I was conceived in that tent.

My mother had only been working for a year so to discover she was pregnant, weeks later, was somewhat annoying. 'Oh, she was definitely pissed off,' Tony remembered. 'I found her once, in the bath, crying that she didn't want you. I told her she did. I think she was just frustrated that having worked so hard to get to where she was, here she was having to be back at home and doing nothing. It was quite different in those days. Having a baby often meant that was it, you were done.'

I get it. In 1967, when I was born, we were forty years away from the notion that women might be able to 'have it all'. Back then, you got pregnant and, that was the end of that. You became a housewife and, if you were lucky, when your kids were in proper school, you might be able to get a nice part-time job somewhere. It was hardly the stuff of dreams for an ambitious young woman.

My mother then, wasn't happily pregnant and Tony recalls the time when, coming back from work and walking across the square of their council estate, she opened an upstairs window, yelled, 'Get me a fucking chop,' and slammed it shut again. Shouting at people from windows again, I thought. She was like something out of a cautionary tale for children.

There was other, more final trouble back at home. Elizabeth was dying. My mother was seven months pregnant when she got the call from her sister that Elizabeth's condition had worsened. Phyllis, still a teenager, had been valiantly caring for her mother all by herself. There would be the occasional visit from Aunty Gerty, but the lion-share of caring fell to the sixteen-year-old. She had left school and got a job in an estate agent's and every day she would travel home on the bus to give her mother lunch but now, Phyllis needed help. So, she called for her sister.

Brenda, heavily pregnant, wasn't much help. She was able to do a bit of shopping, but she didn't cook and wasn't easily given to chores. In any event, she wasn't needed for long. A few days after arriving, Phyllis came into Brenda's bedroom and told her their mother had wet herself. Brenda got up and they set about trying to change the bed but as they were pulling off the sheets, Phyllis realised Elizabeth had stopped breathing. 'It was traumatic,' Phyllis told me. She had died.

As they cried, Brenda told Phyllis to run to a family who had a phone so she could call the doctor, and then to run on to Aunty Gerty, who lived not far away. Phyllis did as she was told and, after calling the doctor, arrived panting at her aunt's house where she found her having breakfast, with her husband, Leslie. 'Can't you let her finish her tea?' he snapped at his niece as she stood, crying, in the doorway. It was a cruelty she would never forget.

Phyllis took to her bed, clearly in a state of shock, while Brenda oversaw the arrangements for their mother's funeral. Phyllis was in such a mess, Brenda told her not to go to the funeral and she was left alone, lying in bed. The other matter Brenda was supposed to deal with was telling their father but with her usual defiance, she decided not to. She blamed him for everything bad that ever happened to her mother. He didn't deserve to know. Bob would find out three weeks later when he arrived at the employment office with his marital support cheque. 'You don't need to send that any more,' he was informed by the clerk. 'She's dead.'

Bob, to his credit, jumped on a train immediately and went to find Phyllis who was now back at work. When he arrived, she was out on her lunch break. He told her boss he was her father, which came as a surprise because everyone at Phyllis's work thought he was dead. Like Brenda, she'd told everyone their father had died of malaria.

Brenda didn't know what to do about Phyllis. She was sixteen, too young for a council house and too old to go into care. Phyllis was adamant she didn't want to move to Corby to live with Brenda, but Leslie wouldn't let Gerty take her in. A school friend's mother said no when she asked if she could live with them. Instead, she stayed in her mother's council house for as long as possible but within weeks, she was sitting on the front step watching as her mother's furniture was sold off. Brenda and Gerty argued over a stair carpet. It was all rather grim.

Help did arrive. Another friend's family took pity on her and she moved in with them. With Phyllis sorted, Brenda returned to Corby. In shock and grieving, Brenda now had to cope with the arrival of me.

'It was bitter-sweet,' Tony told me. 'I was excited about you coming but Brenda was in a state, quite depressed really. Outwardly, she seemed to be getting on with things but every now and again I'd find her upstairs, sitting on the bed, crying. But the odd thing was, she didn't mention her mother. She'd brush it away if I asked. It was like she was switching something off.'

This internalising of her pain doesn't surprise me in the least. Brenda was never one for baring her soul or showing you her underbelly. An admission of despair was, for her, something she wouldn't and couldn't do. Brenda never wanted anybody to think her weak. It saddens me that she had created a hard shell for herself, that she felt unable to properly grieve the death of her mother. God knows, I told anyone within two feet of me how sad I was for the best part of a year. I think at one point I even told the bin men. Perhaps this was how she protected herself. Brenda had, from a young age, learned self-preservation. She was doing what she needed to do.

My birth, a matter of weeks later, was pretty straight forward. After Brenda's waters broke, Tony drove her to the Natal Unit in Corby, where she was walked up and down a corridor for what felt like hours by a thickset midwife. The delivery wasn't complicated and out I popped as my dad, at the coal face, shouted, 'The colours, the colours!' My mother, from that moment, went into something of a decline. For the next four days, all she did was sleep and, unable to feed me, it fell to the nurses on the unit to get me through that first week. I was to have a more profound effect on Brenda than simply stalling her career – this was to be the beginning of a deep-set, post-natal depression.

Brenda was never quite the same again.

Dearest Emmy

Since we arrived in the Var region[1] on Friday the temperature has been 38–42 degrees. It is hotter here than Barbados. Everyone says this is unusual but we can do very little other than sit around. The air conditioning in the Fiesta is useless but we are managing as best we can. We haven't slept for three nights because the temperature was 24 degrees. Poor Tony has been bitten all over, but I used Pears Coal Tar Soap and the blighters left me alone.

The house is charming and in a lovely setting with wonderful views to the Var Hills. The owners are in their 80's and very sweet – Ed and Phyllis. Ed invented a type of X ray which is now commonplace. I had it done. Dye injected into the kidneys. He plays around with isotopes it seems. They have lived in France since the 1960's.

We had a very amusing journey by Eurostar with a family of five from Devon. They were on a day trip to Paris funded by Tesco vouchers! When I asked their mum how many vouchers it took to get a family of five to Paris, she mumbled a reply I didn't catch.[2] My calculation was at least 1000 vouchers. How many years had it taken? I never found out as I didn't ask her to repeat.

We arrived in Avignon on Friday and picked up the car.

---

1 The Var is a French department in the Provence-Alpes-Côte d'Azur region of south-east France. It's on the Mediterranean coast and is crammed with the more glamorous resort towns like Cannes and St Tropez.

2 It was probably 'Piss off and mind your own business.'

Tony had written the route[3] *and we set off. We were trying to get the air conditioning to work and failed. Then Tony pulled over near a culvert. I had opened the windows, the air conditioning was now blowing from the front and the route notes went out the window. As I tried to snatch them back a gust of wind blew the notes into the culvert and they floated down stream at speed.*

Instead of just leaving the bloody things, Tony risked life, broken back and drowning by jumping up onto one wall and straddling the other and then reaching down into the raging torrent to snatch his precious route. I was screaming 'Stop! Stop!' but he didn't listen.[4] *In triumph he put the soaking sheet in front of me. If I hadn't been terrified, I'd have taken a photo.*

We drove off and then the final twist of fate. After risking all, the notes flew out of the window when Tony switched on the air conditioning. I took all this as a bad omen. We'd only been on the road five minutes. Things didn't get any better. While we were having lunch, a fly dive bombed my Fish in Provencal sauce, landed, struggled to the edge of the plate and promptly drowned in sauce. After that, I relaxed. The third bit of bad luck had finished the curse on the start of our holiday.

We thought you would be very interested in a strange phenomenon of the region. There are a lot of Blanchet surnames in the area and I have noticed that quite a few women have those rather staring, poppy eyes. Maybe if she

3 My father's route planning is legendary. He will have spent hours poring over maps, staring at red lines, green lines, yellow lines working out the very best way to get from A to B. What is about to happen will have chilled him to his core.

4 There is absolutely no way, not a chance in hell, that Tony is letting his route notes get away.

speaks to you again,[5] you could ask her if she has relatives in Var.

Nature is just an enigma. Snails in the garden and the lane around have abandoned the boiling hot ground and rocks and have climbed in their hundreds up the trunks of the trees, are clustered on stalks, grasses and twigs. At a distance they look like a strange plant – on inspection small white snails cling to the surfaces. Never seen this anywhere before.

This morning we headed off for the Gorge de Verdon[6] – a spectacular sight. As we approached, it started to rain so we decided to go to Moustiers[7] for lunch. Thank God we did. For an hour and a half, torrential rain raged down the road. In that time, 6 inches of rain fell. We had parked the car outside the old town and were soaked getting back. We were just grateful we weren't on that narrow Corniche sublime in the gorge at the time.

Oh dear! What dramas![8] Will write again soon. Hope the filming continues to be thrilling.

Much love xxx

★ ★ ★

5 I had landed the part of Linda, the English teacher in *Notes on a Scandal*. I was filming all day every day for two weeks. Of course, they cut all the staff-room scenes so Brenda, beside herself at the cast and crew screening, got to see me on the big screen for the sum total of . . . thirty seconds. Ah well.

6 Cracking great canyon carved out by the Verdon river inside the Verdon Natural Regional Park.

7 Moustiers-Sainte-Marie to give it its full title. It's a very pretty village.

8 Which she is loving, of course . . .

Dearest Emmy

Since I last wrote the weather changed dramatically and we had four days of torrential rain and storms. It was an unearthly experience. On one day, the owner's gravel drive was physically raised and levitated onto his lawn. The raindrops were the size of Conran coffee cups. The force of the water was too great for a frail human body to stand. Umbrellas bore the affront as best they could and after fifteen minutes collapsed like pancakes.

The rain didn't stop for 24 hours. We tried to leave the house but torrents of water made it impossible to see the drive. This resulted in our being trapped in a house which was never intended for anything other than a minimum temperature of 30 degrees. The comfort level inside had never been a priority as life was to be lived outside. On one night, the thunder and lightning went on from about 6pm on Wednesday to 10.30am Thursday. We had reached physical and mental breakdown and Tony wrapped a blanket round him and had the shakes.[1] Sadly, as we couldn't leave the house, we had run out of any good alcohol and all I could offer as sustenance was a couple of Aspro Clears. There wasn't much hope of any clear.

After that, we made the best of the gaps in the weather and even drove over the mountains to Bargemon where Posh and Becks have a house.[2] The rain had cleared luckily for the journey but as we found a parking spot the floods started and

1 My father has an abhorrence of storms, which has been well documented.

2 This may surprise you, but Brenda's guilty pleasure was *Hello!* magazine. She loved snuffling through it like a celebrity gossip truffle pig hence being able to conjure up this sparkly nugget.

we couldn't get out of the car for thirty minutes. At one point
we were afraid that we would not make the journey back home
and I was preparing a sad little story in which we found the
Beckham's house and I stood ragged and dripping with water
asking for help and reminding them of the favour my daughter
once did for Posh![3] *It never came to that – we made it to a*
restaurant and stayed for three hours.

Well, I could be perky and say the weather didn't bother us
but the truth was all too evident. Waste of bloody money!
Never had a week like it before. I think the owners were ter-
rified I was going to demand some money back as on the
morning we left, Mrs M rushed out screaming that she 'wasn't
responsible' for the weather.[4]

There is nothing quite so noxious as a particular breed of
English ex pat who think they are Mem Sahibs running the
Empire. She got a cold retort from me and I vowed never to
rent anything from smug, greedy English again. She could have
offered £50 compensation.

We moved on Saturday back into the Luberon,[5] *our old*
stomping ground. Beautiful sunny day. Tried to stop for coffee
in Manosque[6] *which was a charming village five years ago*
but is now a bustling mini metropolis with inadequate parking
opportunities.[7] *At one point a car stopped dead in the road*
while they picked up a friend. Instead of letting him get in
immediately, they kept him outside giving him four kisses,

---

3 I once wrote the script for a show that involved her. I wouldn't call this a 'favour'. I'd call it a 'job'. Having said that, there isn't a doubt in my mind that Brenda would have thought nothing of knocking on their door, dripping wet. I'm almost sad it didn't happen. Almost.

4 This wouldn't have stopped Brenda from claiming she was, of course.

5 A massif comprising of three mountain ranges in southern France.

6 Small medieval town so unlucky it was decimated by the Plague not once, but twice.

7 This will have brought Tony out in a cold congealed sweat.

*oblivious of the fact that a tail back of over a mile had de-
veloped as they blocked the road.*

*Couldn't park anywhere so we drove out of Manosque and
were then assailed by the sight of the terrible forest fires down
here. At least ten miles of forest blackened and still stinking of
that sour, rank burnt smell.*

*Stopped off for lunch. I don't know whether you've noticed
that when you enter a French restaurant and say 'Manger-
deux personnes' a simple statement, they look at you as if you
have told them a filthy sexual joke. They always look horrified,
take a step back, often grasp a nearby chair, give you a final
look of contempt and then show you to the best table in the
room and fawn all over you. Can you begin to understand
these people? No.*

*Well, the bad weather has followed us but the rain in the
Luberon is silky smooth and gentle so we can cope with that.
New apartment is very modern and very smart and we've got
English telly! Hurray!*

The Smoking Room[8] *was on at 1am yesterday but we
were asleep by 9pm. Sorry. Don't forget to get us a tape.*

Love you lots
Mum and Dad xxx

★ ★ ★

---

8 *The Smoking Room* – a sitcom in which I played the ultra-irritating Heidi
O'Connell.

Six

Corby did not work for Brenda. She was at home with a baby and struggling. Dealing with the death of her mother and having to look after a newborn was taking its toll. For the next two years, the woman who had dragged herself up by the bootstraps was stuck, once again, in a small house on a council estate staring at the four walls with nothing to do.

'You never slept,' she would tell me. 'You'd be wide awake first thing in the morning and you never, not once, fell asleep until eleven o'clock at night.'

She became more irritable, anxious, felt listless and her energy levels dropped to nothing. On more than one occasion, she told me, Eric, their neighbour, would knock on the door to see if everything was all right. Eric, hearing me crying, would pop round and quietly lend a hand.

'I sometimes think Eric kept you alive,' she once said, in a rare admission of where she found herself.

It was the only help, other than from my father, she would receive. Postnatal depression was not openly discussed in 1967. Women were expected to just get on with it, muddle through and be nothing but delighted they had a baby. There was no counselling, no medication, no hospitalisation offered. My mother couldn't talk about it or even understand what might be wrong with her. As with so many mental health issues, she would have been alone, wondering what was happening and thinking she was the only person it was happening to.

Like so many women before and after her, Brenda internalised her pain, perceiving it as a weakness that could not be allowed to see the light of day. She had lost her mother, her career lay in tatters and she had no horizons on which to set her hopes. The future, for Brenda, now seemed bleak.

Years later, when I was going through her things, I discovered a small notebook. There was a faded sticker on the front that read *Brenda's Art Ideas*. It's a delightful little thing – full of pictures she's cut from newspapers and magazines to inspire her. There are notes she's written herself, short and precise, quickly written:

Other people's worst memories

CONTROL-FREEDOM
CHOICE-COMPULSION
INTIMACY-DISTANCE

Make a haunted house

What is the point of human beings?

There's a mugshot of Violet Gibson, the woman who tried to shoot Mussolini, a picture of Andy Warhol's wigs, there's the beginnings of an essay on the 'Problem of the Status of Women' but on one page. There's an image of a painting. It's *Architecture 10* by Daniel Cacouault, a faded vision of a person swallowed up in a large chair. The facial features are undetermined and there's a sense that whoever this is, they are disappearing. Underneath it, Brenda has glued a clipping from a newspaper. It reads:

It is clear that depression results from changes in the brain, because it can be induced by chemical means such as high concentrations of the hormone cortisol or the drugs reserpine or alpha interferon. Depression can be thought of as sadness

becoming malignant for a variety of reasons, not least genetic
factors. Heritability of depression is more than 50%

Reading it made me feel desperately sad. My mother never
spoke openly of suffering from depression, and it pains me
that, as with her cancer, she didn't complain. Those times
would be dismissed as 'time of the month stuff', we would
joke that Mum's period was either 'coming, here or she'd just
had it'. In other words, there were only about three days a
month when she might feel normal. I think we all considered
it hormone-related, tied to her period and nothing else. It was
something to be expected and put up with. I certainly don't
recall any serious discussions about anything being done to
alleviate it. If she was suffering from depression, she certainly
didn't tell us, and she wouldn't have been alone. A generation
of women and men were in quiet despair, for whom, certainly
in my mother's case, the only outlet was aggression.

I can only imagine the frustration she must have experienced.
In a matter of months, she'd gone from being a dynamic
woman in charge of her own destiny to a grieving mother out
of her depth. She had done everything within her power to
make a future for herself: one where she had a proper career
and prospects, yet here she was, at twenty-four, when she
should have been forging ahead, locked into a domesticity she
abhorred. I wonder if she resented me and wouldn't blame
her if she did. It would be another nineteen years until I became
good for her and I think it's fair to assume that much of our
difficulties during my childhood were down to the inescapable
truth that I had, pretty much, ruined her life.

Women were yet to be taken seriously in 1967. It would be
four years until *The Female Eunuch* was published. Brenda
couldn't take out a mortgage, she couldn't open a bank account
without Tony's permission, she couldn't have a credit card, she
couldn't be taxed independently, she couldn't expect equal
pay and, even though this beggars belief, she couldn't spend

her own money in a pub. Until 1982, any publican was perfectly within his legal rights to refuse to serve a woman. Women were second-class citizens. They were expected to be dolly birds or mums. The notion of a woman having a serious career was for the larks and yet that was what Brenda yearned for. She wanted to be working.

At some point, and it must have been quite the wait, Brenda made a decision. Here I was, a baby girl, staring up and out at a world dominated by men. In 1967 my prospects were far from glittering, but Brenda wanted something more for me and she made it her mission to give me the very best start so, stuck at home with nothing to do, she dedicated herself to teaching me to read in double quick time. She made flash-cards that were stuck to everything: Table, Chair, Door, Sink, Oven, Stairs, Sofa, Book, Toy, Paint, Paper. Anything that could have a flashcard stuck on it had a flashcard stuck on it. She set a rule – I would be allowed to do whatever I wanted in my own room: if I painted on the walls, then so be it, if I made a mess, so be it. What she wanted was for me to feel free and creative in my own space and by the age of two, she had me reading.

Later, she would repeat to me like a mantra: 'Whatever you do, don't get married and make sure you go to university.' Men, she would teach me, would hold you back. I didn't know it then, but I was going to take what she said very, very seriously.

Luck, which must have seemed in short supply towards the end of 1969, suddenly came calling. Tony had got himself a new job, in a comprehensive in Stevenage. He had driven Brenda down to see the town and have a look round. New towns felt rather glamourous: they were the height of modern chic and aspiration. They were a sparkling start for the working classes, a chance to slide up the scale and make something of themselves. Brenda liked it. Before going back, Tony had to pop into the school to see the headmaster. As Brenda sat in the car, waiting, he casually mentioned that his young wife was an English teacher and that if they needed any cover, could they consider her. The headmaster's eyes widened.

'Oh!' he declared, brightly. 'We need an English teacher!'

Tony, sensing an opportunity, told him she was in the car park, right there and right now. 'Shall I bring her in?'

I can only imagine the fevered steps with which my father would have skipped out to Brenda's open window. 'Quick!' he yelled. 'Get out. You've got an interview. Now.'

The hope that must have soared through my mother's chest in that moment as she leapt out, the quick check of what she looked like, whether her shoes were clean and her top didn't have baby food on it, the nervousness, the sense of astonishment that the perfect opportunity had fallen unexpectedly into her lap. Brenda deserved a break and here it was. All she had to do was not muck it up.

Brenda got the job. She was taken on as a part-time English teacher. She would work mornings only, five days a week.

It was a start.

Darling little Emsie

Shall I start with the journey from Brussels? We arrived at a fairly civilised time in Brussels. You've heard of Brussels? It's a capital city but no one has told the Belgians.[1] Every toilet, café, water source and food depot was shut! It was 10.30 at night! Tony had last eaten at 7.30 and NO FOOD IN BRUSSELS was the menu. We got some water in a café that was determined to close as we stepped through the door – it was not sans gas and was quite undrinkable.

By now it was 11.15 and the station was filling up with the gangster droogs[2] of Brussels, eyeing up the take for the night. Tony through lack of food had by now drifted into a comatose state[3] brought on by our not seeing anyone else on the station who looked as if they might like to catch a train to Berlin – and fear, yes fear!

I knew I had to take charge.[4] I spotted someone in uniform and in indescribable ITALIAN[5] asked for directions

1 And we're off.

2 Droogs is from the novel *A Clockwork Orange* by Anthony Burgess. The hero/villain Alex has a gang of thugs who run around with him committing despicable crimes. He calls them his 'droogs', which, I am informed, is from the Russian for 'buddy'.

3 My father has diabetes and Brenda became quite obsessed with whether he needed to eat at any given time of day. You might think this was an exceptional display of wifely care. It wasn't. It was another of her cunning ruses to eat crisps whenever she wanted. 'You need to EAT, Tony,' she would insist, grabbing a fistful of Doritos and stuffing them into her cheeks.

4 I think it's fair to say that Brenda assumed 'being in charge' was her birth-right/destiny in any given situation.

5 This is even more extraordinary when you know my mother didn't speak Italian.

*to the right platform for the night train to Berlin. Just pause
and imagine the scene. An old lady who is obviously English
speaking to a FRENCH station guard in ITALIAN. I don't
know where it came from. He actually backed away. Instead
of telling me where to go he gruffly shouted
'PICKPOCKETS!' I gave up, went back to Tony and found
the platform. 11.40 – empty.*

*Tony, by now, was taking on a very glazed look so I knew
I had to be brave.[6] Oh, what would I have done for a little
Snowy to help me out! Suddenly a very large man appeared
on the platform. We got talking. He was going to catch a train
to Berlin – but did I know that it went to Hamburg first? We
didn't. Along came a young Peruvian guy. He was going to
Hamburg. Next to arrive was a tall inscrutable beautiful
German girl. Where on the platform should she stand for
Hamburg? Did I look like Tintin? Why were they asking
me?[7]*

*Then – horror! On the Eurostar I noticed a very sinister
looking guy dressed in a grey cap and strange grey uniform.
He looked like the East German stasi. Now he was standing
on our platform. He was so nasty looking I was praying he
wouldn't be going to Berlin. He sidled up to me and the
Peruvian guy. Where did I think coach 95 would stop? My
heart sank, but I betrayed nothing. The Peruvian was in coach
110, the Hamburg coach. Stasi man was in my coach! 95 to
Berlin. Oh my god!*

*I walked quickly away. The train trundled in and I told the
Peruvian guy to run to the right as coach 110 would be up
there. Coach 95 stopped in front of us. I didn't say anything to*

6 *find some crisps to eat

7 Only my mother could turn a dull wait for a train into the start of an
Agatha Christie novel.

Tony. He was in a bad way and I thought it best to keep Stasi man to myself.

Our train had come from Paris and was packed. An American showed me where the toilet was and we got talking in the corridor but not for long as a very large 50ish German woman told me I was 'too loud'![8] Can you imagine it? I thought, shall I fight her? 'Hasn't this train just started?' I said, haughtily.

'Nein, the people are asleep in Paris'

'I'm glad,' I replied and gave her a suitable look – you know it.[9] She shut up.

By now Stasi man[10] had taken off his cap – shaved head! He tried to sleep above me, but I made sure Tony was underneath him. I didn't trust this man and was genuinely afraid of what he might do. Cut to – no sleep tonight. I drifted in and out of sleep keeping a constant check on what Stasi man was doing. I didn't sleep much.

We got up at 5am and had breakfast. By 6am the two Japanese girls in the coach and the Stasi man were awake and we reorganised the sleeping arrangements so we could sit up. Stasi man really was an East German from Northern Ireland! Well. He had family in East Berlin – probably got his cap and uniform from his brother-in-law. Very unpleasant man. Obviously in a neo-Nazi sect. Dressed for the part. Told us at least 20 lies and pretended he was getting off at the station after us in Berlin but he got off at Hautbanhoff with us. Think we got off lightly. I'm sure he broke the top of my glass bottle

8 I'd like to commend this unknown German woman for being the only person to ever knowingly tell my mother to shut up.

9 Yes, I do. It was a look that could turn grown men to stone, a look that seemed like the inevitable result of having been cursed at birth by bad Fairy Godmothers, a look that said, *don't touch that, you'll catch something.*

10 You can't help but be thrilled for her that she's found someone she can pretend she's in a spy novel with.

Bob in his brief stint in the army as a dispatch rider.

Elizabeth, Brenda and a fourteen-year-old Phyllis.

Brenda and Phyllis
pose at home.

Bob on holiday, surrounded by women.

Bob, in his kitchen.
Photo by Rosie Potter.

Tony and Brenda on their wedding day.
She was determined to wear some black.

Brenda at home in Jessop Road, Stevenage.

Jessop Road. The council estate I loved.

Me on Brenda's knee.

We're in Corby here. I found a hole in that fence and crawled off into a road. I was found by a neighbour.

Ah, the seventies. That's not my pint.

Brenda was at her happiest when we were on holiday.

Brenda in pensive mood.

of water. I nearly swallowed glass – I felt something sharp on my tongue and stopped drinking just in time. He must have done it while I was having breakfast. It had been fine before then. I left it under my bed.[11]

My turn now![12] I don't recognise the condition Brenda thought I was in at Brussels! Glazed eyes?

I love Berlin! Despite the heat we've been all over. Our new camera has been a boon, point and go. The batteries keep running down but then Tony bought them in a £1 shop in Hitchin. My lovely fan[13] was so effective, and Tony squashed it in his bag. New German one is not as good.

People are generally very kind and help you, but we've had a few bad moments. A man shouted at me in the street. No idea what he was saying so I just said 'Ich bin English. Thank you for your time.'[14] Walked away and he called me a pig. I took no notice. Then Tony got ripped off in a restaurant. Bastard waiter said he'd given Tony a 5 Euro note when he hadn't. Left in a rush and Tony left his glasses behind. Went back next day – got his glasses and reported waiter. I had to really shout in U-bahn at a young kid who put a hand in Tony's purse! I went berserk and the guy fled. They don't like shouting – everyone notices. Berliners are very calm, very quiet,

11 This is typical of Brenda when she was in paranoia mode. She would have genuinely believed a strange man on the train had tried to kill her by ever so slightly chipping the top of her water bottle. NOTE TO SELF: there are easier ways to assassinate someone on a train.

12 Dad's sudden chip in here is like a man running across a room shouting, 'WOAH, WOAH, WOAH.' In any event, he's been allowed to write one line before the letter is grabbed back.

13 I'd given her a handheld battery-operated fan to help with the hot flushes. When I started menopause, I had a tiny discreet little thing. Few months in and I had upgraded to a handheld battery-operated fan the size of my head. Didn't give a shit what I looked like.

14 That showed him. Having said that, astonished she didn't point at Tony and say, 'He's Welsh.'

very polite. If someone shouts, it's as good as an alarm.[15] *So far so good.*

Hope you've had some good news. Give Poppy a big cuddle. Miss you both.

Big hugs and kisses from your little chickens.

Love you lots.
Mum and Dad
Xxxx

★ ★ ★

15 My mother, in situations like this, was not unlike the Countdown Clowns in the animated film *Yellow Submarine*. Go google them now. No need to thank me.

Seven

In 1971, everything changed.

A book was published, *The Female Eunuch*, written by Germaine Greer who was clever, funny, sexy and uncompromising. It was the clarion call to women everywhere. Its message: you are entitled to have and enjoy sex on your own terms, women have been oppressed for long enough and this rubbish has to end. It was a global sensation. My mother, the lapsed Catholic who had turned her back on organised religion, found in Germaine her Rorschach Virgin Mary. She worshipped her, read and re-read the book until she was shouting bits at my father and it was at this point the quiet regrets that she'd had about getting married, being a mother and doing the 'whole woman thing' came to a crashing crescendo. No more was Brenda going to be told what to do. No more was Brenda going to have her life dictated to and no longer was Brenda going to take a single piece of shit from anyone with a pair of balls.

Feminism fit my mother like a velvet glove. It's hard now to overstate the shoot of change that burst up through frosted ground in the seventies. Women were unimportant, easily ignored. They were a pair of tits and nice legs, something to be whistled at, mauled, abused. Women were not to be ambitious or aspirational. They were the products of their husbands. Single women in their late twenties and above were treated with nothing but suspicion. If you wanted a house, a car, a future, you had to get married. If you weren't married, there was something wrong with you and even if you were married, men didn't take a blind bit of notice, they could have a crack at you any which way. Women were fair game and if you didn't play along, you were frigid. But in the early seventies, there was a seismic shift. Women began to fight back.

There was a rage quietly simmering. Women, gays and Black people were beginning to question centuries-old expectations: be quiet, do what you're told, know your place. Well, no more. The Black Civil Rights Movement began to flourish in the sixties but now, in this brave new decade, gay rights and women's rights were on catch up. It was the decade of Sexual Liberation.

Now in Stevenage, my father and mother were the hot young teachers at school. A former pupil, Linda Whitehead, remembers them thus:

Opinions and thoughts were encouraged. English and Art were subjects that didn't seem to have a curriculum that was set in stone. We could express ourselves. These were 'new young teachers' who had been to 'college and university', they didn't see us as objects, they seemed to see us as individuals. We fell in love and wished all the teachers could be like them. They gave us ideas that (according to some parents) were 'above our station' or 'only for people who aren't like us'. They were teaching us to think. We may have been in the 'A' stream but very few of us could imagine a life much different from our parents.

And then, of Brenda's lessons:

Your Mum's English lessons were amazing. She seemed to be able to weave a spell over us, she mesmerised us, she was so tiny, with her thick bob of hair swaying and her eyes darting as she made a point. Her hands were small, with no-nonsense nails. I seem to remember she sometimes wore thick tights and short skirts, with 'mary jane' shoes, more quirky than fashion conscious. We did wonder how someone so tiny, could ever have had a baby. We also marvelled that someone who had a child still came to work. She loved her subject. I remember taking part in the drama festivals. I remember tackling poetry, and one of my most endearing memories was of our class, dressed in rags, trailing up to Shephall Green Church yard to film a re-enactment of The Pardoners Tale. *The heady mix of doing something so different, being out in costume and stage makeup, and being away from the classroom. She didn't take hostages, if someone wasn't listening or we weren't working, she let us know who was leading the class, a loud voice could come out of that little body.*

Brenda, finally, was in charge. She was an incredible teacher and I have received countless messages over the years from former pupils who were not only grateful, but who adored her. She widened horizons, took kids from council estates to watch Shakespeare at the Royal Shakespeare Company in Stratford-upon-Avon, made films, took them to exhibitions and finally, after all those missed school trips of her own, got to go to Paris. She was looked up to and admired. She had found the thing she excelled at and it energised her. But for Brenda, there was more to be enjoyed in this strange, febrile decade and it was at this point, when everything was finally tickety-boo, she decided, like a character from a seventeenth-century novel set in a French court, that she was going to take a younger lover.

I'm going to call him Daniel. They would have a relationship for the best part of three years.

Daniel was a muscular young man with brown hair that curled at the ends. He wore a brown leather jacket, had olive skin and a square jaw and it doesn't pass me by quite how much he looked like James Dean. Daniel had been having a rough time of it: a member of his family had died and my mother and father stepped up to support him. This brought them closer together and Daniel and my mother began spending more time alone. He would come to the house and chat with her and it was during one afternoon, as they were walking together, that he turned to her and told her he wished she was free. He told me, 'I think she took that as the green light,' and without further ado, she took him to my childhood bedroom where they 'had a fumble'. Now at this point, you might think 'Oh, Brenda, Emma's childhood bedroom? Really?' – whereas all I thought, when told, was, *Not on the eiderdown* in Thora Hird's voice. I really cannot over emphasise how messy my childhood bedroom was. It would have been like trying to get jiggy in a room that had had a head-on collision with a mobile library.

It quickly developed into a full-on physical relationship.

'She was intelligent and beautiful,' he told me. 'I couldn't believe my luck.' They would meet up at lunchtimes and on her afternoons off. 'I was smitten. Madly in love with her,' he said. 'I can't feel ashamed about falling in love with her. I didn't do the right thing but then, neither did she. I feel lucky to have known her. You can go your whole life and never meet anyone as incredible as Brenda and ever since, I tried to find something of her in the people I had relationships with. I wanted her to leave Tony and be with me, but it was never, ever mentioned. No suggestion of it whatsoever. It was an affair and would never be anything more.'

I was enormously grateful to Daniel for agreeing to speak to me. He didn't have to. I have vague recollections of him being around but given how long their relationship lasted, it's amazing how little I remember of him but, my God, the brass balls on the woman. There was one afternoon I do recall when I was at home. Everything had gone strangely quiet, and I went looking for them. Nowhere to be found, I went back upstairs and tried to open the door of my parents' bedroom. It was locked. I tried again only to be told by my mother, on the other side of the door, to 'go away, we're moving the furniture round'. I mean, it's sort of hilarious looking back at this now. Her brazenness is astonishing. She was having sex with a young man in our house while I was in it and I'm forced to conclude that my dear, darling, uncompromising mother was almost certainly a sex maniac.

Today, you can only imagine the frowning. A sexual rela-tionship with a younger man who's not your husband? Affairs, full stop? Nope. Not any more. Never mind she was hot. Never mind he had the time of his life. Never mind it was the seventies when people frequently turned a blind eye – she shouldn't have done it, but she did and there it is.

It wasn't for lack of sex at home – 'all your mother ever wanted was sex,' Tony told me, and their sex life, throughout the years she was seeing Daniel, was as active as it ever was. I don't doubt she loved my father, but I also hope she loved Daniel. Towards the end, she gave him a photograph of when she was a student. 'It was a stunning picture,' Daniel told me, 'and on the back she'd written: *It's a long journey to the right place at the wrong time.* My first wife tore it up.' It's clear, however, she had no intention of leaving Tony. This was, for her, exciting. She loved the danger of it. She loved the audacity, the fact she was doing precisely what she wanted. She loved that she was having sex on her terms. She was living *The Female Eunuch* dream.

The last time Daniel saw Brenda, there was no blow-up, no big this is the end argument. Instead, it was a fizzling out, the air being let out of a balloon. Making arrangements had become more difficult. They would never spend a night together or go away for a weekend. It was always snatched hours here and there. 'I realised it was never going to be anything more. I wanted a proper relationship' – and, to be honest, after the best part of three years, who can blame him? Brenda, however, wanted nothing of the sort with Daniel and they went their separate ways.

Did Tony know? Not at first, certainly. Brenda was brilliant at keeping it secret. In three years, I was only aware of one suspicious visit and even then, was too young to understand what was going on. The game was rumbled during that episode in hospital, when Brenda had renal colic. Daniel had been to visit her and the ward matron, for reasons unknown, took it upon herself to snitch to my dad. Can you imagine the scenes? You're finally found out when you're in a hospital bed and can't move. It must have felt like an elaborate joke. When I asked Dad why he stayed with her, he always said it was because he didn't want to lose me – that was the other problem with the seventies: divorce, and your wife kept the kids. But there's no doubt he was devoted to her and the times lent themselves to not kicking up a fuss when it was 'just sex'. The seventies was such a weird, fucked-up decade where moral compasses went haywire: boundaries were being tested, sexual exploration was unleashed and to hell with the consequences.

It's impossible to understand now, when we live in very different times, that she could have displayed no contrition whatsoever. She never admitted to it and there was no unburdening in later life of a secret long carried. Even when I challenged her on it in her sixties, during an argument where she was accusing my father of having an affair with a neighbour (he wasn't), she remained tight-lipped. I think she thought she hadn't done anything wrong. It was the seventies! I was doing what Germaine told me to! I was just having sex!

My parents, despite all this, were happily married and remained so for forty-seven years. Nobody ever knows what truly goes on between two people and they were able to make their marriage work, but I recall a moment, more than twenty years on from the locked bedroom door incident, when I was a lawyer, standing crying in my senior partner's office.

'What's the matter with you?' he asked.

'My mother's having an affair.'

He looked at me with a quizzical but firm expression. 'So what? It's none of your business.'

I suppose he was right. It was none of my business.

Hang on, you might be asking. An affair over twenty years later? To quote Britney Spears . . . *Oops. She did it again.*

CHATEAU OUTSIDE NONTRON[1]

*Well, we haven't had a holiday like this one for a while now!
It's been quite unsettling I'm afraid.[2] We stopped overnight in
a small village in a non-descript hotel, got up in the morning,
went down for breakfast but no one was to be seen – no hotel
guests and no staff. I went back upstairs to find someone and
noticed a light was coming from underneath all the bedroom
doors in the corridor. Seemed a bit strange. So, I opened a few
doors – empty – then I opened them all – empty.*

*When I came back down and told Tony there was no one
else staying in the hotel, he tried to open the front door, but it
was locked.[3] Here we were in an empty hotel and we
couldn't get out! We started calling 'Madam! Madam!
Monsieur! Monsieur!' No answer.*

*Tony started to look for the key to the front door and I tried
to open a window to call out to a passer-by. The windows were
locked. Then, I noticed a very large kitchen knife on the table
and felt a moment of panic. Luckily, Tony found the key and
we opened the door and went across to the boulangerie and
told the Madam what had happened. She sneered and said
people were always being locked in[4] and then with a few*

1 They're in the Dordogne. Beware when Brenda starts her letters with huge
caps telling us where she is. She has THINGS TO SAY.

2 What did I tell you?

3 I don't say this lightly, but this is the sort of holiday only my parents could
manage to have.

4 Questions, questions . . . I'm quite surprised Brenda didn't try to get to the
bottom of this, but every now and again she'd encounter a French woman
grumpier than she was. In these instances, even Brenda knew to leave well
alone.

'*pouffs*' *she turned her back on us. After that we went back to the hotel, got our luggage and left the money for the room next to the knife. Not a very good start but at least we got out alive.*

I have to warn you that the next part of the holiday was much worse.[5] *We had booked an apartment in the wing of a 17th century chateau. The entrance, down a long lane lined with fields of bright yellow sunflowers, was charming and allowed a full view of the chateau which had three towers and was set in about 15 fabulous hectares of garden and woodland.*

The chateau entrance was very dramatic with two large stone dragons on either side of high wooden gates. Three old style dovecotes were close by and we glimpsed a large paddock in which two beautiful Arabian white horses were gently cropping. We could see it now! A leisurely week here drinking wine, sketching a bit, wandering around a vast estate with tall pines and ancient oaks for shade. Bliss![6] *Ah yes, but it did not quite turn out like that.*

The gates had been opened for our arrival at the prearranged time and we drove towards the chateau itself. As we did so, a very large black mastiff – French – not quite a Rottweiler – altogether bigger – rushed at the car from nowhere, barking ferociously.[7] *We didn't get out of the car – we couldn't. No one was around. We didn't know what to do. The dog was now leaping up, spewing globules of spit which dribbled down Tony's window. Shut tight, of course.*

'If no-one comes in the next bloody minute, we're driving out of here!' Tony was quite shaken.

'Maybe we should keep our finger on the horn – it's a bit of

5 Let joy be unconfined.

6 OR the classic start to a horror film which ends with much running and screaming.

7 We've all seen *The Omen*, right?

an emergency' I suggested because the mastiff was getting fiercer by the second.

As we were about to start calling for help, a figure appeared from behind the stone outhouse. The owner. He took one step towards the dog and called its name. I didn't catch it.[8]

Apologising in a very gentle French accent, he encouraged us out of the car and led us into the chateau. We entered a heavily panelled room with long oak trestle table, high backed chairs and various tapestries on the stone walls. Chatting amiably as we walked, we soon found ourselves outside in a shaded courtyard where a table with glasses and wine had been prepared. I had already forgotten about the dog. I needed that drink. Tony had now relaxed,[9] *and we began the real introductions. When we told Monsieur that we came from Hitchin, he surprised us by saying that he knew Hitchin very well as his wife had grown up there. A coincidence like that always comes as a real shock but we were not expecting what came next.*

'I have a photo of your daughter in the house,' said Monsieur, quietly.[10]

We were speechless. How?

'I have a book about Hitchin Girl's School and your daughter Emma is in it.'[11]

As we had not mentioned you to Monsieur, this was another shock. How did he know your name? How did he know that

8 *idly hopes it was called Trevor or Geoffrey or Ian*

9 Note how Brenda always likes the reader (me) to imagine that it's my father who is in a near constant state of hysteria. In professional circles, we'd call this PROJECTION.

10 OK. NOW YOU HAVE MY ATTENTION.

11 School I went to, obviously. It's a book called *Do You Remember* by Priscilla M. Douglas (needlework teacher) and I am indeed, very briefly, in it. CUE THE SCREAMING.

you had been to the Girls School? An uncomfortable moment. Who was this man?[12]

We both looked at each other and smiled politely, doing our best to hide a certain feeling of panic. First the bloody dog, now a photo of you in a stranger's chateau in the middle of France! I was determined not to let this be a bad omen and kept smiling maniacally at Tony and our host.[13]

He refilled our glasses and went off to fetch the book. We put our glasses down.

'How the hell has he got this book?' Tony was unsettled. 'How does he know Emma's name?'

'Probably through the wife's connection with Hitchin. This explains it. But I wonder where she is? It's strange she isn't here – I expect we'll meet her later. Don't worry about it.' I said, reassuringly.

I wasn't really worried. Monsieur was a gentle man, a bit thickset and small with a standard tan and smart, expensive looking clothes and as always with the French bourgeoisie, he smelled delicious.[14]

He soon came back with the book. Lo and behold he opened the page to the photo of you and the girls in Russia, all grinning. It seems that his wife had kept in touch with some of the staff who had sent her a copy of the book and when she knew we were coming from Hitchin someone at the school who knew us told her that you were in the book. This broke the ice a bit and we laughed about your high jinks in Russia, running off

12 At this point, I'd have surreptitiously taken his pulse to see if he was secretly a ghost.

13 I'm reminded of Kitty, the character created by Victoria Wood, who in moments of panic says, 'We shall have fog by teatime.'

14 Oh well, that's OK then. Know who else liked fancy colognes? HANNIBAL LECTER.

*and catching buses on your own and trying to sell your jeans
to Russians and handing out Mars Bars.*[15]

*Everything was going well. Monsieur fetched another bottle
of very good white wine but this time he was accompanied by
another dog, a very leggy dog with a strange ponytail on its
head. This dog, Sacha, was obviously used to making friends
with strangers and quickly nuzzled up to me and wouldn't
leave my side. As you know I'm not very comfortable with
dogs, so I was a bit cautious about stroking her. Even Tony
commented on the dog's warm affection, but Monsieur
explained it rather strangely.*

*'Your wife looks like my wife and Sacha was my wife's dog.'
He said quietly.*[16] *WAS my wife's dog? What did he mean?
Don't let her be dead, I prayed. But of course, she was
dead.*[17] *She had died a month after we had booked the
apartment – but he never told us. He wanted us to come.
Aaargh!*

*I didn't look at Tony while Monsieur told us the terrible
news. A rare blood disease – it was very quick – he was
devastated – his two young children were motherless. We said
all the right things, we even asked him if he'd like us to leave –
we didn't want to be any sort of burden as it was only ten
months since she had died. Oh no – he was delighted to have*

15 Almost correct – there was one day in Leningrad where a school chum,
Sam Vaughan, and I escaped the clutches of the guide and hopped onto a bus.
Everyone stared at us. We looked very different in our trendy coats, jeans and
trainers. I remember one lady gesturing to me to do my coat up. We went to
Nevsky Prospect, the equivalent of Oxford Street, and stood outside their
main department store. There was one pair of tights in the window display
and inside, a queue for bread. Other girls in our group were asked by
Russians if they could buy their jeans and our teacher, Mrs Creighton, had all
the Mars bars. She gave them out to Russian children who couldn't believe
their luck. Russia, of course, is very, very different now.

16 Hang on. Where IS this wife?

17 Oh God. Oh dear God.

us in his home and he hoped that the sad news would not affect our stay – he wanted everything to be fine for us.[18]

That was it then – no escape! With every moment we realised that the dreams we had for this holiday had been crushed.

First, the chapel. The chapel was in the chateau's grounds and Monsieur walked us over to it and left us to look inside by ourselves. Before his wife died, they had drunk a magnum bottle of champagne together and it had been left on the chapel altar. Her stiletto shoes had also been left on the altar together with her hat. This was a heart-breaking scene but it was also extremely spooky because the walls of the chapel were covered in paintings of blue veiled heads without faces. Why were the faces blanked out?

Quite honestly, we didn't care. We just wanted to get out.[19]

We were then shown up to the wing of the house which housed our accommodation. We were in a tower and had two floors. Our bedroom was in the tower and our sitting room and extra bedroom was on the ground floor.

Our bedroom was up a steep, winding staircase hung with the largest Russian icons I had ever seen: the eyes of the figures large and staring down at you. SPOOKY! On the four walls of the bedroom hung huge gilded mirrors. There were faded paintings everywhere. I knew straight away this was going to be an edgy experience. A woman has recently died in the house and I might see her ghost in one of these bloody mirrors. No sleep for me then.[20]

I went downstairs while Tony was unpacking and walked into the large second bedroom where a photograph of Monsieur's wife was placed centrally. I couldn't miss it. I

18 Before he ate us.

19 Brrrrrrrrrrrrrrrrrrr.

20 At this point I would have burned the house down and left. It's a maxim I live by – leave it, burn it.

looked and gasped. It was as if I was looking at myself.[21] No wonder the dog had been so affectionate. My heart was thumping. I then opened the wardrobe which ran along the length of the wall. It was filled with the wife's clothes, her perfume escaping into the room.

'Tony! Tony!' I called, overcome with superstitious fright.
'What's wrong?' he called down.

I called again. A photo of me and a wardrobe full of a dead woman's clothes and I had to live here for a week.[22]

When Tony came, he looked at the photo and looked into the wardrobe. He went very quiet.

'Shall we just leave,' he asked.

'We can't. You know we can't. What reason could we give? He'd know it was because of his wife.'

'I can't believe our luck. Why is it always us?'

Poor daddy looked as if he was going to cry. We had both been looking forward to this holiday so much. What could possibly happen next? We had a spooky bedroom, a possible ghost and a French rottweiler.

Then there was the first night!

We had left the chateau in the early evening and luckily found a very good restaurant where after a couple of glasses of good red wine we decided we were both being hysterical so we tucked into a very good four course meal and resolved to enjoy ourselves.[23]

A couple of hours later, just slightly drunk[24] we returned in the dark to the chateau. Monsieur had left the gates open, and the Hound had been locked away. How silly of us to

21 BRRRRRRRRRRRRR.

22 I REFER YOU TO FOOTNOTE 20.

23 *get blind drunk

24 BLIND drunk.

panic. We unlocked the door and turned on the lights which were a bit dim, often the case in ancient chateaux. We ascended the stairs to the tower – spooky as the eyes of the icons glared down. We entered the bedroom and more dim lighting cast shadows and our own reflections in the mirrors. Nothing to worry about. Tony went into the bathroom next door. Suddenly there was a cry.

'Brenda, can you come here a minute?'

'Yes,' I said, looking at daddy. 'What is it?'

'Well, it's there on the wall – I'm not quite sure – but I thought you'd better take a look.'

He pointed to some smears on the wall in front of him.

'Does that look like blood to you?'[25]

I was looking at small blood spats spread across the wall – some were quite large.

In that instant, I had already forgotten the euphoria of the restaurant and our foolish confidence. How had these blood stains got there and worse, why hadn't they been cleaned off? Something was not right! I started to feel a strange shaking in my knees. Then I noticed that the bathroom had a connecting door. A CONNECTING DOOR. It was locked from the other side. We were too shocked to speak.

We got into bed, turned out the light – and waited.

'Don't look in the mirrors. We'll sleep with our back to them,' I said, snuggling up close to daddy.

That meant facing the window. We had closed all the shutters so all outside sounds were dulled. We drifted off to sleep – very fitfully and about an hour later I woke up. I could hear a very strange sound. Something was stamping on the ceiling. I shook daddy awake.

'Tony! Something is stamping on the ceiling.'

---

25 LEAVE IT. BURN IT. THEN BURN IT AGAIN.

'What?' He was barely awake.

'Listen! Listen!' I hissed.

We clutched each other as the stamping sounded faster and faster and then – oh then – we heard a terrible panting sound and it was unearthly – it was coming from a group – not a single pant – a number of pants – all slightly different and all coming from the ceiling. When you cannot recognise a strange sound – when you cannot account for it in any rational way – you know you are scared stiff. I was afraid that daddy would panic.[26]

Within seconds, the stamping and panting became blood-curdling screams – screams coming through the ceiling – and now – screams coming from outside – dulled, but screams nonetheless.

Tony got out of bed. He opened the shutters and the screams penetrated the bedroom. I knew I had to be brave. I couldn't let daddy down. He couldn't cope on his own. I got up and dared to look out the window. I didn't know what I expected to see – a banshee – a dead wife's ghost? Whatever, it was much worse. Large white forms were diving and soaring and screaming – a terrifying sound, a sound which wasn't human. I was looking at barn owls hunting in moonlight.[27]

They hunted all night. We closed the shutters again but could still hear them. We tried to sleep but it was hopeless. Eventually I fell asleep and saw the dead wife in one of the mirrors, with the ponytail dog, and both of them were waving and smiling.[28]

In the morning we had breakfast with Monsieur. We didn't

26 *Brenda was panicking.

27 AND RELAX . . .

28 Love how she nonchalantly throws this in. Oh, and by the way, I saw the dead lady with her dog. Whatevs.

mention the blood stains,[29] but we told him about the stamping and the panting sounds. It seems that barn owls make these sounds just before they wake up and start hunting. We were going to have this performance for a week. We couldn't move into the second bedroom as it was occupied by a ghost!

Over the next few nights, the family of barn owls continued to stamp, pant and scream but there was an additional curse. Mosquitoes. We were plagued by them. There were old ponds outside the bedroom, breeding grounds for the bastards who attacked us mercilessly. We slept at night with the bed sheets covering our heads, listening for the tell-tale high-pitched whine as they dive-bombed us for our blood. A few days later on a trip to Cognac a French man looked at my swollen, reddened, bitten face and asked, with great consternation – did I have the petite pox?

We had now given up all hope of sleeping. The stamping and panting started at about 10.30 and the screaming went on till sunrise. The whistling eeeeeeeoowwwwwws of the mossies woke you up just as you were dropping off out of exhaustion and if you had to get up in the night for a pee you studiously avoided glancing in a mirror in case a woman and a dog waved back. We were nervous wrecks.

We never mentioned the blood stains in the bathroom. We were the stars in our own Horror Show. We had really lost the will to live. If Monsieur had come through the connecting door with an axe it wouldn't have been a surprise as we were already in the equivalent of the Overlook Hotel.[30]

We have spent our days getting quietly sloshed in posh restaurants eating far too many haute cuisine meals and being

29 I WONDER WHY?

30 The Overlook Hotel is, of course, the hotel in Stanley Kubrick's film *The Shining*, where Jack Nicholson plays Jack Torrence, the caretaker who goes mad and opens bathroom doors with axes.

*over friendly with complete strangers. French men seem to get
very sexually excited at the sight of an English woman
quaffing red wine remorselessly and asking for three desserts.*

*I suppose you are wondering why we didn't look for alterna-
tive accommodation. Well, in a funny sort of way, I knew that
the Gods had sent us, not to punish us, but to help. We did try
to be entertaining guests and we played with the children and
made a fuss of the ponytail. We hoped that we had brought
some comfort to Monsieur. We learned how to live with a ghost
and I started talking to her in an* Alice Through The
Looking Glass *way. Luckily, she didn't appear in the mirror –
maybe I secretly wished she would.*[31]

Big hugs and kisses Mum and dad xxx

★ ★ ★

31 YE GODS. Everyone go and get a stiff drink.

Eight

If there was one thing my mother gave a damn about, it was making sure I went to university. From as early as I can remember, the mantra was education, education, education. She'd given me the best start possible and, able to read and write before I started school, I was flying.

From the get-go, I had it bashed into me that getting pregnant would ruin my life, the only way I was ever going to amount to a string of beans was if I went to university, and that men were 'awful'. Whenever she said this, I'd look at my dad – the man who did all the cooking, washed the clothes, drove us everywhere, looked after us, was kind and gentle and funny – and wonder what the hell she was talking about, but went in it did and I never did get pregnant and I went to university and I turned out to be a lesbian so I guess I took it all to heart. I don't think all men are awful, though, but don't tell Brenda.

We were now living in a council house in Stevenage. I was having the time of my life and spent every hour it wasn't raining or dark outside playing with kids from the estate. My mother had told Tony she had zero intention of having another child so as far as she was concerned, I was going to be the sum total of her personal output and by God, she was going to get it right. I was allowed one hour of children's television Monday to Friday. On Saturdays, I could sneak watch *Swap Shop* or *Tiswas* for as long as she managed not to notice but other than that it was books, books and more books, with the occasional attempt to make my own pinball machine thrown in.

I loved living on the estate and my memories of it are entirely happy. Brenda was happy too, working again. I was at a primary school I adored, collecting caterpillars from the willow tree outside it so I could watch them turn into butterflies, waiting for chicken eggs to incubate and hatch and running everywhere wearing my coat like a cape. I liked painting on the walls in my bedroom, I liked the mess I was allowed to make, I liked the book *Dougal and the Blue Cat* being read to me every single night. I liked looking at the pictures in books called *Ann in the Moon* and *The Beast of Monsieur Racine*. I liked my dad letting me make things on his potter's wheel. I learned to ride a bike. I learned how to hide behind the sofa when the Rent Man came, to pretend we weren't in. I learned how to butter a crumpet and how to gargle salt water when your tooth fell out. I learned when Dad made a fruit cake, if I hung around at the right time, he'd let me lick the spoon. I learned that boy rabbits sometimes turn out to be pregnant female rabbits and I learned that teachers' children in costumes aren't the actual Wombles. I had friends, I had freedom and I was happy.

Post-war Britain, in the meantime, was struggling. We had strikes galore (which my grandfather was all for, natch), power cuts, no money and a sense that we had hit a wall. It wouldn't be until we joined the European Common Market that things would start to improve but probably the less said about that the better. One thing, however, was that teachers had been given a significant pay rise and out of the blue, my parents were suddenly able to buy our council house, but the purchase came as something of a poison pill because shortly after, they sold it on at a considerable profit and we left the council estate I adored and moved to the posher town of Hitchin.

The move coincided with me going to a junior school which, conveniently, was at the end of the road we lived on. No longer would my parents have to dash across town to pick me up – I could just walk home and let myself in with my own key. I was so disgustingly well behaved that for the two years we were there I would arrive home and go straight upstairs to my room where I might read or draw or try and work out where the goldfish had gone or whether my hamster was still alive and wait the half hour it took for my parents to arrive home. In the seventies, you could leave a child tied to a tree and nobody would bat an eyelid. If it wasn't dark or after six, being home alone was entirely acceptable but then 'child-care' in the seventies mostly consisted of being left in the car while your parents went to the pub or being watched by a passing dog. There would be no radio on, no light to read by. Occasionally, you might be brought a bottle of Coke and a packet of crisps you had to salt yourself. If it was your birthday or your parents were drunk you might get super lucky and get a packet of pork scratchings. In a nutshell, your only entertainment was staring silently at all the other children sitting in the parked cars around you. It was like being in a zoo of the terminally bored.

Brenda was rather pleased with her new house. For the first time in her life, she was no longer living on a council estate. It must have felt an astonishing accomplishment. It's strange for me to look back knowing this was when she embarked on her first affair, but it was also the time she started regularly taking me to London and when we began our odysseys to France. There's a sense here, then, that Brenda was enjoying life. She was expanding her horizons, shopping in Biba, taking me to plays, giving me books to read that were way beyond my years, pointing at avocados and telling my father to buy them. She started hosting dinner parties where Tony would do all the cooking and she would do all the laughing. She wore coloured clogs, got her furniture in Habitat, put art on the walls, drank Assam tea, occasionally smoked a cheroot, read *Cosmopolitan*, bought *The Joy of Sex*, discovered wine and European cheeses, re-read *The Female Eunuch* (again). She climbed over hedges to get into the Knebworth Music Festival, took me to see David Bowie and the Rolling Stones and would have conversations with people while staring at herself in any available mirror. She took me to museums, bought me a three-piece suit and tie when I was going through a phase and held on to the back of my bikini bottoms to stop me going into any sea beyond my knees. At this point, my memories of my mother are entirely positive. She was happy, fulfilled and getting all the sex she could cope with. No wonder she was in a good mood.

Matters improved again. One early summer evening, Brenda decided we should all go for a walk. She chanced upon a lane that reminded her of the one that stretched away from Ashley Lodge and, going up it, she discovered an empty house with an enormous garden. She fell in love with it on the spot. Fate was shining down and the very next day Tony saw a picture of it in the local estate agent's window. They crunched the numbers. If they pulled in the purse strings here and made savings there, they could just about afford the mortgage, so an offer was made. It would be the house she died in but like all good fairy stories, it became a cautionary tale.

It was bliss, at the beginning. There were long hot summers, we had an orchard and a hammock stretched between two apple trees. Friends would come and gasp at the size of the garden. There were secret passageways, nooks to turn into dens, an old, World War II air raid shelter that still had bunk-beds in it. Endless wildflowers filled the beds alongside poppies the size of your fist. It all smelled delicious. Everything about it was a million miles from the council house Brenda had thrown herself from because she wanted to die. Life gets better. No hard day lasts forever. She was instilling in me the cast iron belief that whatever your circumstances, you can do better, things can improve, you can fight your way out.

Brenda would tell anyone who cared to listen she'd been to university, but we know now, she hadn't. It was of vital import-ance to her that people thought she was worth more than the teacher training certificate, which was her only qualification, Brenda was embarrassed by her lack of credentials and it was that, in part, that fuelled her obsession when it came to me. Besides, she should have got into university and that's what mattered – what Brenda deserved would hang over her all her life.

Instead, she would fill my childhood with all the cultural riches she could muster. I can't fault her on this. What she gave to her pupils, she gave to me tenfold: plays, musicals, concerts, books. She took me to see Q and As with film directors like Francois Truffaut at the BFI on the Southbank, and encouraged me to stick my hand up. She took me to see obscure Korean films, prog rock, promenade plays at the National Theatre, outrageous jazz musicians, the artist Kit Williams, the animator Chuck Jones. She walked me around Cambridge, let me get lost in Foyles on Charing Cross Road, and always laid a place for me at every dinner party she had. I was to learn to be sociable, to hold my own with adults. At this point, I wasn't even ten.

The net result was that I was confident, mature beyond my years, and if there was any downside, it was that when it came to school friends, I was perfectly happy to mix and play but could never understand the small things children got upset about. It felt alien to me and utterly inconsequential. When I wasn't at school or out playing, I would be perfectly happy in my own company, up in my bedroom reading, drawing or practising kissing Christopher Reeve. Everything felt pretty steady and unremarkable and then one day, I heard some shouting from the garden, and I looked out of my bedroom window to see my father running down the garden being chased by my mother holding a long hoe.

I watched as he ran round in circles trying to get away from her and then she swung it at him, catching him on the back of the head. He fell down and, for a moment, I thought she'd killed him. She dropped the hoe and stood, shoulders heaving. I opened the window and she looked up at me. 'I've hit your father with a hoe.' The most shocking thing about this was the supreme calm with which she told me. It was like she was saying, 'Oh hello, we might go to the supermarket and buy some J cloths' or 'Have you seen the pegs?'

'Is he all right?' I asked.

He moved.

'Yes.' Then she turned and marched back to the house.

I'm not sure what sparked the sudden outburst, but staring down at my father, who was pushing himself up onto his knees, I was not to know that this was something I was going to have to get used to.

Dearest Emmy

Now for the prologue.[1]

    The journey. Paris – would we get there? Scene at St Pancras at 6.45 pm – a re-make of a WW2 movie. Chaos![2] People milling everywhere. Suitcases, trolleys, panic-stricken faces. Eurostar attendant calls out 'Paris!' and suddenly everyone is fighting to scramble UNDER the barriers which have been placed like a labyrinth around the entrance.

    An atavistic memory suddenly took over and I was one of the first under that barrier, hauling bags and Tony with me.[3] First in the queue – new tickets issued for 9.25 train. We wait 2 and a half hours. Arrive 3 hours later in Paris. Lovely afternoon and evening.

    Catch train to Montpelier – 1st class this time. 2 large armchair like window seats alone. Opposite, a rather plump man in a black striped shirt with wide grey stripe and a glaringly vulgar white kipper tie. His laptop was small, white with a silver TOSHIBA emblazoned on the lid. Something apart from the tie made me look harder at him. I thought I knew his face. Was he from Hitchin? Had I met him with you? The familiarity made me struggle hard to remember. Then I saw his hands, the nails short and beautifully manicured. A chef's hands.

    Who else could it be? Of course! It was Heston Blumenthal

1 This feels like a gauntlet thrown down in the sand.

2 And lo, she doesn't disappoint.

3 If Brenda thinks I'm believing she's hauling bags anywhere, she can go whistle at the moon. In this scenario, I feel confident in directing you to disregard this nonsense. She would have been trotting, bagless, elbowing people out of her way while squealing, 'Tony, hurry up!', as if it was the last helicopter out of Saigon.

– the Merlin of Chefs.[4] Luckily, he obviously hadn't brought his chemistry set. Was he going to Barcelona to attend to his cauldron of concoctions? I secretly passed a note to Tony – 'Don't stare! The guy who poisoned Sue Perkins is sitting opposite!'[5]

When it was 12 pm we couldn't wait to see whether he would set out gold lettuce and silver tomatoes for his lunch. No – it was a ham baguette[6] and a lemon curd tart! He thoroughly enjoyed them both.

When we got to Nimes, a major drama on the platform. A brutal sort of man was manacled to a Gendarme with a back-up team of 6 other gendarmes forming a phalanx around him.[7] Tony and I speculated about the crime. Must have been a murderer. Too heavy police presence for a theft. We both went very quiet thinking that we had looked a murderer in the face. He slightly resembled Hannibal Lecter – Ooooh!

Arrive at hotel in Montpellier.[8] Very charming old palace in splendid area. Tony's French was up to GCE Grade C. Bastard receptionist wouldn't speak any English – would only say 'Pas de tout' when he was expected to have a bit of English. Wait till I tell Sarkozy.[9] Montpellier is a University

4 I am astonished she didn't attempt to chum up with him.

5 Brenda is mistaken here. I rang Perks and asked whether this had happened. She told me, 'No, I had norovirus. I was not poisoned by Heston Blumenthal.'

6 Who among us doesn't quietly love the fact the Wizard of Food likes a ham sandwich?

7 I have never seen a man in cuffs at a train station. If you have, do write and tell me.

8 Montpellier is a rather beautiful ancient university town in the Occitanie region of Southern France.

9 At time of writing, Sarkozy has just been convicted of corruption and sentenced to three years in prison, two of them suspended. Brenda would have been scandalised.

*town – hundreds of them expecting to be doctors and lawyers –
they must speak English.*[10]

*We have discovered a lovely long drink – an alcohol-free
cocktail for Mediterranean hols. It is called a CJ – Coke, ginger
beer, lime juice and ice. Very nice. We had a couple sitting in the
sun with all the hundreds of students who study in cafes.
We felt the stress of living in Hitchin seep away – a long way
away.*[11]

*Set off in evening for restaurant hunt. Found a
charming place in a suitably ruined Roman Temple. Pillars,
Roman carvings, stone floors, trees growing up the walls.
The menu – Tony had terrine – I had gazpacho. Tony's terrine
– excellent. My gazpacho came in a large glass bowl and
looked suspiciously like apple sauce. It was pureed cucumber –
no spice, no garlic, no tomatoes – pureed cucumber. When
I only ate 3 spoonfuls, knowing that my holiday would be
ruined by distemper if I continued, the patron had the
cheek to complain loudly. I just gave him a cold schoolmarm
look.*[12]

2nd course – lamb – just about edible.

*3rd course – only thing I could eat was pineapple. It came
in two small dishes, chopped into tiny fragments and tasted
disgusting. The pineapple had small bits of green aniseed leaf
mixed in. Pineapple and green aniseed is something you*

---

10 Or, Brenda, you could learn French?

11 A small telling moment. My mother retired early, at fifty-two, and her life
in Hitchin was anything but stressful. They had a decent pension on which
they could live comfortably, a house and garden she loved, a daughter who
was doing just fine. Brenda, until she got cancer, had no major worries and
yet her perception of the town she lived in was one fraught with anxieties and
imagined plots against her. It's why she loved travelling so much. She allowed
herself to be the person she could have been.

12 By now you will be in no doubt as to the severity of this glare.

experience in Heston's kitchen, probably mixed with potassium
salts. Starving – go to bed with a plum.[13]

BACK ON THE ROAD AGAIN

Trepidation as hire car experience approaches. I have my
map, I have been told how to get out of the Europcar parking
and out of Montpellier.[14] *We manage to get the ticket pass to*
work, we leave Europcar and make our way to correct street
which will take us out of Montpellier on the road to
Millau.[15] *Millau is signed straight ahead – but there are two*
signs – one in each lane. Quickly I tell Tony to take the left
lane as the right lane doesn't look as if we can get far. Tony
ignores me and takes the right lane which forces us into going
back into Montpellier on the wrong road. Disaster. Now we
have to find our way back to the left turn to Millau without a
road map of Montpelier. Much screaming.[16] *20 minutes later*
we are back where we started, this time in the left lane.

Suddenly windscreen wipers start flicking – Tony can't turn
them off. I told him to go through all the new switches before
we set off in the Twingo[17] *– but I was ignored. Hell of a*
journey. Sign to Millau appears without warning and we have
to negotiate a sharp turn to the left. Just miss a car. Six

13 A trait I have inherited from my mother is the ability to feel crushed by a
disappointing meal. I was brought up to love food and savour every meal.
When that meal is shit, it's devastating.

14 Tony will have done all these things, handed her the paperwork, pointed to
the destination and said, 'Just read that.' NEVER, EVER give directions to a
woman who can't drive.

15 Town in the southern part of the Massif Central.

16 The problem here of course, is that you have a man who will study a
roadmap until he's cross-eyed and a woman with an, at best, lackadaisical
approach to signs. It's a recipe for disaster. If my mother ever told my father
which way to go, he didn't believe her. And here we are. Screaming again. The
inventors of Sat Nav don't know what a gift they gave the world.

17 Made by Renault, the car's name is a portmanteau of the words twist,
swing and tango. I'm amazed it didn't come covered in sequins.

French horns blast us on our way. Must light a candle in the
first church we find, I think to myself.[18]

Journey into a lunar landscape of strange-shaped rocks
jutting out. On route now to Millau. Stop for excellent light
lunch in Clermont and continue. Reach the bridge.[19]
Camera ready for best shots. The experience was slightly less-
ened for me as I was seeing it through a camera lens but
despite that the beauty of this bridge is heart stopping. And
the English designed it.[20] Thank God we can still make
something.

Journey continues after photo shoot session from beneath and
side of bridge. Start heading into mountains now, not knowing
what to expect. Quieres – yes – that was its name![21] A tiny
medieval village and then a long winding track going high and
high until we reached the farm. 3D views all around us. But
now the moment of truth. Tony fetches key to our room. I am
expecting cootie covered walls and green-eyed spiders running
amok. But no – a charmingly decorated little room – tones of
earth reds in the bed linen – hand carved beds and chairs and
wardrobe. Remember Heidi? So far so good.

Now for the meal – served at 7.30 in the big house. For

18 For someone who couldn't drive, my mother had an extraordinary capacity
to make any journey ten times as stressful as it needed to be. Every time she
saw a car coming from another direction she'd suddenly scream 'LOOK
OUT!' which would make you jump out of your skin and think a juggernaut
was speeding at you from a side road. She would regularly scream when overtaking lorries on the motorway. To conclude: get into any car with Brenda and
you will emerge a shadow of your former self.

19 She refers here to the Millau viaduct. It's a whopper and spans the gorge
valley of Tarn.

20 Not QUITE correct. It was designed by a consortium headed up by
French structural engineer and bridge specialist Michel Virlogeux and Norman
Foster (the famous British architect) and was made by Eiffage S.A., a French
civil engineering construction company.

21 It's not. It's called Masquières. You're welcome.

about an hour, people had been arriving – all very posh. 2
guys from Pool on motorbikes – an organist and his male
friend – a consultant and his chatty wife – Dutch couple and
French couple.

We go up to the house, enter through a huge Oak door with
wonderful lock contraptions into a stone flagged room with a
raised wood burning fire, oak settles, tables, huge modern lamps
and antiques to weep for. It was wonderful.

Then the meal. My God. First course – Salade de Rustique
– green salad and preserved onions – scrumptious. 2nd course
– a wonderful Navarin of lamb.[22] *I have never eaten a meal*
that was so delicious – the lamb was reared on the farm, the
vegetables grown in the garden. 3rd course – cheese board. 4th
course – cherry sorbet with small redcurrants in it and served
with fresh figs.

Had long chat with young chef afterwards. He spoke good
English and so I told him about the cucumber experience in
Montpellier. Never eat out in Montpellier. According to this
young man, Montpellier was built on swamps and marshes
and consequently is a very damp, humid town. As there haven't
been any frosts for two years, the town's restaurants are
crawling with large black COOTIES – COCKROACHES!
Ah! I could smell them in the restaurant we visited – you
know the smell – like a pair of pants gone rancid. He was so
charming, I told him he was the premier chef dans le monde.
He was very pleased.

Long drive down to St Remy Provence – our old stomping
ground. Staying in a typical Provencal Mas[23] *– beautiful*
grounds and state of the art tasteful. Had lovely meal in

---

22 If you're wondering what a navarin of lamb is, it's not unlike a hotpot. It's
a rich lamb ragu in a wine sauce, cooked until the meat is pull-apart tender.

23 Traditional farmhouse.

S. Remy last night – restaurant packed with French – always a good sign.

Off to Menerbes[24] now. As this is a road holiday we haven't had many funny encounters. Oh, we did meet a woman who had lived in Hitchin! Scary, eh?[25]

Back Monday
Big hugs and kisses
Mum and Dad. Xxx

* * *

24 Ménerbes is in the south-east of France, down in the Côte d'Azur, so they're really zooming about.

25 Sadly, Brenda would have thought she'd been sent to spy on her.

Nine

I'd done well.

We'd been given an IQ test at school and I'd come joint top with a boy whose name I no longer remember. It meant that I was off to Hitchin Girls' School, the ex-grammar that was now a single sex comprehensive. I was rather sad to be leaving junior school, not least because a lot of my best friends had been boys: there was James with the silky-smooth skin, Simon who gave me warts and Christopher who once had fleas and looked like an extra in *Oliver!* Boys and I would not collide again for the best part of six years.

It was at this point, as I entered puberty, that my relationship with Brenda began to deteriorate. This doesn't strike me as unusual – most teenagers and parents knock heads – but it wasn't for bad behaviour on my part: I loved going to school, I always did my homework, I ate all my vegetables, I didn't nick money, I wasn't trying to smoke, drink or have underage sex. Instead, as is entirely normal for a child living with an unpredictable adult, I did exactly as I was told, so quite why we started not getting on is more of a mystery. Perhaps it was more down to me starting to see my mother for what she was – a deeply complicated, flawed woman who suffered bouts of depression – but lacked the maturity to understand that much of this was beyond her control. In short, I was starting to resent her and the consequences of her behaviour on my day-to-day life.

I became wary of her and embarrassed. Her outbursts increased: mortifying when they occurred outside the home, exhausting and upsetting when they didn't. I'd go to friends' houses and be astonished by the sense of calm, marvelling that mothers were something other than fuses in danger of being lit. It felt amazing to be with families who weren't walking on eggshells, or tip toeing round trying not to get anything wrong. Living with someone with a mental illness is draining: you lose sight of yourself and your own needs. Every waking moment is devoted to appeasing and cajoling. In many ways, you become invisible. You forget you matter.

The shift is reflected in my diaries. Arguments are meticulously recorded. 'Another terrible row with mum' is the constant refrain but something else was going on with me: I had been raised to be confident, but my self-belief was slipping away. No longer did I have any sense that I might be likeable or worthy. My diary is filled with moments where someone has complimented me – I get word a boy called David fancies me: 'He must be mad'. A girl in an upper year tells me I'm pretty: 'She doesn't know what she's talking about'. A teacher tells me I'm special: 'Bonkers'. And I'm told, repeatedly that I have talent as an artist: 'Must be blind'. It saddens me, reading it back, and if I could go back and take hold of myself I would. I had lost all confidence because I was living in a state of constant fear. I wanted to be invisible. I filled my days with escapes to other people's houses, worried about subjects I was no good at rather than enjoy the ones I excelled at. I started going to a church, despite not believing in God, and sought friendships with older girls. What I was looking for was stability and comfort.

It was around this time that Brenda's affair with Daniel would have been coming to its end and I suppose part of her increased agitation may have been to do with this. My mother could never tolerate being bored or quiet or ignored. She thrived when she was the centre of attention and had a visceral need to be the burning candle in any circle. I do wonder, thinking back, whether some of her outbursts were down to boredom: she had an uncanny knack of turning entirely normal domestic days into living hells. She could also catastrophise anything. Broken glass? End of the world. Lump of coal on the carpet? You've ruined everything. Everything had to be done precisely how she wanted it and every moment of our lives was controlled. It's a struggle not to consider her behaviour a form of abuse. Today it would be called coercive control, but the single reason I am able to look back at my mother's behaviour and not hate her for it is because there isn't a scrap of doubt in my mind that she couldn't stop herself. Each and every time she would lose it, it was like watching bad weather rolling in from nowhere. She was like a tornado touching ground and, when she was in those moments, deaf to all sense or reason, trying to talk her down was about as much use as trying to control the direction of damage. I think it was her way of coping.

As to what she might have been suffering with was another matter. Was it depression? Did she have a personality disorder? Was she bipolar? Did she have Attention Deficit Hyperactivity Disorder? Something else? Or was she the sum total of her difficult start in life? These were the questions that I needed to answer.

This isn't to diminish what my father and I were subjected to. There were days where it was unbearable and the only thing to do was escape to separate rooms and wait until she'd calmed down. It was like being under siege, but I also don't want to lessen how much fun she was. It's a balancing act for me, telling her story here. It's easy to remember the bad bits but the good bits, the brilliant bits, outweighed the madness and we both loved her very much.

Phyllis loved her too, but she still dreaded seeing her. 'It was never a pleasure,' she told me. 'I'd come to see you but it was never a case of, oh, I'm going to visit my sister, I'm really looking forward to it. Instead, it was always, what mood is she going to be in this time? So often she was hyper and looking for a row. It was exhausting.'

Having lost her mother at a very young age, Phyllis would have adored a big sister with whom she was able to have a loving relationship, but Brenda just wasn't capable of it. 'She didn't look after Mummy. She didn't look after me. She didn't look after Gerty when she was dying. I don't think it was because she didn't care. It just didn't cross her mind. She couldn't do it.'

It's a strange, inexplicable facet of Brenda's personality. She had the capacity to care a great deal and yet, when it came to Phyllis, it was like a switch turning itself off. She often told me Phyllis didn't want a relationship with her but that's not quite true. She did. She'd suggest shopping trips only to be told 'I hate shopping'; she'd ask to meet up in London only to be brushed off. From Phyllis's perspective, Brenda was not interested. 'We never did things as sisters,' she told me. 'She missed out on that.'

Brenda did what Brenda wanted and what she most wanted was not to be a devoted sister, mother or wife but to have a fulfilling career. Work, for Brenda, was the thing that gave her purpose, and it was going well. She was respected and had been promoted to school librarian, a position she loved. What it didn't change was her inability to get up in the mornings. Day in, day out, Tony would stand at the bottom of the stairs shouting up at her to get up 'or we'll be late'. Every morning, without fail, she'd totally ignore him and would only rattle down the stairs when she was good and ready. In her head, the first lesson of the day began at nine and that meant she didn't need to physically be inside the school gates until five minutes before.

'There was one morning when Mr Johnson, the headmaster, was standing out at the front of the school,' my dad recalls, 'and as we pulled up, parked and got out of the car, he was waving his arms and shouting "GET IN. YOU'RE LATE. HURRY UP." And it was only as we got closer, we realised he wasn't shouting at kids. He was shouting at us.'

My father is the sort of man that if he knows he's got to be somewhere by midday, he'll be standing with his coat on, jingling the car keys on the end of a finger two hours before he needs to leave. If he tells me he's coming to see me and will 'be there at eleven', it means he'll arrive at nine. He's always had a thorough approach to life: before Sat Nav, he'd memorise maps, he'd write out arrowed itineraries and, crucially, if he discovered there would be no reliable parking, he'd call the whole thing off. My mother was the polar opposite. People who like things to be organised will feel the depth of his pain, but she never changed. Brenda was a bloody nightmare when it came to giving a single rat's arse about anyone else.

'I think I spent every morning of my entire working life breaking out into hot sweats simply because your mother wouldn't get out of bed. I started taking her breakfast in bed to try and hurry her along. Worst thing I ever did. She worked out she could now get breakfast in bed. She was like an evil genius.'

You had to hand it to her. Breakfast in bed, chauffeured everywhere because she couldn't drive, she never had to cook (she couldn't cook), all dusting was now done by me as was the interminable spinning of the washing that was done in an ancient, clanking machine that was operated BY FOOT PUMP. My dad was right – she was an evil genius if 'evil genius' meant somehow interpreting feminism to mean she never had to lift a finger at home ever again. As far as she was concerned, the work she did at school was more than enough, thank you very much. She was like a Roman empress. She didn't even make cups of tea.

People often don't believe me when I say my mother never made me a meal, but she really didn't. She didn't even make me toast. There has only been one week of my life when I've had to do without my dad. He's deaf in one ear and it was decided, in an attempt to improve matters, that he was going to have a bit of bone taken out and a bit of Teflon put in. He was going to be in hospital for a week. Reading the situation precisely for what it was, I had gone into school, pondering quite how I was going to survive on my own with my mother.

I simply could not comprehend how she was going to keep me alive. As luck would have it, on the same day, my French teacher announced we were going to be embarking on a special project and she told us to 'ask your mums to get you a scrapbook'. My hand shot up.

'I won't be able to do the project,' I said, in all seriousness, 'because there is absolutely no way my mum will be able to get a scrapbook.'

I genuinely believed this. The thought of my mother, who did not carry money, like the Queen, being able to a) go to a shop and b) find a scrap book and c) buy it, was beyond anything I could comprehend. Nope. Never going to happen.

My French teacher took this the wrong way and misinterpreted me as confessing to coming from an impoverished family running a strict budget for whom the price of a scrapbook would be onerous. The next day, she called me out of class and handed me a scrapbook she'd bought herself. It was the only time I ever cried at school. Kindness has always floored me.

On day one of my father being in hospital, I stood, hockey stick over my shoulder, PE kit hanging off the end of it, and stared at my mother. I was like something out of a Spaghetti Western except we were in the hallway and I was about to walk to school. 'This is your big chance with me,' I began. I was eleven. 'Do you understand?'

She nodded, solemnly. 'Yes,' she said. 'I understand,' as if we were going over the final arrangements for a very important military assault that would result in many dead but might turn the tide in any given war.

'I am not cooking for you,' I added. 'Do you understand?'

She nodded again. 'I understand.'

Off I went to school where, to cover myself in case of the inevitable, I had double lunch because, to be brutally honest, I didn't believe a bloody word she said.

I came home to discover her beaming, at the doorway. 'Are you ready for your first course?' she trilled.

First course? I thought. There's a *first* course? What alchemy is this?

I was ushered through to the dining room. There was to be no further delay. There was a first course, and we would be having it immediately. I sat down.

'*Ta daaaah!*' With a flourish, she plonked a jar of pickled cockles down on the table in front of me.

I stared at it as she handed me a fork. 'I can't open it,' she added. 'So, *you* can open it.'

She said this as if she was surprising me with the greatest gift known to man, a proper treat. It was up there with the time she forgot it was my birthday when we were on holiday in Suffolk, so she ran into a bric-a-brac shop and bought me an antique doll of a little soldier with real hair that looked as if it were haunted. Occasionally, I still get it out to show people. It is the single most terrifying object you will ever see.

I took the jar and twisted the lid. Nothing. I tried again and hurt my hand. I handed it to Brenda. 'No,' she just said, shaking her head. So, I put the jar back down on the table and we stared at it for a bit.

'Oh well,' she shrugged. 'We'll have to forget the first course.'

'What's the main course?' I asked, in the same tone that might be used if you'd arrived in a village in the middle of the night and you're not entirely sure the man who runs the only pub isn't a cannibal.

'Rice and garlic,' she announced, proudly.

I pushed myself up from the table and made myself a sandwich.

'Can you make me one too?' Brenda asked, and I did, because she *is* an evil genius.

The following evening, I found her hunched over a boiling pan. She was stirring it.

'What's that?' I was almost too afraid to hear the answer.

'Broccoli,' she announced, with the confidence of someone who's just invented breadsticks.

I peered in. It was parsley.

Anyway. You get the point. My mother could not cook and that week, as Dad lay in hospital, she got me to ring round my friends and cry down the phone: 'My dad is in hospital and can I come for tea?' Then, when their mum replied, 'Of course she can,' I had to add, 'And my mum, too.'

My mother took all of this in her stride. We'd arrive, I'd be mortified, my friend's mother would look mildly surprised Brenda would also be having fishfingers and beans and then, to cover my embarrassment, I would offer to do the washing up. At one of these moments, with my mother sitting cackling with glee at the table, I turned to her and asked, 'Aren't you going to help wash up?'

To which she replied, 'I can't pick up a pan, Emma. My womb will drop out.'

When my dad came home, he had to lie very, very still for three days. He gave Brenda a twenty-pound note, told her to walk into town and 'get some things for the family'. She was gone for three hours and came back with a candelabra and a bunch of grapes.

She'd eaten the grapes on the way home.

GAETA[1]

Dear Emmy

Thankfully had an uneventful flight to Rome, picked up a small Fiat and tried to get out of the airport. It was the plastic card device. We[2] put it in the slot but the barrier wouldn't go up. Tried again – and again – and again. We couldn't get out of the airport. Luckily, we were alone while struggling with the card and not causing an embarrassing build-up of people trying to leave like us. Unluckily, there was no one around.

There was an office looking building to the right of the barrier, so Tony left the car and walked over. No-one to be seen. Tony shouts 'Scusi! Scusi!' a number of times hoping to attract attention. No luck, so he switched to a stronger 'Assistanza! Assistanza!'

I watch him from the car. It is a very hot afternoon in Italy. We can't expect anyone to come because it's mangare time.

'Bang on the door!' I shout. He starts banging on the door. 'Scusi!'

While he is doing this, another car turns up and parks behind us. Tony continues banging on the door of the office building. The driver and his passenger sit and stare.

'Buongiorno,' I shout from the car window.

The driver of the car shouts 'Que il problema?'

'Parla inglese?' I respond with a big smile.

Tony now comes back and shows the driver his useless piece of plastic.

1 Uh oh. We're starting with a town in capitals. You know what this means . . .

2 *Tony

'*Il carta che il non Bueno, signor.*' *The driver gets out, takes Tony's ticket, turns it over, flips it in and the barrier goes up.*[3]

'*Molto gracie*' *we both shout waving and smiling at a slightly contemptuous Italian driver.*

Our journey to Castel Gandolfo,[4] *our overnight stop en route to Gaeta*[5] *was very pleasant. Driving down the evocative Via Appia*[6] *was a surprising thrill. It was very easy to imagine the Roman legions who built it and the stocky Italians in their red plumed helmets, probably practising their Sinister Dexter Sinister Dexter*[7] *as they strode so confidently forward for imperial conquest.*

A bit different from the more modern version – Italian drivers. Terrible – the worst in Europe. They still do Sinister Dexter but without any signals – they drive in the middle of the road, honk loudly as they are about to overtake and drive precariously one handed while the other hand adjusts the vanity mirror, the sunglasses, combs the hair or lights a cigarette.

By late evening, we had reached Castel Gandolfo where we had booked an hotel near the lake. Castel Gandolfo is the Pope's Summer Residence, and we were looking forward to visiting the Renaissance palace and village.

Castel Gandolfo is on a hill and we knew we had to go down the hill to get to the lake. This should have been straight-forward, but we weren't in luck for straight-forward.

3 This is precisely the sort of low-grade and entirely self-induced scrape my parents were forever getting into.

4 Town sixteen miles to the south-east of Rome.

5 City in central Italy, on the sea. You're about to find out what it's currently best known for.

6 Appian Way, one of the most important Roman roads. It went from Rome to Brindisi and was built specifically to transport troops.

7 Left, right in Latin. If you've read *The Tent, the Bucket and Me,* you will recall my father marching me along Hadrian's Wall saying, 'Sinister Dexter'.

There were no directions to the lake and in a panic, Tony shot across a red light.[8] A carabinieri just happened to be around at the time and we were pulled up with a series of aggressive whistles (is he whistling at us?), surprisingly threatening gestures and a lot of shouting.[9] Tony pulled in and the carabinieri strode across – he did not speak English and we did not have much Italian. We ended up with a fine.

'Just throw it away,' I said. 'We haven't got time for this.' I snatched the slip of paper and threw it out of the car window.

'Now you've done it' said Tony.[10]

Twenty minutes later, after travelling down the hill and up the hill, we found the right turn for the lake. By now it was dark, and the empty lakeside was strung with fairy lights. A few restaurants were still open but as this was October, the season was over. We were hoping to get a meal as we were starving.

Suddenly I spotted the name 'Mongolfiera'

'There it is' I pointed to what could only be described as a very run-down Spanish style Ponderosa. It looked like a suitable setting for the Maltese Falcon. Shady.

The door was opened by a dark-haired man, beyond him the walls of the bar and lounge were crammed with garish paintings of undressed ladies and bulls. Bulls horns were displayed on extravagant wooden stands. I can tell you Emsy, my heart sank. We were staying in a set for a 1950's B Movie.

A small man took us to our room. Its most noticeable feature was the wallpaper which had been casually ripped off in a number of places. The bed was comfortable, and we had a

---

8 No doubt induced by another stunning round of 'Directions from Brenda'.

9 Not entirely clear here whether the shouting is from the carabinieri or Brenda.

10 This will have terrified my father to his very core.

useful adjoining terrace with views over the lake to the Pope's palace on the hill.

After hurriedly tidying ourselves we set off to find a restaurant. By now it was 9pm. We parked the car and walked beside the lake hoping to find somewhere open. We could hear a lot of noise coming from near-by so headed towards it.

The restaurant was full of people, young and old, milling around. The place looked like a school canteen, plastic topped tables, no tablecloths and chairs. There were no curtains on the windows. A trestle table was covered with bowls of salad, bread and an amazing suckling pig which was being carved as we arrived. There was noisy appreciation of the suckling pig and large glasses filled with wine were being drunk around us. We thought we had walked into a private party, but we were okay – it was for everyone. With a paper plate filled with salad, focaccia bread and suckling pig accompanied by a half pint glass of rough Chianti, we stopped worrying about anything.

An hour or so later we left with our tummies full, already very drowsy. On the way back to the hotel we were quite surprised to see about twenty cars parked away from the meagre lights around the lake. As I peered into the darkness it was fairly easy to register that the cars and their occupants were parked up for sexy business![11]

In the morning when we passed the spot again, it was littered with pieces of toilet paper and used condoms. Disgusting! This was meant to be the Pope's Summer Residence![12] After seeing so many Fellini[13] films we were not

---

11 REMINDER: my parents, in their courting days, were not averse to a bit of In the Car Hokey-pokey so Brenda's shock here is entirely put on.

12 Given Brenda's loathing of all things Catholic, it's surprising she's had an attack of the prudish vapours here.

13 Federico Fellini, great Italian film director and screenwriter, winner of four Oscars. His best-known film is probably *La Dolce Vita*.

surprised at all. In fact, there were Felliniesque scenes all around. As we drove around the lake, a number of men in very, very small bathing trunks were offering their wares – much posturing and flapping of towels. The Roman legacy had not been crushed by Catholic Popes.

The Pope's palace and the village were charming, and we were very lucky to be there when a glorious Italian wedding was taking place. The bride wearing an extravagant dress for a ball and the family and friends all resplendent. Lovely!

From here we carried on to Gaeta which is near the Bay of Naples and another adventure – but this time we couldn't have guessed what lay in store. We were booked to stay in Gaeta residence – a Renaissance Palace offering self-catering apartments. The view from the Palace shown in the brochure from the apartment terrace was of Gaeta Bay with mountains in the distance and the sea at our doorstep. We were so looking forward to staying in this beautiful spot.

When we arrived, we realised we were booked into a large modern looking hotel not a Renaissance villa. That was the first disappointment but as the apartment was stylish and the terrace was large, we accepted the compromise. However, within 30 minutes of doing our quick appraisal of Gaeta we had to accept that all was not as we had been led ourselves to expect.

This time it was my fault.[14] I had suggested a quick trip to Gaeta before going back to Rome: sea before the city! This was the first time I had used a posh brochure instead of finding delightful places to stay in The Lady *magazine.[15] I had not*

---

14 If you have a marker pen to hand, highlight this sentence. Even better, rip this page out and put it in a frame. It is the only known admission by Brenda to anything having been her fault.

15 Even more shocking, Brenda, determined feminist, hater of Margaret Thatcher and all things Tory, here admits to being an avid reader of *The Lady*. In two sentences, everything I thought was true has been smashed to smithereens.

done my homework because a trip to an Italian coastal area should have been without complications. The sea is the sea. Not here!

Gaeta is famous – not for its charming fishing village character, not for its lovely old mellow stone buildings. It is famous for being a NATO headquarters housed in the castle at the top of a cliff and a USA Naval port.[16] The main entrance to the Naval Port was right outside our apartment window and the helicopter pad, a mere 40 yards away. When we sat on our terrace the view to our right was the brochure image – the mountains and the sea. The view opposite and to our left was a helicopter pad, a working military Navy port and moored in that area a grandiose and somewhat intimidating large grey US Navy supply ship. Milling around everywhere were hundreds of US sailors in blue work fatigues and white hats.

Enough? No! Our hotel – remember that brochure description of the Gaeta residence – the Renaissance Palace? Well, actually, it was being used to house US Navy personnel. Every day we were passing uniformed staff officers on the stairs and in the lift. Young men and women in whites were in the bar and at breakfast we would be lucky to get a table. We realised to our horror that we were part of a US Naval barracks.

After two days, we started to accommodate ourselves to this unexpected experience and would have shrugged our brown shoulders and thrown ourselves into the ever merry companionship of the naval crew if this had been a just a naval backwater.

But Gaeta was the hub – the centre for CIA intelligence, for international meetings, for secret agendas.[17] Everyone involved with the US military and their allies came to Gaeta.

16 And now the story begins . . .

17 Oh God. Here we go.

The helicopter pad was never out of action. At least 8 times a day and all night, naval and government personnel were brought in and taken out of Gaeta.

We could not sit on our terrace. Apart from the excruciating noise there was a real risk that we would be cut in two by the helicopter blades if we stood up too fast. After two days your Mum went into revenge mode.[18] We had been sold a turkey and friendly smiling navy boys would not make up for the huge amount of money we had spent on this holiday – the flight, car hire, the petrol, palatial rent.

After a few pointless complaints to the manager who resolutely denied responsibility – 'People who come to Gaeta know about the US Navy' – I decided that stronger action was needed.

Okay. I would prepare my evidence starting with a photographic record. I[19] took photos of the naval base, the helicopter pad, the navy personnel in uniform at the hotel. I walked across the road to take close shots of the grey supply ship and smilingly snapped as many guys in blue uniform that I could. Of course, my activities with the camera were being observed.

One morning, coming down to breakfast a very large American woman officer stopped on the stairs to greet us. 'Hi!' she said. It was the sort of 'Hi' you might hear in a thriller or a ghost film in which the evil one pops out unexpectedly and then kills you quick!

'I think you've been taking a few photos of us.' She stared hard at Tony, obviously going for the weakest link.[20] He looked at me flummoxed and did not reply.

---

18 You know when the T-Rex is brought back to New York by idiot businessmen in *Jurassic Park Lost World* and it gets out and loses its shit? Like that, but worse.

19 *told Tony to

20 Probably because he was the one being forced to take the photos but excellent use here of 'weakest link'.

'*Yes, we have*' *I managed to step higher up on the stairs while I spoke to her.*[21] *I was taller than her now.*

'*Yes, it's photographic evidence.*' *I said in a determined way.*

'*Evidence?*' *She looked equally suspicious and annoyed.*

'*Yes. For court.*' *I said in a deliberately flat voice.*

'*For court?*' *More suspicion.*

Tony was shifting down the stairs, preparing to run.

'*Tony! Just wait!*' *I said. I had not moved from my stronger position.*

'*Are you taking us to court?*' *she half jested.*

'*Not you personally. Just the hotel*' *Same flat voice.*

Leaving it at that, I stepped down around her and followed Tony who was already out of the door.

'*Bye! Lovely day!*' *I waved from the bottom of the stairs.*[22]

We made the best of Gaeta, the weather was glorious and on the far side of the bay the fishing village atmosphere was charming. I can't say that I'd recommend Gaeta as a holiday destination: there was very little to do and inevitably we got into a lunch time habit of drinking too much. I don't like Italian wine, so I got our regular taverna to make me Manhattans – they were very good. Too good, I'm afraid. Tony was mortified with my public displays of drunkenness – they were on a par with the drinking ability of the US Navy.

I couldn't understand why Tony was so annoyed. After 3 Manhattans[23] *and lunch, all I did was giggle a lot, kiss Tony on the street and walk into other bars for drunken chats with the navy. Nothing extraordinary. We did make one friend – a tiny nun who we saw and spoke to every day when we passed the magnificent church in the village square. Our conversations*

21 Good grief, I wish I'd seen this with my own eyes.

22 It's at this point I realise my mother is like a character out of *Napoleon Dynamite*.

23 THREE! AT LUNCH!

were in Italian, but we seemed to understand each other. She would greet us with 'Ciao Brenda and Tony. Come sta?'

'Multo bueno' we would reply, every day the same. Tony made sure we made a detour round the church after the Manhattan lunches. He didn't want the sweet nun to see the real Brenda!

Off to Rome next but I am really looking forward to the fight for full compensation, I have to admit.

Lots of love and kisses
Mum and Dad.

* * *

Ten

In 1983, Shephalbury School closed – there was a lack of demand for school places across Stevenage – and the site of the school was set to be taken over by North Herts College. It would be the home for the Arts Foundation Course and Dad, being an art teacher, was offered a position. He would be teaching life drawing.

Brenda, on the other hand, was shuffled sideways to another school in Stevenage, Barnwell, where pupils and teachers who agreed to it were being transferred. She wasn't particularly happy with the new arrangement, so when a position for someone to teach history of art came up at the new college, she was able to persuade the powers that be she'd be perfect for the job and just like that, both of my parents were back working together in the same place again.

She made an immediate impression. A student there, Anji Archer, remembers her:

She had a very strong presence. When she arrived in a room, you knew it. She had incredible energy, was incredibly clever. I learned so much from her. I admired her. I was scared of her too. On a personal level, I'd been going through a hard time and had confided in Tony. He was such a generous man, always smiling. I had gone to see him in his office and Brenda was in there and she picked up on the fact I was having a bad time. To try and change the subject, she got me talking about Biba, a shop she'd loved to shop in in the seventies. It worked and then, totally to my surprise, she found me a few days later. She'd bought me a book about Biba. It was so kind. The other thing, of course, was that she was the person who taught me what a phallic symbol was. You remember these things.

Well. Quite.

This was a happy and fulfilling time for Brenda. She had walked into the new world of further education, looked around and worked out what she needed to do to stay in it. She preferred the older students, enjoyed their company and conversation and so decided, there and then, that she would never return to teaching in schools. This is where she wanted to be and, spurred on to make the most of herself, she decided, at last, to get a proper degree. She enrolled herself in a part-time film studies course in London and began the odyssey of improving herself yet again. Brenda was a woman who never gave up.

She threw herself into her studies. Her thesis would be about government propaganda in wartime films of the 1940s. Here she was, like her father before her, embracing the dark arts of politics. She would hold forth at the dinner table about psychological warfare, controlled disinformation, the bleeding of political objectives into advertising and women who were being quietly subjugated to wartime needs. She became obsessed with a 1945 drama, *The Way to the Stars,* so much so, that every time she mentioned it, I would pretend to fall into a coma. I shouldn't have been so ungrateful: when I sat at friend's mothers' tables, I'd be lucky if the most challenging thing I was asked was whether I watched *EastEnders*.

The Way to the Stars, directed by Anthony Asquith, written by Terence Rattigan and starring John Mills, Michael Redgrave and Rosamund John, is about a pilot officer posted to a squadron at a new airfield. On one level, it's exactly what you'd expect of a wartime film about pilots: there's the green rookie, the gnarled Squadron Leader suffering from battle fatigue, the stolen romances, the inevitable deaths. What sets it apart is that, for a war film, there are no combat sequences and there are only three very brief shots of anyone inside a cockpit. The film is really about the Home Front, maintaining relationships during wartime and, crucially, the ramming home of the emotional resilience of the British and how the welcome arms of the girls at home can reboot a burned-out pilot. For all its robustness, it's a film that drills down to one thing: the love of a good woman will save all men and it's women's patriotic duty to deliver it.

You can imagine, can't you, what my mother might have had to say about that. As far as she was concerned, it wasn't a woman's duty to do anything other than make the best of herself and improve her own prospects. The thought of abandoning every hope, wish or dream in order to prop up a man, was an outright affront. If you ever stop and wonder why so many men have been so very successful, she used to argue, it was invariably because they've got an unpaid slave at home making sure they don't have to worry about a thing. In our house, that role was reversed.

My mother, then, was still holding the flame of feminism aloft. She was a suburban Boudicca, leaning into the front of her chariot, whipping on the horses, and Tony, the most mild-mannered man you'd ever wish to meet, was, I think, just happy to let her get on with it. He was extraordinary, really, especially for the times. He was the only man I knew who did the cooking. Friends would actually be startled by it. 'Your *dad* does the cooking? Your *dad*?', as if this was like me telling them I'd been grown in a lab by aliens and my entire existence was an experiment. I may as well have told people I was being raised by wolves. Nobody other than me had my home set-up.

I can look back now and marvel, I suppose, that I was brought up in what was an enlightened household. I wasn't bound by societal norms, I was encouraged to think, to carve my own way, to be whoever I wanted to be but at the time, I didn't have the foresight to see that this was all rather good for me. Instead, it was simply mortifying. Why couldn't my mother be like Helena, the farmer's wife I stayed with every Wednesday when Brenda was at college and Dad was sitting outside the Greek takeaway, behind the BBC, eating a shish kebab? She had an aga and wore a skirt and sensible shoes and spoke with a soft Irish lilt and cooked sausages for breakfast. She lived in a house in a village and if you stood very still, all you could hear was the thick ticking of a grandfather clock. Everything about it was calm and peaceful and ordered and safe. There was no chaos, and it felt amazing.

Yet now, I understand my upbringing was the making of me. It's the reason I am who I am and at times it was difficult, but it was also a den of riches. 'Who wants to be boring?' Brenda would yell. For her, being dull was the worst thing imaginable. Life was to be experienced, poked at, provoked. She would make mistakes, terrible ones too, but who wants to spend a lifetime not making any? Mistakes, for Brenda, were opportunities, failings were motivations to do better.

Doing the research for this book, I finally got round to reading my mother's thesis. She used to beg me to read it when she was writing it, but I was doing my O Levels at the time, now known as GCSEs, and would use that as an excuse: I was revising, I had homework, didn't have the time. It must have hurt her. Here she was, finally achieving a long-held dream and nobody at home was the blindest bit interested. I certainly wasn't, and all Tony enjoyed was the amazing kebabs he got to eat during the weekly trip to London to drop her off and pick her up. She had nobody to bounce ideas off, so she held forth at the dining room table when we couldn't escape and while she chattered away, overflowing with ideas, we rolled our eyes and feigned yawns.

Her thesis is excellent, by the way, revelatory even. The film, I discovered, was part of an extensive propaganda campaign ordered by the US Office of War Information. It was designed to produce a sympathetic acceptance and understanding of the American Alliance during World War II and it screws down to how the British relinquished authority on propaganda to the Americans. I was reminded of a moment when Brenda burst in through the front door. She'd submitted an FOI request for documents on the Film Division and had come up trumps.

She had discovered a memorandum dated 3 September 1943 to then president, Roosevelt.

> *It would be preferable to have one supreme authority on propaganda policy in one place . . . Such an authority should make its decisions in global rather than local terms. The seat of this authority should be Washington . . . so that propaganda policy may be directly integrated with military and foreign policy. Churchill recommended Govt. to concur.*

In other words, Churchill gave up British control on messaging.

She was triumphant. At the time my mother was writing her thesis, the anti-American mood in the UK was growing: the Greenham Common Peace Camp was in full swing, CND were making a stand against US cruise missiles and protestors were peacefully walking onto US air bases to make it quite clear their presence wasn't wanted.

Brenda felt as if she had uncovered a historically significant event and one that tapped directly into the mood of the moment. She was ecstatic but her enthusiasm wasn't encouraged, a fact I now regret. My mother was a creature of passions that burned bright: whether it was teaching or her MA thesis or the views she held, everything had to be intensely felt or else what was the point and here she was, jumping up and down for joy at home and neither of us felt sufficiently interested to celebrate it. Brenda was having to do the same thing she'd had to do all her life: just get on with it by herself.

At the same time as Brenda was widening her horizons, two things of significance took place: Phyllis gave birth to Ben, who was to become one of Brenda's best friends, and a French family moved into the house at the end of the lane. On both counts, Brenda was beside herself.

Brenda got on better with boys. There was no doubt about it and in Ben, she was to find someone she adored and who adored her back. 'She was the first person,' he told me, 'to take me into a sex shop.'

Of course she was.

For Ben, Brenda meant one thing: fun. There would be Christmases where she would spend the afternoon dressing him and his little brother, Tom, up and make them put on a play. Later, when he was older, it was Brenda who would meet him off the train at Waterloo and take him off to the South Bank and Soho.

'We'd always go to a new bar for cocktails, see the latest art film,' Ben recalls. 'She introduced me to so many things. She bashed feminism into me, liberal views, gave me perspective on how women are treated. And then, when Tom and I were older, the roles reversed. It would be us who were taking her to the new bars, the new exhibitions, the new films. She thrived on being around youth. It kept her young. She always wanted to know everything.'

At this point in the story, though, Ben was a baby. Perhaps this was the point where Brenda might buck up her ideas about playing the role of the big sister?

'She was absolutely useless,' Phyllis responds. 'I'd had to have a caesarean, Ben was in intensive care and all Brenda did was sit at the end of the bed showing off. She didn't even ask me how I was. Mind you, I wasn't surprised. She'd been exactly the same at my wedding. She turned up the night before, didn't lift a finger. I spent the entire evening making sandwiches then found her eating them.

'What a day it was. Paul was so pissed from the stag do I have no idea how he made it up the aisle, I had a wedding dress made from an eiderdown cover, you fell in mud, Bob was trying to have it away with my friend Linda over the boiler, Paul's mother did nothing but cry and told me she'd never forgive me for stealing her son and Uncle Leslie impaled himself in a rose bush. Brenda spoke to nobody.'

So, that's a no.

Ben was right though: Brenda fed herself on new things. Our new French neighbours were, as far as she was concerned, fabulous. Brenda had never up until this point, shown any interest in or got on with her neighbours and as her mental health deteriorated, it would be our poor neighbours who would bear the brunt. But foreign neighbours? Who'd only be there for a few years? She couldn't roll out the red carpet quick enough.

Michel and Mado were very, very French. Michel was tall and lean with a prominent nose and the deep, dark eyes of a poet. Mado was the short, bob-haired, immaculately turned out, Cleopatra-eyed wife. She didn't believe in feminism AT ALL. She was a housewife, she smoked and she couldn't give a shit. Brenda adored her. Brenda loved how she'd fly off the handle at the slightest thing, throwing her arms in the air and shouting, 'BOUFFF!', swearing with words Brenda didn't understand. It was like watching someone being mesmerised by a snake. They were polar opposites yet something about them was unmistakably familiar: they both liked to laugh and shout a lot.

My father and Mado began to have cooking competitions until Mado became incensed because my father had made a better crème caramel than she had. As far as she was concerned, it was akin to a national humiliation and so we entered the phase of the Over-The-Top Dinner Parties, which culminated in an eleven-course meal so rich my father had to go and vomit in the garden.

There was flirting, of course, and Brenda was convinced that Mado was madly in love with Tony but then Michel was clearly madly in love with Brenda, and I can only be grateful that neither Tony nor Brenda were prepared to quite return the feelings. These were the good days: Brenda was properly fulfilled, intellectually and professionally. She had a new nephew to love and exotic friends and things were about to get even better.

I'd passed all my O Levels and had decided to aim high.

'I want to go to Oxford,' I told her.

The game was on.

Dearest Emmy

We are in the second apartment which is very like the house where we first stayed together in Siena.[1] It is very beautiful, and we have hundreds of acres of olive trees and vines to look at. You should come here for complete relaxation. The place is full of Germans, but we don't see them or hear them. It is like being in a retreat: everyone's come for rest, solitude and calm. We have a magnificent terrace – high up – with spectacular views of the valley and mountains.

This is the Maremma[2] – the valley leading to the sea. We have access to hundreds of acres of woods, rivers etc and special keys to open secret gates. It is very romantic. You would love it. This morning we had a long walk in the woods, but we were a bit frightened of coming across wild boar who are definitely around but worse, we came across a strange, large footprint which we didn't recognise. Is it a bear, a wolf, a badger? We didn't know – but it was enough to make us go back. As there are a large number of Germans here, our apartment had a few Der Speigel *magazines which I flicked through. To my horror, I came across an article about wolves*

1 I had just turned sixteen when I first went to Italy with my parents. The villa we stayed in was outside Siena, up a hill, no garden to speak of, just straight out into an olive grove and, of course, no pool. I remember feeling utterly irritated that I had nothing to do other than traipse round beautiful churches and amazing Siena, visiting incredible ice cream parlours and watching the Palio, a once in a lifetime experience everyone should enjoy. Cultured travel is wasted on teenagers. What an ungrateful wretch I was.

2 Maremma is the beautiful coastal part of western central Italy. It includes parts of northern Lazio and south-western Tuscany.

being reintroduced into Tuscany.[3] We then decided that the strange footprint in the wood could have been a wolf. No more walks that way.

Anyhow, we are really enjoying it here. Tomorrow we are going back to Punta Ala[4] for a sentimental journey. My Italian is much better now. I had a conversation with a complete stranger in a Co-op about the price of this strange small car the old men drive which is a small cabin for one with a large truck behind. It's nearly a motorbike. Anyhow, I couldn't believe that they were nearly £2,000. Tony is jealous now. He's too shy to speak to people and I'm not. I can understand them now. Italian is much easier than French.

Glad I spoke to you tonight. Tony says you can't be paying for our calls when we rang you. Anyhow, he's got to sort out how to pay more at this end.

DAD – Mum just asks questions and nods and says 'Si, Si' but she hasn't got a clue what anyone is saying to her.[5]

★ ★ ★

3 Please note my mother cannot speak or read German. She's seen a picture of a wolf in a German magazine. That's it.

4 Small seaside resort in Tuscany. It's best known for sailing regattas and being a firm favourite with well to do Italians. We had been there, once before. It was my only day on a beach that holiday and I went mad and didn't apply a single drop of sun cream. I spent the next two days covered in vivid pink camomile lotion.

5 It's like he knows her . . .

Monteciano
Wednesday

Dearest Emmie

I am sitting on a bench facing rolling wooded hills, listening to a golden oriel which has just come into the garden. The only other sounds are greenfinches, bees and the tinkle of the sheep in the distance. It is May 1ˢᵗ and everything is shut so we intend having a quiet day in these perfect surroundings.

The house and garden are so lovely that we can only leave it out of a sense of duty to visit the stunning hilltop villages around. We always come back by 3pm to flop around enjoying the view and the weather. We have green/black lizards, a potential grass snake and scorpions. We haven't seen the snake or the scorpions – yet! There's a deep pond in the garden which is full of frogs! Tony throws stones into the water to watch them disappear. The weather is glorious, and the garden is full of very tall mauve flag irises and I am sitting under a bower of wisteria, the petals gently falling around me. Perfect. I feel very calm and I wish I could always feel like this.[1]

The neighbourhood cat has just come to visit, and we couldn't believe how he looks just like our Pooter[2] with

1 I think one of the reasons my mother loved travelling around Europe so much was for precisely this: finally, she felt relaxed. She may have been retired, she may have had a husband that did the shopping, the cooking, the washing, the cleaning, the driving and who took care of all the boring admin, but she was forever on edge at home, constantly alert to every imagined slight or threat. It must have been exhausting to be inside her head.

2 Pooter was the first-born tom cat of Buttons, the evilest cat that ever lived. One very cold Christmas Eve, Buttons badgered me, with her mewing, to let her sleep indoors. I relented and allowed her into my bedroom because it was

*the same markings. Yesterday he spent at least twenty
minutes eating soldier ants – huge things. You don't have
to go to Australia for exotic insects – Italy has its
share.*

*Last night we drank two bottles of the local wine which is
very good and watched the stars. I got very drunk, tried to
move my deck chair which collapsed and in a drunken state I
fell flat on top of it. I didn't feel anything at the time but when
I woke up, I had a very stiff sore hand which obviously bore
the brunt of the fall. Teach me to get drunk when I'm 60. I
intend staying sober from now on.[3]*

*We had a long, weary journey from Paris to Milan on Friday
but had a good night with two Americans in a restaurant in
Paris. I think the four of us were a bit loud and we upset the
French. Oh well.*

*We travelled with two men from Hong Kong from Paris to
Milan. They were in the fashion business but felt a bit nervous
about Milan. They were very sweet, but I found out a lot about
China. China is the future – no middle class – rich/poor –
that's it. Back to feudalism. Milan was fine. We looked at the
Pirelli building[4] and caught the next train.*

*We are driving a brand-new purple Fiat Punto which has
been okay so far. It's very stylish and Tony loves driving it. We
had a small incident with a moped in Florence, but it was his*

Christmas. She thanked me by pissing all over my head at three in the
morning. And a very merry Christmas to you too! Pooter, on the other hand,
was sweetness itself. He was the size of a large ham.

3 Brenda would continue to enjoy all the delicious wines and cocktails until
she was diagnosed with gallstones. From that moment, she was teetotal until
the day she died.

4 The Pirelli Tower is a skyscraper and isn't particularly stunning one at that.
Given all the visual delights on offer in Milan, it's something of a puzzle that
this is what Brenda chose to go and gaze at.

fault. He overtook on the wrong side. We nearly hit him, and I was furious.[5] *Driving around here is okay. We hardly see anyone on the roads – very relaxing.*

Will write again soon.

Lots of love Mum
Xxxx

★ ★ ★

---

[5] There would have been much gesticulating out of her window with feeble attempts at Italian swear words or she would have shouted, 'ATTENZIONE!' at him while pointing her finger accusingly. Nobody did righteous road rage better than my mother.

Eleven

Here it was then, the culmination of everything Brenda had ever dreamed for me: I not only wanted to go to university, I wanted to go to Oxford. I have written about this before but it was as much Brenda's story as it was mine so forgive me for repeating it here.

I had read the Thomas Hardy book *Jude the Obscure* and become mesmerised by it. The hero, Jude Fawley, a baker's boy living in a village with a view of the spires of Oxford, dreams of going there to study. He has, realistically, no chance of doing so. There is a moment in the book that etched itself into my heart: he is sitting, staring at the city in the distance and sees a finger post pointing towards Oxford. 'Thither I go', it read. We have no way of knowing what is going to start a fire within but that did. *Thither I go*. It was to be my mantra for the next two years.

I was reasonably clever but not exceptionally so: I was very good at English and a hard worker, but I don't think I was anything out of the ordinary. The one thing I did have going for me was determination: if I set my mind to something, it got done. My schoolteachers, when I announced my intentions, were somewhat baffled and I was greeted with the sort of unencouraging shrugs delivered by car mechanics when you say you don't want the new clutch even though you haven't been able to shift the gears in weeks. There was another problem: I had decided I wanted to do a history degree, not English which I excelled at, which, looking back, is up there with one of the single most stupid decisions I ever made. It wouldn't be the worst.

Brenda, when the letter landed on the doormat with the Oxford college crest on the back, held it in her hand with a solemnity as if she was bearing a gift from the gods. 'This,' she said, staring at me, 'is the greatest chance you will ever have.' There will be some families for whom such things are to be expected but for my parents, both from working class backgrounds, this was nothing short of miraculous. Somehow, their child had a stab at going to one of the country's best universities and Brenda was giddy with it.

It astonishes me now, thinking how little preparation I had for that interview. I'd met up with my form teacher on only two occasions in an obscure cupboard of a room I'd never seen before in my six years of being at the school. It was the sort of room that might be reserved for delivering news so terrible it couldn't be done in the headmistress's office or somewhere you might take a student if they'd been mauled in a hockey match and you wanted them to die quietly, out of sight, before having to phone their parents. It had an anonymous smell you couldn't quite put your finger on but both times I went in there, it was so noticeable I visibly sniffed before wondering whether something genuinely was rotting or whether this was just the stench of doom.

Brenda spent the days leading up to the interview striding me round the garden and pumping me up. She was like the gnarled boxing trainer in *Rocky* but without the half-chewed cigar and the damp hand towel drenched in sweat slung over one shoulder. This was going to be the fight of my life, she told me. I would be up against people who had been to *gasp* public school, people who had been tutored for this moment to within an inch of their lives, I would be up against privilege and boys, boys, boys. What Brenda did in those days was instil in me a sense that I had as much right as anyone to be trying for a place at Oxford and I wasn't to forget it.

'I wish I could come with you,' she said to me, 'but I'm worried I might punch someone.'

I didn't need to dissuade her. She was more nervous than

I was. This would be her crowning achievement, the great Fuck You to her father: look what I made without your help, look what my child is capable of.

As it was, it fell to Tony to drive me to Oxford. I was to be interviewed by two tutors at St Catherine's, a college it was suggested I might apply to by my head of year, purely on the basis they had once taken someone from our school, and they thought that might 'shorten the odds'. It's fair to say that my school wasn't holding its breath.

I remember the morning well. Brenda had clutched me in tears, as if I was going to war, then shouted, 'Be brilliant!' at me, as she waved me off. I was forced to consider, if I didn't get in, there was a very real chance it might kill my mother. Tony, on the other hand, was sanguine. Dropping me off at the porter's lodge on a grey, dull day, he leaned towards the open window as I stood on the pavement. 'Do you think there's parking?'

I heaved a sigh of relief. If my father had been as worried about me as he was about finding an adequate parking spot, I'd know I was in trouble.

There was another boy lingering in the lodge. I would later work out this was Richard Herring, now a comedian, writer and podcaster. He was to become a lifelong pal, but I didn't know that then. Back then, I just stared at him and he stared at me and both of us looked a bit nauseous.

Meanwhile, back at home, Brenda was pacing. She told me later she spent much of the time making noises like a wounded badger and if she could have put herself out of her misery with a spade to the back of the head, she would have. The interview itself was quite unremarkable. I remember a plate with some biscuits on it, the languid way my interviewers leaned back into their chairs, the brown brogues, the hefty weave of a jumper. We discussed the rise of fascism in the 1930s and the likelihood of it ever happening again. I thought it unlikely but not impossible. 'History has a habit of repeating itself,' one of them said, taking a sip of the rather bitter coffee we'd all been served.

Two weeks later and another letter with a college crest landed on the mat. This time my mother was crying before I'd even opened it. It was so intense I had to retreat to my bedroom to read it. I did, then ran to the hall and screamed down the stairs.

'I've got an offer!' I yelled. 'They've offered me a place!'

The scream from Brenda that followed was on a par with the one yelled to the sky by Tim Robbins in *The Shawshank Redemption*, having crawled through a sewage pipe, after carving an escape hole with a tiny spoon for ten years. Everything in that scream was the expulsion of all the terrible shit my mother had ever had to put up with. It was like an exorcism. She'd done it. I'd done it. We'd done it.

'Two As and a B,' I announced, having another look at it.

She took the letter from me and stared at it. 'You can do that. That's doable. What are your predicted grades?'

'Two As and a B.'

'Well. There you go. Now you just have to make sure you get them.' She stared at it again. 'Can you even believe it?'

'No, I can't believe it.'

'But you can get those grades, you think?'

'Yes. I can get those grades.'

It must have been hard for her. The memory of her own fall at the last hurdle will have preyed on her mind, but this time, the prize was so great, so within reach that a form of terror took a grip of her. Brenda, to her credit, did not suddenly clamp down on me like a ton of bricks. She didn't have to. She had raised me to be self-motivated and focused and I knew that, while it was going to be tough, if I knuckled down, I could do it.

Then disaster struck.

It was the era of the village disco. Most weekends, someone would be having a birthday party. They'd be held in village halls, lights off, two boys from the Upper Sixth doing the DJing, with every other song being a slow number so the snogging could get properly underway. I was clamped on to someone, I can't remember who, but was indulging in the usual tonsil hockey that was par for the course at these events. Back then, it would be a tap on the shoulder, a lad would ask you to dance and off you'd go, put your hands round his neck and your head on his shoulder and then, following the protocol that around thirty seconds was as adequate a courtship as any, the lad could then start pumping on your face as if you were a blocked sink. Nobody ever did anything more than snog apart from one head girl two years previously who was literally head girl one day and disappeared the next. That's what happens to girls who get themselves pregnant, we learned. YOU DISAPPEAR.

One week later and I'm sitting in a Latin lesson at a desk at the front. I'm feeling a little peculiar and I'm having trouble concentrating. Outside, the sun is trying to bleed through a gauze of cloud. It feels as if there might be thunder on the way and I am consumed with the need to put my head in my hands.

'Are you all right, Emma?' my Latin teacher asked.

'I feel a bit odd.'

I was dispatched off to the nurse who, taking one look at me, sent me home.

It was at this point that I made another idiotic decision. Rather than walking straight home, I decided to idle in the sweet shop on the way and buy a Wispa. I ate it and then, for other reasons I will never understand, I decided that instead of going to bed, I'd stick a few records on and have a sing song. Two hours later and my parents arrived home to a dark house. They found me, crouched in the dark and hallucinating. I had a raging temperature, my throat was closing up and my scalp felt as if the skin had been peeled off. As Brenda put me into my bed, my head so sore I had to have a duvet under it instead of a pillow, Tony was dispatched to call the doctor. I could tolerate nothing but complete darkness and when he arrived, I cried because the light in my bedroom had to go on. The news was not good. He thought I had glandular fever. He was right.

I've never been able to eat a Wispa since.

The next month was awful. I remember very little of the first two weeks other than sleeping and not being able to eat. I felt like the statue of Achilles in *Jason and the Argonauts*: all my strength drained out of me in one fell swoop. Walking to the bathroom was like scaling a mountain, getting dressed a thing of the past, friends from school sent notes and cards, I had a visit from the head girl. She sat on a chair at a distance, and I stared at her, unable to speak. When I'd had chickenpox, two weeks before O Levels, a rumour had gone round school that I was off because I'd had an abortion. Not this time. Three weeks in and Dad started taking me downstairs and putting me in a chair in front of the television where I would say goodbye to them as they went off to work and then promptly fall asleep. I'd be woken at lunchtime with a bowl of soup and, if I was lucky, I might manage the occasional spoonful. Every scrap of energy I'd had was gone. It was like living suspended in a bell jar.

For all her foibles, I can't fault Brenda when it came to my being ill. She was always kind and patient and caring. She would wash my feet and hands with a cold flannel, keep my forehead cool, sit with me and stroke my hair and tell me not to worry, but there was everything to worry about and she knew it. This was the one time in my life in which Brenda didn't make a fuss and behaved. There was no yelling, no flying off the handle, no bad behaviour. It would be a pattern that was repeated throughout my life: when I was unwell, Brenda became brilliant.

It would be another year until I was properly fit again but the damage was done: the rest of my time at school was watered down and muted. I bumbled along, crawling from day to day, and it was clear to Brenda that the future that sat in the distance ready for me, was slipping from view.

'Are you sure you want to take your A Levels this year?' she would ask me, more than once, but I didn't want to listen. Like her, and her father before her, I had a stubborn streak and the thought of not finishing school at the same time as my peers was impossible. Again, it's to her credit that she didn't try and force me to defer or read me the riot act. I think she could see in me the determination she had encouraged. I was going to finish my schooling and take my exams when I was meant to take them. I had worked hard but the majority of the work, prior to my illness, was surely in the bag? All I had to do was stay awake.

Sadly, I didn't manage that bit and during my two-hour paper on British history, my forehead nestled softly into the crook of my elbow. I was nudged awake by the invigilator, but the damage was done. I managed one full essay and two half-cocked scribbles, and my results would reflect the slip up.

As my mother had done before me, we stood, staring down at my A Level results and realised I would not be going to Oxford. We sat together for ages on my bed, her arm around me. This is the Brenda I had forgotten, the woman who was kind and understood and got it. These were the moments of calm amidst the turmoil, the times she was able to see and feel clearly. Perhaps it was because she had been in the same spot, when she had been my age; perhaps it was because my succeeding was inextricably linked with her own sense of worth but whatever the reason, and for all her faults, Brenda was always able to muster up some empathy. She didn't patronise me with platitudes. We knew I'd fucked up. I was crushed and exhausted. What I needed, she knew, was to just do something else entirely different for a bit.

I had a school friend who had been working at a hotel in a local village. Perhaps, Brenda suggested, I might like to see if I could work there too? I'd be earning some money over the summer and I'd be with people who weren't obsessing about university. I could do that and then think about what I wanted to do. It was amazing, really. At no point did she force me to go into the clearing system. She recognised that something had died inside me and she was just going to have to wait for my pilot light to reignite itself, so off I went. No longer would

I be drifting among the dreaming spires of Oxford, instead I would be shifting steaming piles of dirty dishes.

I was good at washing up, so much so that within a short space of time I found myself promoted to peeling vegetables. My mood lightened and people started to like having me around. I made friends with an Irish woman in her forties who had four children. She taught me how to drink alcohol without throwing up. When you need people to hand down life skills, that's one of them. I was promoted again and became a waitress. What had started at the beginning of summer as an occasional evening job now became a full-time occupation. Not a day went by without me being at the hotel from break-fast until the end of the evening. I learned how to serve vegetables with a fork and spoon, how to carry three plates on one arm, how to chat merrily to anyone who walked through a door, how to make a perfect French coffee, which cheeses to recommend, what wines might complement a meal and when I wasn't serving food, I'd help out with cleaning the rooms. At one point, I volunteered to do the gardening. In a matter of months, I had gone from being downcast and depressed to getting my mojo back. I loved it so much, all thoughts of going to university, any university, slipped away.

My mother, watching this slowly unfurl, kept her own counsel. I was earning money and was back to my bouncy self. I was enjoying my days and had regained a sense of self-worth. She encouraged me to open a savings account and be sensible with my wages. I was doing well. I liked working in a hotel. 'You should be running this place,' the barman said to me one evening. Perhaps I should, I thought. The environment suits my personality. I like meeting strangers and making a fuss of them. It's rewarding and physically demanding and it's fun.

These then, for my mother, were the dangerous days but she knew she was the wrong person to help me back to the right path. I might be making another of my bad decisions, but she had to let me work it out for myself. I had thrown myself into life at the hotel, the people there had become a second family. It didn't matter whether I was clever or good at English. All that mattered was that I was competent and likeable and just like that, Oxford was gone.

It was September and school friends were calling to say their goodbyes. I wished them well and pushed down the small nagging pangs of regret that had been buried deep under a pile of napkins waiting to be folded just so. My mother, I was well aware, was itching to say something, to ask what I might think I was doing, but I pushed it all away. I had failed and the pain was too much to bear. It was easier to turn away from the ruins and build a different wall, but luck was about to throw its hat into the ring.

Whenever we revisited this moment, my mother would clasp her hands together, close her eyes and tell me it was the one time in her life when she truly believed there might be a God. I was in town, wandering about in search of a new top. I had my own chequebook now and could afford skirts from Jigsaw. I was living the dream and then, outside a shop we used to gather outside as schoolgirls, I bumped into my old English teacher, Mrs Graebe.

Mrs Graebe hadn't had the love she deserved during my school years. She was a vicar's wife, a Mrs Tiggywinkle of a teacher, thick specs and rather goofy looking front teeth. She'd been one of the older members of staff and while she'd been respected, she wasn't granted the adoration enjoyed by younger teachers. Seeing her coming, I felt my stomach sink. There was no avoiding it. I was going to have to talk to her.

'You must be off to university!' she said brightly.

I heaved a small sigh. She'd left before I'd gone down with glandular fever and didn't have the first clue what had happened.

'No.' I was chewing my lip. 'I'm not. I'm not going.'

She let out the sort of gasp reserved for a sudden and unexpected anal exam.

'Why not?'

I then went into the long by now boring explanation of

what, precisely, had happened. 'I can fold napkins into swans now,' I added, as if that made everything worthwhile.

I will never forget the stare she gave me in that moment. It bore right to the core of me. It was a stare that said, 'What the fuck is wrong with you?' It was then that she opened her mouth and changed my life forever. 'Anyone can give up, Emma,' she said, without blinking. 'Easiest thing in the world. Don't give up. Never give up.' She then reached into her handbag and gave me a card with her number on it and told me if I wanted to try again, I could go and see her, and she'd be very happy to help me.

As she wandered off, I stood, staring at that number and felt nothing but horror. I had set myself one goal in life and let it go at the first hurdle. This wasn't who I was. This was not the girl my mother had raised me to be and so I went home and told Brenda and showed her the card and without saying a single word, she handed me the telephone and waited for me to spark up the rest of my life.

Once a week for two months I rode on a bus to the village where Mrs Graebe lived, and she'd have tea and biscuits and sometimes cake waiting for me. We'd discuss plays and poems and novels and, on a chilly day in early November, I found myself back in Oxford, sitting in an ancient wood panelled room at St Edmund Hall with six other people, staring down at a Robert Graves poem, 'Lion Lover'. Writing about it for one hour changed my life entirely. I still have it, covered in scribbled thoughts. At the bottom, in bold blue ink, is my mother's handwriting. She'd asked to see it when I came home. It reads, 'This is terrible!'

It wasn't terrible, because on 17 December 1985 I received another letter with a college crest. It read:

'*I am very glad to be able to tell you that the College has decided to offer you a place to come into residence in October 1986 to read English.*'

It was the greatest achievement of my life. Brenda couldn't have been prouder.

Dear Emmy

We are safely settled in our new house. It is part of a large Mas[1] in Tarn which is very beautiful. The owner of the house was a dancer with the Paris ballet who now has two young sons and a sister who is the Director of Marie Clare magazine! As you can imagine the owner's house looks like a Sunday supplement special. Stone floors, wooden beams painted white, dramatic iron surrounds to massive stone fireplaces and a particular sort of mise en scene in the bricolage of fabrics, sofas, antique and rustic furniture and the odd whimsical 'thing' that only the French can produce.[2]

Madame is very young, early 30's, very pretty, fluent English, very friendly and luckily for me likes a good discussion![3] Her husband is a handsome hunk who used to be a ski instructor and now works for the Stock Exchange. How he made that transition I can't imagine. In the course of our two-hour getting to know you conversation we learned that they decided to leave Paris because of the pollution and the dangers of the city which wasn't suitable for young children. The Parisiennes en masse, Mado and Michelle[4] included, seem hell bent on mass exodus and seem to favour a new pre-revolution, romantic, neo-Louis XIV existence in large rustic houses with a new style aristocratic pretension. They

1 Traditional farmhouse.

2 Brenda loved a fancy interior and had fantastic taste. She would devour any interior decoration magazine she could get her hands on.

3 That's Brenda code for, 'Oh good, I've found someone to argue with.'

4 The French couple who lived in the house at the end of the lane for a while.

*regard France to be economically doomed and they are starting
'new' lives with their carefully made millions to start a new
trend. The evidence of good taste is without question – the
product of the new courtier's money.*

*But they are very nice with it – they are not snobby. It's a
tempting lifestyle and we could afford it – but there is nothing to
do here. You have two choices, learn French and hope to break
into the tribal system or live a reclusive existence. The English
who have settled here have brought a strange colonialism to
France which seems more in keeping with the English in India in
the 19th Century. E. M. Forster's* A Passage to India *must be
required reading. You can imagine them all cooing sycophantically
round the equivalent of the Collector and establishing a pecking
order which is straight out of a Mason's manual.[5] They are
ghastly Tory voters who hate Blair but have all the advantages of
French socialism – better healthcare – French pensions etc. Most
of them have very little to do with the French they don't even
speak French. They are mean, getting every penny out of you – if
you used 12 francs on a few light bulbs, they want it! Our
French hosts on the other hand give electricity for free. So nice.*

*Apart from the social history this is a very gentle part of
France – rolling hills, old 14th Century hill towns and nothing
much else. Spring and summer is idyllic but the suicide rate in
winter must be horrible.[6] We'll keep coming for holidays. I
chose well this time.*

*I had a terrible accident in the first house. They didn't have a
shower mat and I slipped getting out of it. You know how clumsy
I am! Well I caught my right leg outside the cubicle to stop
myself falling and I whacked it really hard against the tiles. It*

5 Not sure what she means here. The only *Mason's Manual* I can find is the
official parliamentary authority of state legislatures in the United States.
shrugs shoulders

6 That lands from nowhere, doesn't it?

hurt horribly and I have black-red bruises from mid calve to my toes. I just hope I don't get gangrene.[7] I couldn't remember the bloody word – all I could think of was 'greengage' Since having the menopause I have looked at certain older women in English literature, particularly poor Mrs Malaprop in The Rivals *and realised that she wasn't stupid, she was menopausal!*

My beard[8] is growing well and the sister from Marie Clare who is about thirty four stares at it without embarrassment, barely disguising her 'orror'. I engaged her in conversation/debate about the invisible older women in Female magazines but she had probably never seen one before with a beard and anyhow, older women were outside her remit. I asked her whether she was a feminist and all she said was that her marriage was termine and she was starting a new story. Her make up is a work of art.[9]

Well, I can really recommend this place – beautiful swimming pool[10] and great style.

Will write again soon. There will be a lot of mileage in this place. Tony is fine. He is going to show Madame how to make profiteroles.

DAD 'No I'm not'

* * *

7 If ever any of us had a bruise, Brenda would often warn, like a doom-laden character in a morality play, it might 'go gangrenous'. She would always say this with an air of great authority.

8 Had a good look at mine this morning. Thanks for the genes, Brenda.

9 I wish I had witnessed this conversation. It feels like something that could quite easily have appeared in a Woody Allen film.

10 Which she would have looked at and not got into.

Darling Emmy

Well. Here we are again in Bella Italia. La casa me piace moltissimo (like it very much) It is a small version of an alpine retreat – pine floors, ceilings and chestnut beams with wonderful views from the bedroom window of the wooded hills.

    The mountain air is so clean it rasps out the muck from your lungs. No traffic sounds apart from the odd farmer's tractors – otherwise perfect peace. Usual suspects of creatures – lizards, big buggers of flying saucer black beetles, a whole army of soldier ants – and you've guessed it – our old friends the wild boar. They run up and down outside the fence every night – but by 9pm we are asleep – the air knocks you out – so we know they are there, but we've been asleep when they come. We had a bit of a fright on an evening walk – we thought we saw a wolf.[1] I was convinced it was a baby wolf – light grey and vicious looking so we did a runner. Won't be walking out there again.

    The driving is as hairy as ever. Italian men must have FOUR testicles – they are so testosterone charged. White lines on the road don't apply to them – God forbid – only to old tourists. We've been taking the back roads and avoiding red routes. Vespa drivers and motorcyclists are the worst – if they see a straight line that lasts 50 yards they do a ton on it. Poor Tony is an old man now – we are both very nervous little mice. Had a very stressful day trying to find the Co-op in a nearby large town. You can picture the scene – round and round avoiding one-way streets getting constantly lost asking a dozen people for the name of the street – all to no avail and all conversations in Italian. Then I asked an extremely fat tramp for directions – thought he

---

1 She's obsessed with seeing wolves.

didn't understand my Italian but then in perfect English he gave
us careful directions and we found the Co-op. Tony now in his
element. Tony only happy when he's in a Food Shop. We haven't
had too many rows so far.

    The house is so nice, and the weather is lovely – not too hot
– so we are staying put at home. We have had a few trips to
new places, but we don't wish to go to Florence, Sienna or
Arezzo again. We just pootle around the hilltop villages. Good
job our legs are still up to it as most of these hill towns have a
mountain to climb to get to them.

    The countryside is stunning in May – all the wild-flowers are
blossoming – the poppies, buttercups, lovely grasses, a stunning
type of orchid and a purple clover like flower that is something
you only see here. The trees are dripping with white blossom and
the perfume from them is glorious as you drive along with the
windows open. This is the best time of year to come – but then
as Gerald Manley Hopkins said 'May is Mary's month, long
live the weeds and the wilderness yet.'[2] Fecund Italy – the old
pagan religion always beneath the surface. I bet you didn't know
that Piero d'ella Francesca – Arezzo's famous artist son was a
follower of the cult of Mary Magdalene.[3] His paintings are
full of symbols relating to this cult and the pagan fertility cult. I
don't think Catholic Italy is aware of this! For the first time I
have seen a reference to ST. Mary Magdalene in his art. I don't

2 Of course this made me wonder if this was the Gerard Manley Hopkins
poem she'd wanted read at her graveside. The quote here is mangled though.
The first 'May is Mary's month' is from 'The May Magnificat' which includes
a reference to spring as the 'mighty mother' from which you can draw your
own conclusions, but the latter half, 'long live the weeds and the wilderness
yet' is from his other poem 'Inversnaid'. Neither were read at her funeral.
Sorry, Brenda.

3 I'm not sure this is true. There's no evidence to support this claim. Piero
della Francesca was renowned for one thing: his geometric perfection when it
came to perspective. He was the master of it. Google his Montefeltro
Altarpiece and marvel at the marble ceiling he's depicted.

. *think the Pope would have canonised a prostitute! Very inter-esting. Dan Brown ought to follow this up.*[4]

Well, I've started the letter with the good things. Now I'll give you the flip side.

First, our overnight at Gatwick. Terrible hotel. Scene 1 – the reception area. Large group of Beck clones – Beckham haircuts, exotic tattoos over both arms, tight T shirts, very loud. Large pink suitcases blocking the reception desk – kids screaming, running around feet, tripping old people up. Brenda forced to use teacher voice – can you imagine – it's my holiday and I've got to start a fight.[5]

Well, the receptionist got it first. We had been told that a cour-tesy bus would pick us up from the airport and take us to the hotel. No bus to be found – had to get a taxi – it cost £8 for 200 yards. Major complaint to receptionist. Followed by major shout at Becks gang to move their huge pink suitcases so we could get into the corridor to our room. Next, the meal. Couldn't get into the dining room – all tables already booked. Ended up with a smear of lasagne calling itself a meal for £12. Had to eat it in the bar surrounded by the Becks clones and their screaming kids. Drinks balanced precariously on shelf above head – expecting it to tip down my new clothes any minute. Meanwhile ghastly kids try to put their sticky fingers on my new jacket.

The alcohol consumption that was going on would bring an A&E doctor to sobbing tears. They were boozing hard enough to pass out on the carpets, oblivious of the children THEN the match started on the television. God help us – I've never eaten

4 I refer you to my previous statement on my mother and Dan Brown. Basically, she just wanted to be his pal.

5 This is one of those situations that brings me out in hives and if I'd been with her, I'd have slunk off and stood outside until it was all over. Brenda thought nothing of shouting at strangers if she was ever so slightly inconveni-enced and given her background, it never fails to astonish me what a snob she could be.

*a scrappy lasagne so fast. It was like the Roman Games –
alcohol splashing everywhere – grunts from the tattoos, hoary,
half sexual comments about the players and the inevitable
trouser rubbing started. Have you noticed the way young
drunk lads rub their crotches when they watch football?
Hideous! We make a run for our room. Never again!*

*Always interested in what is happening politically in Italy
now that Berlusconi wants to create a Fascist state.*[6] *Italian
TV full of Berlusconi's decision to pass a law to prevent any
black people entering Italy. Here we go again – 1939 repeat.
The timing of this statement comes just as the G7 meeting is
taking place in the earthquake area. Now that's sensitive but
the worst bit is that Obama will be staying in the building
where Mussolini was held prisoner in 1943. Berlusconi has said
that as there was a security problem for the American president,
this El Duce building would be the best place and remember El
Duce didn't have a great love of black people, Jews, gypsies et
al. I think there might be an international upset over this.
Berlusconi is a midget – they're always dangerous.*[7]

*Give Poppy a big cuddle
Love you dearly.
Mum and Dad
Xxxx*

★ ★ ★

6 It's impossible not to admire the seamless segue here.

7 Oh, dear God. I mean, where to even start? Thank GOD Brenda was
NEVER on Twitter.

Twelve

I found out only very recently that on the day I left home to go to university, Brenda sat under an apple tree in the orchard, opened a bottle of wine and cried for two hours.

It's easy, isn't it, to remember the bad bits, the days mistakes were made, the words you're not sure can be taken back. Everybody gets it wrong sometimes, without exception. It's not possible to go through life with a perfect score card however open minded, thoughtful or kind you might imagine yourself to be. God knows I've been an arsehole of epic proportions at moments in my life: I've said and written things I'm ashamed of, I've been mean, I've been cruel, offensive, I've made jokes at other people's expense. I've punched down not up. It's embarrassing. Is this the sum total of who I am? No. These are the dark moments, the mistakes made during the course of a life. When Brenda died, it felt as if rooms would always be full of her shadows, but the more I remember her, the more I discover the curtains were always open. People are not the sum total of their problematic edges or their missteps. Sometimes, good people do bad things.

This was a happy time. Brenda used to say, 'It was like we all went to Oxford', and she was right. Any excuse to see me was grabbed with both hands. My parents would turn up, grinning from ear to ear, bearing a chocolate cake made with Guinness by Tony that would be devoured on touchdown. Rumours of its excellence spread to such an extent that the merest sighting of them striding across the front quad would result in a queue of people appearing at my door.

My mother was thrilled by it, of course. My friends adored her. Here was Brenda in her element, holding forth, prepared to be shocking, being entirely different from every other parent who came to visit. To contemporaries who had grown up in restricted households, she felt like a breath of fresh air. She lavished me and hard-up pals with lunches at Browns, took us for posh cocktails, invited any passing undergraduate to 'come see us' back at home during the holidays, parcels would arrive, heaving with goodies. She was conviviality itself and not once, during these visits, would there be even the slightest whiff of trouble.

Well, I say that, but my friend, Mouse, had a rather vivid memory of her.

I had come to stay for the weekend, and we were upstairs watching a video. Your parents were off somewhere else in the house and then suddenly, your mother burst in, look of thunder on her face and bashed her hand down on the top of the telly. Up to this point all I'd ever seen of your mother was sweetness and light, always smiling and sociable. 'That's it!' she yelled. 'I'm divorcing your father!' I was terrified, properly scared. I felt mortified that here I was, at your house, at the moment their marriage disintegrated and then you, without batting an eyelid, just said, 'Oh shut up, Mum, we're watching a film.'

I forget now how unusual our set-up was. 'That's it, I'm divorcing your father' was an every-day occurrence.

. . . Nobody had outbursts like that at my home. Ever. I think the first time I met her was at matriculation. I thought she was a student. She looked so young, not like a parent at all. She was rather childlike in her manner, over excited, fizzing and cackling. I will always remember her cackle: joyful but slightly deranged. When you told me she was a teacher, I was astonished. I couldn't fathom it.

He's described Brenda perfectly. Joyful but slightly deranged. There was no doubt, in the visits to our family home, that everyone would be treated like kings. '*Sunday lunches were amazing. You knew you were going to have a brilliant time. Filled with endless laughter.*'

Brenda, then, was in her cups. This was the high life she had always dreamed of and here she was, walking the cobbled streets of Oxford, enjoying a punt on the River Cherwell, surrounded by young, intelligent people she could bounce off. Every time she came, she wanted to know what I was up to, what books I was studying, every last scrap of my daily routine. She was hungry for it, her delight in every aspect of my university life visceral.

I was loving every minute: studying in the Radcliffe camera, lectures at the English faculty, riding everywhere on an old sit up and BEG bicycle with a wicker basket; it didn't matter what I was doing, I was just delirious with joy to be there. I don't think a single day went by without me feeling astonished I had actually managed to get in. Every second was to be savoured but it was this love affair with university life that was to be a breaking point with my parents and my past.

A diary entry after my second term is telling: '*Just had my first harsh words with mother.*' I was home for the holidays and ploughing through my reading list. '*Her anxiety and paranoia un-nerves me completely.*' This was in 1987, she was forty-four and still teaching, and it's the first time I have a reference to the paranoia that destroyed her but there are other entries where I talk of her making me 'cry laughing'. It was the eternal juggling act: she was awful, she was great.

There comes a time in everyone's lives when, to be perfectly blunt, you're no longer that into your parents. It's the moment you become a proper adult, see the world with grown-up eyes and begin the slow, torturous process of peeling yourself away from your childhood home once and for all. The tragedy, in our case, was that Brenda and I had had just over a year of getting on again and now here I was, drifting away despite all her efforts. We were going to have to find a new way of being but in the summer of 1987, I had news.

'I'm going to be performing at the Edinburgh Festival,' I said. 'The Seven Raymonds are going to support the Oxford Revue.'

As luck would have it, my tutorial partner at St Edmund Hall was a young man called Stewart Lee. He'd met another young man, Richard Herring, who was reading history at St Catherine's (he had got in) and they'd started doing comedy sketches together at the Oxford Revue Workshop. This has forever struck me as one of the oddest strands of fate: which-ever path I'd taken, I'd have been with one of them. Stewart had a delicious, thoughtful quality and an esoteric curiosity unlike anyone I'd ever met. He was terribly polite. Richard liked baked potatoes. During the early weeks of our first term, I had made a joke about Nana Mouskouri, which I now can't remember, but it made Stewart laugh so much he asked if I'd like to come and be a goldfish in a sketch he'd written. We were off and by the end of that term, we'd joined up with two other undergraduates, Mike Cosgrave and Richard Canning, and become The Seven Raymonds.

Having quickly established cult status, we were the obvious choice to be that year's second comedy show to be taken to Edinburgh with the Oxford University Drama Society. We were the fresh-faced underlings to that year's Oxford Revue, a student production going into a minor venue. We had zero money.

My mother gripped me by the upper arms. 'Edinburgh FESTIVAL?', her eyes widening.

'Yes, the Edinburgh Festival. I'll be there for all of August.'

'So, you won't be coming home at all for the summer?'

'No.'

She paused for a moment then whispered, 'You've made it now, you realise. Edinburgh Festival? You've made it.'

God bloody bless me, but I believed her. I genuinely thought I'd hit the big time. THIS WAS IT! THIS WAS MY CRACK

AT FAME AND FORTUNE! I'd done the whole getting into the super university thing, why the hell not pop the cherry on the cake and become famous as well?

For reasons I still don't fully understand, it was decided I would journey to Edinburgh on the sleeper train. Brenda told Tony to get me a First-Class Ticket, thinking she was bestowing on me an act of magnificence that would get me accustomed to Hollywood and having to go to the BAFTAs. I'm laughing while I write this, but I cannot emphasise how much Brenda genuinely believed this. Anyway, the bottom line was, I'd never been on the sleeper train to Edinburgh, and it turns out it has beds in it, and they are cheaper than a First-Class Ticket in a stupid seat. What a bunch of amateurs.

The assembled company of the Oxford University Drama Society, of which I was now an esteemed member, were staying in a Masonic Lodge at the top of the Royal Mile. By the time I'd lugged my rucksack up there from the station, it was around seven in the morning. I knocked on the door. Nothing. I knocked again. Nope. I stared up at the door, looked again at my piece of paper. Masonic Lodge. This was it. The problem, of course, was that the other members of the Oxford University Drama Society were students and were all hung over bastards and incapable of answering the door. I had to wait for two hours before the face of Mike Cosgrave appeared above me.

'Oh, hello.'

'Hello.' And down he came and in and up I went.

It's amazing what you're prepared to put up with when you're twenty. I was led up a long flight of stairs to a large open room. On the floor were a mass of bodies in sleeping bags. It was like looking at the aftermath of a natural disaster. There was another room beyond, with more bodies. One actor, Ewan Bailey, a bona fide university heart-throb, had managed to build himself a den. I was impressed. Off the main room was one tiny kitchen with two black plastic bins in it – one filled with pasta, the other with cornflakes – and one toilet with a small hand basin. There were no other washing facilities.

There were around sixty of us. With no patch of floor to claim in the smaller room, I went back to the larger room and threw my rucksack on the floor by a coffin. It would be my home for the next six weeks.

Brenda would see this with her own eyes five weeks later. It was the only time in my life I recall her being speechless.

In that six-week period, I only had two baths: one at the old Victorian Public Baths, after which I contracted athlete's foot, and the second when Brenda frogmarched me into the bathroom on the landing where they were staying. They'd taken a room at Edinburgh University, something they would do every time they came to the festival, and I can remember vividly the feeling of having that bath followed by the horrified scream of my mother when she saw the state of it. I'd pulled the plug and returned to their room to find something suitable to scrub the sides down but Brenda, in an uncharacteristic moment of domestic knuckling down, took a flannel from her washbag and set to it like a woman possessed.

They would stay for four days. In typical fashion, they'd had an eventful journey up. Rather than take the train (no doubt deterred by my own shattered experience) they had decided to drive, which was all well and good, but had broken down outside Peterborough.

'We were towed all the way to the Scottish border by the AA man.' Tony shook his head. 'And then he had to hand us over to a Scottish recovery driver because he was only allowed to go as far as the border and then the Scottish fellah drove us all the way to the university and then he took the car to the garage. Your mother, despite the hellish journey, was in a surprisingly good mood. She only complained about fifty times.'

Every day they were there, they would come and see me in our show. 'I think the largest audience was five,' recalled Tony, wistfully.

I remember this time as one of the happiest of my life: joyous memories of playing cards with Richard, dancing till dawn at the Gilded Balloon, destroying the Death Star, finally, on a Star Wars games console, eating baked potatoes (Richard was right), drinking beer and laughing, laughing, laughing. I developed a crush too, on a blond-haired lad who I would later kiss in a bush at Magdalen College. He would go on to become a Sweet Historian and all-round marvellous eccentric. If it hadn't turned out I was a raging gay, he's the man I would have married, but I hadn't quite worked out yet why I couldn't fall in love with boys. That would come much later.

I was dazzled by student life, with my new friends, with the days that were never dull. It would be harder, from now on, to ever spend time at my old home again. The gears were shifting, and Brenda knew it. She needed a new project.

Dear Emmy

Here we are again. We had a good journey down, one night in Paris but it was freezing then TVG to Avignon with a French family of four, the brother and sister arguing for four hours – tears, petulant slaps, mother on the edge, father oblivious. We sat opposite unable to hide our tight smiles. Fetched hire car in Avignon. Tony couldn't park it properly – much annoyance from other French drivers because he was blocking an exit from a multi storey car park. I'm sure you can imagine the flow of traffic, speeding down the runway to be unexpectedly slowed by Tony with the right wheel on the kerb. Despite numerous efforts, he couldn't get the car to straighten up. I ended up shaking my fist at them all. So much for my French lessons. Hated the lot of them.[1]

Arrived in St Remy d'Provence, very pretty town, very chic. Lovely hotel, lovely lunch. Felt much better. Post prandial saunter round St. Remy – discover much to our amusement that it was the home of NOSTRADAMUS! There was even a fountain dedicated to him and Rue Nostradamus. Took many photos to show you, bought little book of his predictions, plus the card. Will send book separately as it needs packing. Later had 2nd splendid 3 course meal – soup au pistou, poulet et olives vertes, chocolat fondue and Arabic sauce – all for £7 each!

Why can't we eat so well so cheaply in England? We would have paid £30 for this.

Left St. Remy, took wrong turn at Aix (not my fault[2]) and

1 Super! The holiday is off to the perfect start!

2 She would have been the navigator, so yes Brenda, it would have been your fault.

ended up in Marseille. Nightmare. It is a terrible place. Took country route – saw no one until we arrived in Hyeres then straight on to Bourmes. Very pretty Provencal house – very stylish. Magnificent hill village, beautifully restored – parks on different levels, lovely small shops, cafes, restaurants. Very select. Great walks around village. Went to Le Lavandon but the old village no longer exists. Good walks round port. Today the bloody mistral started – 80mph winds! Very exhilarating but scary. Had to watch trees and flimsy signs flapping frantically. Very tired. Too much fresh air and exercise.

DAD 'it is a bit windy'[3]

★ ★ ★

3 Just reading this letter exhausted me.

Thirteen

'Your mother was as mad as a snake's eye,' an ex-colleague, Val, tells me. 'She had an opinion on every subject known to man. She was confrontational, argumentative and never stopped moaning that everything, and I mean everything, was entirely the fault of the Masons or the council.'

It's true. My mother, despite never knowingly having met one, absolutely HATED Freemasons: everything was their fault. Planning permission granted for a neighbour. Freemasons. Dad missed out on a promotion. Freemasons. There shall be rain next Tuesday. Freemasons.

'She was obsessed with them,' continued Val. 'And she was constantly writing to the council. "I'M GOING TO WRITE TO THE COUNCIL," she'd yell, every five minutes. I've never known anyone more ready for an argument at the drop of a hat, but I'll tell you this, she was never, ever boring company.'

I remember Val well. She was one of the very few women my mother liked.

'She fell out with everyone. There was always someone who wasn't speaking to her. She was a total Drama Queen. Forever shouting she was leaving Tony. Yeah, right. She wouldn't have lasted five minutes. I did love her though. She was always interesting, even if she did drive you crazy. She'd come up with some mad cap theory that would raise your eyebrows as far as they could go, and I'd tease her by asking her to explain how she'd come to that conclusion. She'd fall about laughing. She just loved being outrageous.'

I think Val's hit the nail on the head. It might seem mystifying at this point as to why anybody put up with her. She was provocative, she loved fighting and she never, ever apologised but, and this really was her saving grace, she was fun. It was also, up until very recent times, entirely acceptable to simply think someone was 'nuts' and not give it a second thought. There must have been so many people like my mother, crashing through work and relationships, struggling without a diagnosis, unmedicated with little or no support. My mother was just a bit 'mad' and we all accepted it.

'There was one time,' Val remembered, 'when I properly fell out with her. It was around the time we'd been told there was going to be redundancies at the college, and we'd been asked to put ourselves up voluntarily. I wasn't interested but the place was rumbling with it. I was in my office and in ran a male colleague telling me to come quick because Brenda was holding forth in the library telling anyone who cared to listen that I should be the first person to put myself forward for voluntary redundancy because I had "a hundred grand in the bank". He told me she was in "full flow". I didn't need telling twice. I didn't have a hundred grand in the bank or anything like it. She'd totally invented it.

'I was FURIOUS so up I jumped, stormed to the library and tore a strip off her then for ages I refused to speak to her unless she apologised. We'd be in the cloakroom, side by side, me applying lipstick and completely ignoring her. Anyway, your father called me in to his office and told me Brenda was upset I wasn't talking to her to which I think I told him, "Your wife is crazy." He didn't disagree. She never apologised but I ended up forgiving her. She had charm.'

Two things strike me here. Yes, Brenda never apologised. She was incapable of it. Apologising would mean admitting she was wrong and that was never going to happen, but she clearly did know she was in the wrong because she got Tony to do the heavy lifting for her. It was a rare thing for Brenda to tell anyone she might be upset and I'm struggling now to think of a single occasion in which she ever admitted being upset to me. She'd let us know she was angry loudly and often but upset is a different thing entirely. Upset suggests wounded feelings rather than annoyance or irritation. Upset strikes at the heart of who we might imagine ourselves to be. Upset has standards. Upset is sensitive. Upset wants to feel better and happier. Upset feels guilty. Upset cares. She was upset because she liked Val and she'd fucked it, but she wasn't able, despite clearly wanting to, to say sorry.

I often wonder whether, when she sat on her own staring down the garden or stayed in bed pretending to read a book, she was thinking about her life and what she had made of it. I have always said, when it comes to the cold hard truth that everybody, lying in bed looking up at the ceiling, knows the exact shape of it, precisely: everybody fibs a bit, glosses a bit, doesn't want to be the bad guy but each and every one of us knows, deep down, what really happened. Life, for many, is like sitting in a dodgem car, careering from one bump to the next. Mistakes are made, reputations forged but what do you do when you're stuck with what you've got, and you can't extricate yourself from it? Phyllis said it perfectly – 'it was as if she was playing a part' – Brenda liked being controversial. She liked to be the centre of attention. She liked stirring things up but as to whether she liked being that person is another matter.

At work, my mother was a contradiction: on the one hand, she was the much adored teacher but on the other, she was the consummate maker of enemies. There was no grey for her, anywhere, whether it be in politics, love or everyday life. You were either with her or against her and it's easy to see how she would have rubbed people, for whom her abrasiveness would have been intolerable, up the wrong way. Most people like a placid life. They like compliance, consideration, an adherence to societal norms. My mother was the hand grenade to all that and people who had to work with her had to put up with living in her rubble.

Yet for all her bad behaviour, it was still only myself and

Tony who saw her at her very worst. 'I never saw that side of her' is a refrain I've heard again and again from friends of mine or people she liked when asked if they ever saw her properly lose it. She had it in her to hide her darker impulses and was careful not to spiral out of control unless she was on safe territory. It's an aspect of her I find hard to reconcile. I saw her again and again, unable to stop, but perhaps she could control it. Perhaps it was a choice?

'There were three Brendas,' Phyllis told me. 'The amazing Brenda who turned it on for lovers and students, the lovely Brenda on her best behaviour with her nephews and people she admired and then for you, me and Tony, we got the Bitch. Brenda needed to be in control. And when she couldn't control people or was questioned or had to deal with anyone who disagreed with her, she'd lose it.'

What was going on? Here is a highly intelligent woman, someone who validates herself through sex, whose self-esteem was forever focused on proving to herself she was somehow better than her beginnings. She had capacity to be exciting, electric, fantastic company, fizzing with ideas and vibrant conversation but all of it could be shut down in a moment, like a heavy door slamming. It might be easy to label this up-down behaviour as evidence she may have been bipolar but having looked into it, I don't think she was. What might be called her manic phase was never quite manic enough. In fact, I don't think she was manic at all and her down days, which a clinical psychologist would be looking at, never lasted for more than a day at a time. Brenda's issue was about control. She was disruptive: she had impulse control issues; her conduct was disordered.

There is a recognised disorder, Intermittent Explosive Disorder, which might be a fit. The diagnostic criteria, according to the *Diagnostic and Statistical Manual of Mental Disorders*, Fifth Edition, requires recurrent behavioural outbursts that can include unpremeditated temper tantrums and physical aggression which seem out of proportion to any provocation that might have sparked it off. However, as recognisable in her as this might seem, it's a diagnosis that is only given if other mental disorders are not better fits. Elements ring true but I came to the conclusion that we weren't at our journey's end quite yet.

My mother though, for all her brashness, was forever keen to be liked. Val recalls one of their many college trips to Paris. They were in a restaurant, with a clutch of students, and Brenda was holding forth about how awful it must have been to be French and in Paris during the Occupation. 'Imagine it,' she said, shaking her head, 'it must have been terrible. The Nazis were diabolical.'

At this point one of their students admitted that her grandfather was German and had been in the Hitler Youth as a child. Brenda paused for a moment, realised she may have caused the student to feel uncomfortable and added, 'Oh, he was a *nice* Nazi, was he?'

'Did she ever tell you about the Renoir thing?' Val was laughing. 'I think it's one of the maddest ideas she ever had.'

Yes, I had heard of the 'Renoir thing'. She had sent me a solemn and serious letter glued onto a piece of black card. On the reverse was stuck a grainy black-and-white photocopy of a photo of a bearded man in a hat. He bore an uncanny resemblance to Bob. It was the famous painter, Renoir.

My dear love, the letter began, *We have never really talked about the secrets of your family tree and since my last meeting with Bob your erstwhile 'gramp', I feel compelled to reveal all.*

What a start to a letter. Never let it be said my mother didn't know how to be dramatic.

The man you see before you is Renoir, your great-great grandfather. He fathered your great-grandfather, Bob Payne with a chambermaid in London circa 1880. Bob Payne is Bob's father.

I have enclosed a photo of me, your mother (I presume this was in case I'd forgotten who she was) *visiting the family pile – Renoir's house in Cagnes Sur Mer. I am holding his wheelchair, the closest I would ever get to giving my own dear great-grandfather a cuddle.*

The creative gene has firmly embedded itself in both sides of the family – sadly it missed Phyllis (RUDE) and Bob! But they have other talents.

Do not disown your heritage

Ps Do not put this on the internet – Phyllis would find out. My God! I intend being B.I.R.Williams from now. (Brenda Irene Renoir Williams)

Love and kisses.

I should add that there is zero evidence of Renoir having been in London at the right time and zero evidence my ravished chambermaid relative was ever a chambermaid or, indeed, ravished. In short, my mother found a picture of Renoir which, admittedly, is the spitting image of Bob, and thought to herself, oh lovely, that'll do.

God bloody bless her. I love that she underlined the order that I must not, under any circumstances, reject a lineage to a world famous painter because that's exactly what you would do, wouldn't you, if you suddenly discovered you had a valid claim to a multi-million pound estate.

The photo she mentions was not, more's the pity, included. Instead, there was another picture of Brenda, grinning away through the gap in a statue of a rather voluptuous and naked woman, peeking through an arm with hand on hip. On the back she has scrawled, *I've got my eyes shut in ecstasy on the other one so sending this one instead. I think my belly is rather like hers.*

Here she is again, then, dreaming of being something she's not. It's a thread you can connect all the way back to her as a young teen, telling people her name is Becky, hanging out with richer kids, playing that part.

'I do wonder,' Val confided, 'whether she should have been an actress.'

It's a thought that keeps popping up but as I've already established, she'd have been a nightmare and besides, she was a brilliant teacher: nobody else was allowed to talk, she was in charge and everyone looked up to her. She'd found her perfect calling.

The next thing she needed to think about was whether I'd found mine.

Dear Emmy

I managed to contain my terror in the plane but I was glad when we arrived safely. We had a very muscular gentleman at the end our row who spent most the flight flexing his arms and engaging in a form of calisthenics which involved standing up regularly. Since Tony was safely tucked into the window seat he didn't have to endure this but as you can imagine, I gave the guy various hard looks and let out the occasional gasp of irritation but he carried on.[1]

We had a small nightmare getting out of Rome airport. Europcar gave us an electronic card to get through the exit barriers but it didn't work.[2] *After three attempts at three different X-ray barriers with Italian drivers expressing murderous hate we reversed and drove round various admin buildings looking for a friendly face. None. Parked behind extra super car driven by extra smart Italian woman and off we went.*

The journey took three hours and took us through a surreal wasteland of shack towns and tumbleweed. Our hotel is perched on a hill so drove in circles coping all the time with crazy Italian drivers. By now it's getting dark, and we still haven't found the hotel. Does it even exist we think? Drove and drove past shabby hideaways, pizza restaurants and bars all the time

---

1 Strangers fell into two categories for my mother: people whose entire life history she was hell-bent on discovering in five minutes or less or people who she decided she was going to loathe from the off. Clearly, man with bad back who needs to move about on the plane is firmly in the latter category.

2 It is astonishing, isn't it, given how many times this happens to them, that they haven't worked out by now that they might just be putting the card in upside down.

feeling more depressed with the end of season shabby feel. Then Psycho like a large hotel sign leads up a very sharp bend to a building which had seen better times and was a dead cert copy of the Alamo. We looked at each other with restrained trepidation knowing that we didn't have any choice but to spend the night there. The patron was a large man – jowls, big head and hooded eyes under 2 black wigs for eyebrows. An Asian woman appeared and we walked up stone steps, tried to unlock door but the handle fell off. Lights didn't work. Had to leave bathroom light on all night as we didn't feel very secure with broken door handle and busted lights.[3]

Walls covered in faded blue velvet – large white piece of metal in corner which was the air conditioning unit. This peaceful haven for travellers was 3 star no less and cost £40 a night. In morning we felt differently. Opened shutters to fabulous view and lake now looking sage and spectacular. Off we went again. We won't talk about Italian drivers. No, we really won't. it's best you don't know. I'll just say that on the journey I did not see any of the places we went through. I only saw the cars in front, the 2 cars behind, the cars overtaking at any opportunity, the cars that crossed the road across our path with no signals. Don't think about it![4]

We have a lovely apartment with a superb view, well sort of. Our holiday has been ruined. It hasn't really but we have a cast iron argument.[5]

[3] So far, so entirely normal Pezzer Family Holiday.

[4] She will have alerted my father, the long-suffering driver, to every single one of them too. 'TONY! LOOK OUT! CAR! LOOK OUT!' For as many tedious hours it took to go from A to B. It's a wonder my father didn't stop the car, get out, phone for an ambulance and have himself taken to the nearest medical retreat.

[5] Sadly, we don't get to discover how the holiday has been ruined but I rather adore the half confession that it 'hasn't really' but, as has now been well established, if there was the merest whiff of a battle with an establishment that had even slightly irritated my mother, the game was ON.

Hope People Like Us[6] *went well. I'm sure it did. I bet you were wonderful, and we are both pretty upset that we missed it and that we couldn't be with you when it went out. But we look forward to seeing it when we get home. Little Emmy is a very, very famous gal now.[7] Hip Hip hooray.*

★ ★ ★

6 *People Like Us*, the TV series written by John Morton. I was in two episodes. They are, without exception, the best I've ever been at acting. Two unfortunate things to say here – on the one day the casting agent, who was starting to regularly put me up for things, came to set, I had my once-a-month brain freeze during a long scene that required one take. Basically, if I was filming on the first day of my period you could forget it, and words I knew inside out and back to front slipped away on the wind like a dandelion shedding seeds. I looked like a lazy bastard who hadn't learned her lines. I wasn't, my brain was in the maelstrom of hormonal fog. The casting agent never asked to see me again. The second thing to say is that these series are never shown any more because the lead actor was sent to prison for a while. Never has the phrase bitter-sweet felt more resonant.

7 I am really not famous.

My dear love

We had a good night in Paris, caught the TGV to Dijon, picked up the car and headed south for Cluny[8] which is approx half an hour from Trambly where we are staying for two nights. It is in the middle of forested hills and quite isolated with only farms and a few cottages spread miles apart. The chateau is magnificent and we have a suite of rooms, including a music room, a library and a luxurious bathroom. The antiques are wonderful and Messieur is a famous mason who has built and restored some of the most distinguished sculpture etc in Paris.
The apartment is filled with beautiful art and pottery and various marble mantles and fireplaces which he has made. The bathroom is filled with soothing, perfumed unguents, strangely shaped tools for massage, oils, candles, a luxury indulgence which can only be matched by Harrods. Since I never use such things, I've been squeezing bits on my hands to give the impression that I have not ignored the generosity offered.

　　DAD: Bathroom tour lasted half an hour[9]
　　Well. Then the drama began.[10] We were both very tired and in need of showers and hair washings etc. I couldn't have a bath as it was a hip bath nearly four feet high but I managed to use the shower fixtures to wash my hair. I then went into the bathroom to dry my hair. All I was wearing was a white T shirt which had some nylon in it and clung rather tightly

8 Cluny – in the Saône-et-Loire region of eastern France.

9 Reminiscent of the shattering ennui he would experience being dragged around clothes shops by my mother for hours on end.

10 Jolly good.

around my Jordan[11] bosoms. As I had the hair dryer going, I was unaware of a woman, a stranger, entering our apartment.

Tony, by now was in the shower. The shower must be clearly visualised. It was enormous, bow shaped and fully see through. Tony being deaf[12] couldn't hear that a strange woman had entered calling 'Excusez moi, excusez moi' until she stood with mouth agape at Tony in the shower. Just as she started to back out, Tony turned – full frontal – cottonbud on display and froze in terror like a museum exhibit.

I meanwhile suddenly aware of an intruder clapped my hands over my Jordan breasts (luckily I had my knickers on)[13] and stood behind her. The poor woman's head was spinning like something out of the Exorcist *between the Jordans and the cottonbud.*

I stepped back, allowing her an escape: meanwhile Tony is still frozen, but hands are disguising the cotton bud. The poor girl, having committed the worst privacy faux pas, is mortified. To ease her predicament, I laugh hysterically and rush into the bedroom closing the door. First, I shut out the vision of Tony in the bathroom. I dress hastily, come out, she is standing shocked by the piano and offer my hand. 'Enchante Madam' and laugh hysterically again.[14] No one under 60 should see my Jordans.

It seemed that our ever so slightly eccentric hostess had previously shown this young couple around our suite of rooms as theirs and had taken their luggage which now could not be found and so you have a French farce.

11 Reference to Katie Price, formally known as the model Jordan. I met her once at *Hell's Kitchen* and she was utterly charming.

12 Not entirely deaf. He has a piece of Teflon in one of his ears. At least that's what he told me. It was put there by a surgeon on purpose. He didn't just ram a bit of broken saucepan into his lughole.

13 Never have I felt more grateful.

14 Why is this woman still standing there? What's the matter with her? Surely anyone with half a notion of sensitivity walks in, takes one look and LEAVES?

Madame came and collected them and some shrill sounds were heard. We, of course, could not be expected to move after being discovered en flagrante.

Our hostess was a charming copy of Edith Piaff. She spoke fluent English, was an artist and a philosopher and everything concerning the house was organic. This did not narrowly relate to growing and eating food but was a complex philosophy which included not locking doors. 'Nothing is locked here'

Now, that is obviously the thinking of a higher mind but for guests staying in a large and rather spooky chateau overlooking a large garden and forest, not being able to lock your doors becomes an obsession. We could lock our bedroom but nothing else. Two outside doors, the bathroom and the doors to the balcony leading to the forest. We didn't like it. Then things took an Alice in Wonderland *turn when we discovered a connecting door to another guest's room – but it had a key – on our side.*

By now it was 10.30 and we desperately wanted to go to bed but the thought of all these open doors prevented us. With a leap of hope we started to quietly turn the key to the connecting room. But madame was a sadist! The key did not function – it was a malevolent trick!

We had been quietly trying to turn the key and were bent over our task when the door opened from the other side. We were horrified. A man, 6 foot tall, the twin of Nosferatu (Werner Herzog version)[15] stood silently in the doorframe.

'Pardon,' we said. 'We are trying to lock the door' (In French)
'Nein' came the reply. 'Das ist mein zimmer'
'Parlez vous Francais?'
'Nein'
As we couldn't remember any German under the circum-

15 Google this immediately.

stances, Tony tried to explain our worries about the locks.

'Ya. Nein clef.'

'Parlez vous Francais?'

'Nein.'

Then followed a strangely sinister one-sided conversation in German which obviously had something to do with locks. He held us in his gaze, body slightly bent and head to one side then quietly closed the door on us. We then looked for at least two chairs to put in front of that door.

We didn't sleep well. We had a suitable array of possible weapons by the bedside – torches, the iron[16] etc. With every creak we expected Nosferatu to grope his way around the bedroom door.

But the dawn came, and everything was fine. Organic was not a problem. We had a lovely time there and Nosferatu was a charming man (no English). We were sad to leave.

Have now arrived in Hotonnes in Ain.[17] Wonderful views over mountains – simple house – Chickens and cows outside the window.

Will write again soon.

Mum and Dad.

★ ★ ★

---

16 I would pay money to see my mother chasing someone off with an iron.

17 They're still in eastern France.

Fourteen

I wasn't sure what I wanted to do when I left university. I ran away for a bit to America but when I returned, I was at a loss. 'I feel completely worthless and useless' I wrote in my diary. It still astonishes me to this day that it didn't even occur to me to do the thing I was good at – namely writing – but no, it was I Think I'll Do History all over again. Nobody in my family was in the creative industries and I'd had it banged into me from day dot that nothing was ever going to be handed to me on a plate. Despite Brenda's wild claims, there was no family money hidden in a pot to save me and I was going to have to get a *proper* job by which my parents meant in an office, Monday to Friday, answering to a boss in a freshly laundered suit.

I was heartbroken to be leaving Oxford: matters made worse by the fact many of my closest college friends, all medics, were staying on. I was consumed with the fear of missing out and, while they would all be carrying on as normal, I was drifting into a land of the unknown. All in all, I was pretty miserable. I'd had to return home too. Without a job, I was in no position to be able to afford to share with pals leaving for London and the sudden shift from being somewhere that was constantly on the move to the dripping quiet of my childhood home was nothing short of crushing.

Brenda, with her usual blanket belief that nothing was impossible, kept shoving the *Guardian* Jobs page in front of me and pointing at things I had absolutely no relevant experience for. We were at an impasse and life that had felt so buoyant was starting to resemble a slowly deflating balloon. The best thing that was ever going to happen to me had been and gone, now what?

I wasn't sure Brenda enjoyed having me home again. When you've lost something, you get used to it but here I was, the fledgling back in the nest but I was now an adult and rattling round the house with nothing to do. It was not something to get used to. It was a difficult time for the pair of us: I was now a fully formed adult with opinions and no time for putting up with her nonsense. She too had shifted. I was the listless daughter, lacking ambition. It was easy for the respect she had had for me to slip away. My diary of those first few weeks back from America make for pitiful reading. 'Another downer evening,' I wrote, 'had to retire to bed for yet another weeping session.' Brenda was having none of it, she didn't have time for moping. Your life, she would always insist, is precisely what you make of it. If you want something to happen, put yourself in charge.

'Don't look at anything unless it's in London,' she would say to me. 'Don't get stuck *here*, you'll go nowhere.'

She was someone who had made a successful career for herself 'here' and yet, for me, she clearly wanted a wider horizon. It always surprised me Brenda never wanted to live in London: she was made for it, but the rebel with a cause had settled herself into the home counties and had no intention of leaving. The real problem wasn't that I lacked drive or ambition, the problem was that I didn't know which direction to head off in. I had set myself one goal in life – to get into Oxford – and now I'd finished with it and I hadn't a clue what the shape of the rest of my life looked like. There was no point thinking about pathways into careers because I had no burning desires to be something. I was standing in the middle of a field shrugging and lost.

These were the days before mobile phones, emails and social media. I had very little idea what anyone else was up to or doing and so I sat at home, flailing around, waiting for the once-a-week creative job ads in the *Guardian* and writing letters to friends I was missing in the hope they would write back. It was hard to make choices, but a severe lack of money was about to sharpen my mind.

Having had my mother wave me off to America at the start of the summer telling me I was going to make my fortune, I had returned months later, rather desperately, with five cents in my pocket. Every advert that had the word 'Graduate' in, Brenda pushed my way. Her attitude was: get out there, start earning and work out if you're happy later.

I got lucky. The very first interview I went to, I got a job offer. I was to be an assistant editor for a new legal directory at a small publishing house near the Barbican. I was more than happy to accept. I would begin my office life in a wonky looking building on the edge of Smithfield's meat market where men in bloodied white coats and hats would carry carcasses over their shoulders as I was coming into work. There would be the occasional trotter in the gutter and blood on the pavements. If you didn't know there was a meat market tucked away under the Victorian arches, you'd think there'd been a murder.

The job failed to grab me from the off. 'I hate Mondays like there is no tomorrow,' I wrote. 'Hated every minute of being at work. Yuk. Yuk. Yuk.'

'It was an absolute pain,' said my dad, holding nothing back. 'I had to take you to the train station, pick you up and make sure there was food for you to eat. Every day,' he then mumbled, shaking his head. 'Every bloody day.'

I don't blame him. Commuting was a bore, and I was very fortunate to have a devoted father to give me a lift to the station, but I quickly realised living at home was not a viable long-term option and when a pal from university got in touch to ask if I wanted to find somewhere to live in London, I leapt at the chance. Rent prices, though, were not easily within our reach and so we found a third person to be our flatmate, someone I worked with, and in March of 1990, six months after I'd come back from America, I finally moved to London.

For the next four years, in the two flats I lived in (we always needed three people to pay rent for a two-bedroom flat), my *bedroom* was the gap between the sofa and the wall in the sitting room. I was like a Borrower or something out of a Dickens' novel and I'd lie on the floor on a thin mattress, trying not to mind if I wanted to go to bed and nobody else did. I recall one occasion when a flatmate's boyfriend started having a go at me because I'd asked him and two other lads I'd never met before if they could leave the room. It was three in the morning and I wanted to go to sleep.

'But it's my room,' I said, staring at him.

'No, it isn't,' he'd replied and pulled the ring on another beer can.

Despite all this, something momentous was on the horizon, something that was to pale my 'I Think I'll Do History' into insignificance, shoot it into outer space and hurtle it to oblivion. A medic friend was studying at St Barts and I'd been to spend the evening with her. Sitting on the edge of her bed, glass of wine in hand, she'd asked me whether I was going to stay working at the small publisher. I'd finished work on the directory and had slid sideways to the legal recruitment section. I was now an assistant to a tremendous woman from Preston who I liked very much. We got on and I was enjoying the work, but I knew it wasn't going to be permanent.

'I think,' I said, after giving the matter two minutes of thought, 'that I'm going to go to Law School.'

'Excuse me?' My pal spewed her wine back into her glass. 'You? A lawyer?'

'Yes.' I stood, the cape of destiny furled itself around my shoulders. 'I am going to be a lawyer! And I'm going to go to court! And I'm going to HELP PEOPLE!'

Well.

You can imagine what Brenda had to say about this. She was THRILLED.

'A lawyer, Tony. An actual lawyer. It's marvellous. You can sue EVERYONE.'

My mother often fantasised about a day in court against any number of suitable adversaries (all of them would be Freemasons or Tories, preferably both to kill two birds with one stone) so the prospect of having someone close at hand to be her personal consiglieri was causing her to rub her thighs with glee. In her mind, we would be carried aloft on righteous wings, swooping in to dispense all the law, all of it, and then stand, on clifftops, wind in hair, breathing in nothing but the sweet smell of justice.

Before all that though, there was the nutty inconvenience of actually having to go to law school and, before I could go to law school, I had to be offered a position as an articled clerk and so I began the next merry-go-round of hauling myself off to firms who might be persuaded to take me on.

I got lucky again. The very first one I went to, a medium-sized law firm off Chancery Lane, liked me and made me an offer and just like that, I stepped onto the treadmill of Sensible Job Central. I was told later, by the partner who interviewed me, she had considered me a 'bit of a maverick' and had pushed for me to be offered a clerkship based on the fact there was nobody like me at the firm. She would live to regret this, but I'll get to that.

So here I was, about to commence the epic journey to become a bona fide solicitor. Brenda dipped into her savings and helped me buy books. I had a brand-new notepad, a file for coursework, a pack of pens and a shiny ruler. This was it! The start of the rest of my life! I positively bounced down Moorgate, leapt in through the big front doors of college, ran up the stairs and found the room where my odyssey would begin. I smiled at a few people. Some of them smiled back. In walked the lecturer, a grey-haired man in a brown tweed suit that had seen better days. He gave a light cough, and we were off.

Within five minutes of my first lecture on my first day of Law School, I knew I had made a terrible, TERRIBLE mistake. You might think I'm exaggerating here. I'm not. The enthusiasm which had carried me on a crest of hope came crashing onto rocks. This was the DULLEST thing I'd ever sat through – mind-numbing procedural nitpicking was not, it turned out, my bag, and I'd had to suffer Anglo-Saxon translation tutorials which I'd thought would never be beaten but here's the thing – there was no reversing it, no getting out of it. My new law firm had parted with cash – cash I did not have to pay them back so here I now was, stuck, staring down the barrel of the two most tedious years of my life. It was like I'd been sent to prison. I shouldn't have been there. I should have been out in the world scrabbling for the odd sketch or two on Radio Four. I should have been trying to scratch a cast together for obscure plays, writing things that were rubbish and not being afraid to make mistakes. Instead, I was staring down at a book that had the catchy title *Elements of Land Law*, eyes crossed with boredom. It was so big you could have used it as a murder weapon.

Trust law, contract, criminal, land and tort – my days were filled with egg-shell skulls, snails in bottles, carbolic smoke balls, *mens rea* and *actus reus*. The tone was dry and serious, the mood plodding and methodical. I was surrounded by boys with plummy accents and young women with their eyes set to the horizon. I had made a catastrophic mistake and my only option was to see the whole thing through to its tedious conclusion. It wasn't just a matter of passing exams and leaving Law School, I was also going to have to qualify. I was looking at a four-year stretch.

I'm going to give myself some credit here. I stuck with it. I also did not tell Brenda. Every phone call was greeted with the same response: 'It's great!' I would lie and then spend the remainder fending off all the legal questions she'd written down on a piece of paper.

No, we had not got to the bit in law where a neighbour might be interfering with your drain.

No, we had not got to the bit in the law about how to stop a neighbour secretly selling their garden to a developer.

No, we had not got to the bit in the law about how to stop Freemasons being quite so Freemasony.

You get the drift. My mother had been catapulted to a joyous shore where, if I'd been caught unawares by a wave, she'd have shouted, 'Help! Help! My daughter, THE LAWYER, is drowning!' Brenda was convinced that, now she had a legal brain in the family, NOBODY would dare mess with her. Nobody dared mess with her anyway, of course – she was the greatest friend and the absolute worst enemy. She was perfectly capable of taking care of herself but her glee at my progression to the top of the professional tree was that she now believed she would have back up, with Writ guns and Solicitor Letter grenades. With me behind her on the chariot, she would be undefeatable and unstoppable.

My mother loved a fight. If she'd come from a wealthy family, she might have made a great barrister. Nothing would have made her happier than tearing strips off men she considered corrupt or sexist or mentally weaker than herself, but she would also have been given to grand theatrics, would have laid into the judge and been rude to everyone so it's probably for the best she was denied the opportunity. Instead, she had me and she couldn't wait for me to qualify.

My time at Law School was an odd time. I had spent my time at Oxford absorbed by my subject but now it was like eating food for fuel rather than enjoyment. In my diary, I considered a 'rare highpoint' a moment where 'two people dissolved into coughing fits and our dry tutor raised an eyebrow and asked them kindly not to expire during his lecture because it did nothing for his reputation.' That was as good as it got. I often wonder now whether the only reason I went to law school, which was such a wrong fit for me, was simply for Brenda. Perhaps subconsciously I was keeping the peace or tapping into the deep need to always please her. Whichever it was, the only way of making it bearable was to start partying.

I was now living in a basement flat in Highbury Fields, still sleeping behind the sofa and sharing with two fellow law students. Our next-door neighbour was a seminal bluesy pop singer who I would occasionally see in the street. Above us lived a tremendously well-heeled couple. I'd like to apologise to them now because that year was going to turn into a never-ending revolving door of parties. My diaries are rammed with people coming to dinner, trips to restaurants, cinemas, theatres, lunches, all-nighters watching films and booze, booze, booze. I became the sort of person who would collapse on any available carpet at five in the morning, wake up and declare, 'Hey! I'm already dressed!' and go off to work. From 1990 through to the beginning of 1993, there isn't a single day in my diary that doesn't have a social event. How I am still alive, I will never know.

Our landlord was a mysterious figure who, we were to discover, was wanted by the police. Occasionally, they would turn up looking for him, thumping on the door at dawn while shouting, 'Police, open up!' I assumed it was a joke but no, they wanted our landlord for suspected mortgage fraud, and we spent the rest of our tenancy expecting to be turfed into the street at a moment's notice.

By this time, my contemporaries from Oxford were starting to make some headway into the world of comedy: Lee and Herring were becoming respected jobbing writers at Radio 4 and had landed themselves a sweet gig working for Armando Iannucci on his new show, *On The Hour*. It would be the precursor for *The Day Today* and would help establish my old sketch troupe pals as the next big thing. Brenda would ring me up and tell me every time she saw a name she recognised in the *Radio Times*. 'Aren't they doing well?' she would say, proudly. I was delighted for them and, despite my pursuing a career devoid of larks, it still didn't occur to me that their path might have been mine. As far as I was concerned, having fun for a job had disappeared into the mists of Brigadoon.

Brenda, in the meantime, was making full use of her daughter having a pad in London. She began referring to it as 'our flat' and set about making sure all my flatmates adored her. There were gifts, cards, flowers, cakes made to order by Tony, there were invites to 'weekends in the country', as if her house in Hitchin had magically become a location in an Evelyn Waugh novel. There was no end to her largesse. She had become the Magnificent Hostess with the great big garden where all the fun was to be had. She bought me a salmon-pink suit, in anticipation of my beginning work at a law firm, and started making pointed references to the fact that friends of mine were starting to get married and here I was with nobody in sight. Well, yes, Brenda, because you told me never to have anything to do with men. Go figure.

Brenda's garden parties became the stuff of legend: sun out, bodies strewn across the grass, a seemingly never-ending supply of food, booze on tap and Olympic standard showing off. My father, always the bridesmaid at these gatherings, would quietly get on with making everything happen while pals would slowly but surely get him cross-eyed pissed. I have enormously fond memories of one such gathering when Brenda appeared at a door asking where her husband was. A young man, who is now a very important professor, pointed to a cistus halfway down the garden. 'He's lying in that bush, Brenda.' Nobody batted an eyelid.

My mother enjoyed a drink, but rarely got drunk – she was at the fun with a bit of fizz in her end of the alcohol scale rather than someone for whom drink meant turning mean. The worst I think I ever saw her was entirely my fault. It was one Christmas towards the end of my time at Oxford. Inspired by *Brideshead Revisited*, I decided to make Brandy and Champagne cocktails. With no idea what I was actually doing, I forced three of the things down my parents' throats before we'd even thought about sitting down for lunch. The carving of the turkey was like something in a medieval tableau, the entire meal consumed in minutes and before the pudding could appear, which was traditionally brought from the kitchen aflame by my rosy-cheeked father singing, '*The boar's head is held on high and here we are to eat it up*,' followed by much cheering, things took a turn for the worse: my mother was so wasted, her forehead was on the table and Dad had disappeared. I found him, face down in the hallway, with one hand on the front door as if he'd tried to make his escape but hadn't quite managed it. I then tottered into the sitting room only to find myself locked in from the outside moments later by my mother who had woken suddenly at the dining room table and decided it must be bedtime. It wasn't. I was trapped and had to pee in a vase.

I had, in the end, had fun at Law School, made some chums, got a few snogs in, enjoyed some wild weekends, but my heart wasn't in it. I was going through the motions and six months later, on my knees on the cobbles in front of Charing Cross Station, I discovered, staring down at the sprawled *The Times*, flattened so everyone could see the Law Society results, that my name was not there. I had failed my business paper.

Brenda, of course, was furious. 'What do you mean you've failed?' She then set about blaming this entirely on my flat-mates. It wasn't fatal, thankfully and, because I'd only failed one, I had a chance to redeem myself.

'Don't you dare fuck it up,' said Brenda, in one of her more direct moments. I didn't have to pass for myself. I was having to do this for both of us.

Meanwhile, of course, I had started as an article clerk. I was in the property department, sharing a room with a female partner who liked to smoke while slowly dictating letters and staring out the window, legs crossed and misty-eyed. As a trainee, I was handed a file representing a large developer of new houses. It was my job to see the conveyancing over the line, straightforward stuff where I used to enjoy telling estate agents they were authorised to hand over the keys but, if truth be told, it felt a million miles from that moment on my pal's bed where I had declared I was going to 'help people'. Property then, was not going to set my world alight but I got a decent report for my first six months.

'You're doing well,' commented the partner who had recruited me all those years ago, shooting me a wink.

I smiled and then the male partner also giving my assessment, added, 'But perhaps you'd like to smarten up a bit,' at which point I stopped smiling. I remember, in that moment, giving serious thought to 'doing a Brenda'. She'd have torn him a new one and wouldn't have blinked doing it but that was the thing about my mother: she was fearless, especially when it came to dyed-in-the-wool sexism. There were lads in my intake of trainees who came into work covered in yolk smears and wearing socks that smelled of mice. Were they asked to smarten up a bit? No, they weren't. I wore a skirt suit and loafers but wasn't stick thin and my tits weren't under my chin. What he was really saying to me was 'lose some weight so you're more attractive'.

To my eternal shame I didn't do a Brenda. Instead, I clasped my fingers together and pursed my lips and said not a word. There is a power deficit in these moments, and I was painfully aware of it. To her credit, the female partner looked at me then told him to 'Shush' and I was so grateful, I made myself a silent promise that if she ever asked me to do anything, I'd work my socks off for her.

Brenda, meanwhile, was telling anyone who would listen, that her daughter was now a very important lawyer at a very important firm in London. This was, of course, her usual nonsense. It was Edinburgh Festival all over again: you've made it kid, with nothing to qualify it. The truth being I was far from important. I wasn't yet qualified, I'd failed one paper in my exams and my immediate horizon was nothing but misery: not only was I going to have to retake it, but I'd been moved to the company department where I was now sharing a room with a near silent forty-five-year-old tax lawyer with zero conversation and the personality of a squashed aubergine.

On the personal front, I'd met a woman who looked like Madonna who had taken me to Whitstable and seduced me. I didn't know what to do about it.

Hell was here.

Dearest Emmy

Am sending you this so that you can check out a few things.
Maybe it would be worth finding a safe hair dye, particularly
since I have got a persistent bladder infection.[1]

    Don't use Henna products, they've been withdrawn for some
time now. I probably only used them every three months,
approximately, but I can't help thinking the dye, despite being
non-chemical actually contained some very nasty things indeed.

    Check with your hairdresser and ask around. Also check out
your shampoo, deodorant and bubble bath. Tony has been using
green bubble bath for years with sodium sulphate[2] as the first
ingredient! That's gone in the bin! God knows what I'm going
to use. Try not to use deodorant too often. I know it's difficult,
but a good wash should suffice when you're not on TV. Don't
use too much sun block either.

    Don't want to panic you but it's best to ration use of all of
these things. NEVER use mouth wash!

    Looking forward to hearing your show tonight. Tony and
Ben said it was one of the best and that you were marvellous.
Ben said he didn't realise you could do so many voices.[3]
Wish I'd been there but I can't move out of the house in these
temperatures, and I was pretty bad yesterday.

    Hope the garden is still looking good and that you've

---

1 WHAT A START TO A LETTER.

2 I think she's in a lather here over a scare story about sodium lauryl sulphate being a potential cause of cancer. There is no scientific proof that it is.

3 This must be a radio show I was in. No idea which one because I used to do loads. I can do a lot of accents, hence my being on Radio 4 for many years, but never ask me to do Newcastle because I am useless at it.

remembered to water the plants. Do it before you go to work.
Hopefully you can come up soon for a weekend if you aren't
doing Soap Fever.[4] *Hope to see you before you go to*
Edinburgh.

Take care on the scooter.
Xxxxxx

★ ★ ★

4 I bloody loved presenting *Soap Fever*. It was a weekly chat show, super
irreverent, every Sunday on ITV2 before anyone had ITV2. We were allowed
to get away with murder and, under the brilliant eyes of producer Rachel
Ashdown, we all had quite the high old time.

Fifteen

'Do you think you should have been a barrister?' Brenda would occasionally say to me.

She'd watch legal dramas and perk up when the wigs turned up. The truth was, there was nothing remotely glamourous about being a solicitor. For those of you curious – barristers are the ones in the gowns and the wigs, the ones who get the glory of standing up in court and prosecuting and defending. Solicitors do the paperwork. For the first two years, all you're really doing is photocopying, putting files together, doing the grunt work on research, taking notes and providing reports on contracts people far more important than you can't be bothered to read. I was required to hang around in the dead of night, waiting for negotiations to grind to a conclusion and guard the sandwiches (don't feed your opponents until they've caved).

And then I was moved to litigation.

Sometimes, you walk into a room and it's like a spotlight hitting you full in the face. Suddenly, I was being dispatched to the Royal Courts of Justice at the top of the Strand, court document in hand, running to file things before deadline. I would prepare submissions to be signed off by counsel, I got to spend afternoons in the Inns of Court, in QC's rooms, tea and biscuits, jotting down their considerations. Everyone was clever, everything was urgent, every outcome vital. This was it, I realised, the cut and thrust I'd been waiting for. Finally, my days had a purpose.

I would be sent off on day trips, often meeting opposing solicitors, where we would pore over disputed evidence or, even better, try and find some. Brenda would want every grisly detail. 'I'm not allowed to tell you.' I'd respond.

'Oh, don't be mean,' she would whine. Client–solicitor privilege, she had decided, also meant 'And Brenda too', but I never told her a single detail. It would drive her to distraction.

Having said that, there were days where I'd have given a limb to be able to tell her what I'd been up to. A family was disputing the will of an elderly man who had unexpectedly left his entire fortune to a young fellow he'd known for a very short space of time. They were calling shenanigans, so off I was sent to the deceased's flat to see if anything might turn up. Our opposite was supposed to be meeting us but failed to do so. We took the view we would continue without her – we'd travelled a long way and our client was being charged for our time and, in any event, anything we discovered would be disclosed. So, in we went.

Well.

I was with a junior solicitor, a rather sombre chap who wore an old school tie, the dictionary definition of prim and proper. 'Do you want to do the bedroom?' he asked in a tone that meant, 'Please do the bedroom', so I took the challenge and set about sweeping the place for forgotten documents, diaries, anything that might point to evidence of undue influence. I stepped in and stood for a moment, glancing about the room. I was looking for a writing desk or tucked away boxes, bedside tables where notes might have been left. To my left there was a large built-in wardrobe unit and, with an absence of any other furniture that had drawers, I opened the two largest doors.

'What the actual fuck,' I murmured, my eyes widening, for there before me was a veritable smorgasbord of sexual paraphernalia. I was now required to meticulously note down every single thing I found or touched, irrespective of whether it was pertinent to the case. Everyone will have their predilections; everyone will have secret fantasies they might indulge from time to time but not everyone expects those things to be laboriously listed and then faxed for inspection after their death. The list was lengthy but included:

Cock ring (large, silver, engraved Hello Big Daddy)
Anal beads (black)
Large penis dildo
Dildo with a face on it. Don't know who. Looks like Ian McShane.
Not sure – thick wand snake head thing – I have no idea what this is but can guess where it goes
Leather head gear with large dummy
Mister magazine (34 editions)
Wrist restraints (leather)
2 lengths of rope
Pair of leather shorts with hole in rear
Wizard outfit with hat

Not only that, on my return to the office, I had to dictate a report which had to be typed up by my secretary.

'Jesus Christ,' she muttered to me, as she handed it back, all done.

The day after, the partner came in, ashen, and sat down. 'I read your report on the tube this morning. The woman next to me told me I was disgusting.'

This was more like it. This was making my blood pump. Litigation, I decided, was my pathway to a life that would never be dull, but it was at this point that my maverick status was about to bite me in the arse. A few months earlier, I'd been put in charge of the in-house magazine. It was a straightforward affair – restaurant and film reviews, legal round-ups, a gossip column on the back (which I did not write) and every now and again, special inserts designed to have everyone laughing. I produced a fake brochure for graduates thinking of applying to the firm, an illustrated re-write of *A Christmas Carol* filled with co-workers and partners – you get the drift. I was pushing the boundaries of deference and I was starting to get quite the reputation but the upshot of playing fast and loose was that it was decided they'd shunt me off to another building for the last six months of my clerkship. When I was told I was moving to the tax department, a deathly dull mausoleum of sorrow, I visibly baulked. 'I don't want to go,' I told them, very clearly. 'I'd like to stay in litigation or, if I can't, I'll go back to company.'

'All right, calm down,' a male partner said to me, as if I was thrashing on the floor, wetting myself.

I've never forgotten that moment. I hadn't raised my voice, I wasn't trying to be difficult, I was expressing a preference. I had zero interest in tax law, spending six months there would be a total waste of my time. I knew precisely why they were doing it: they wanted me out of the way.

It was at this point, finally, I found my inner Brenda. Fuck them, I thought, walking away and out of the office. Fuck. Them. I rang Brenda and told her.

'Fuck them,' she said.

And so I picked up a copy of the *Law Society* magazine and saw an advert for a small law firm called Stephens Innocent. Brilliant name, I thought. They were looking for a newly qualified solicitor to join their litigation team. Small problem – I was not newly qualified, but I only had six months to go. 'Who cares?' Brenda said, with her usual nothing's impossible breeze. 'What have you got to lose?'

She was right. Fuck it, I thought. I'm going to apply.

Mark Stephens is one of the Legal Legends. He is, without doubt, one of the most wonderful people I've ever had the pleasure to know. He's entirely mischievous. This was going to be a match made in heaven. The thought of stealing a trainee from a whopping great law firm on his doorstep was too good an opportunity to pass up and so, after a rather raucous interview, he offered me the position. I would finish my clerkship and qualify under his eye.

Telling the whopping great law firm I was leaving before the end of my clerkship was one of the greatest moments of my life. Brenda asked if she could come with me and pretend she was on work experience. Sadly, I didn't allow it. They were absolutely FURIOUS, but I'd played them at their own game. Waste my time and you can forget it. Never in a million years was I going to sit learning the precise sum of nothing for six months. Never again was I going to be pushed over. I stood out on the pavement in front of my old office, cardboard box in hand and realised I was, finally, my mother's daughter.

'That told them,' Brenda said, with a degree of glee. Brenda would now think nothing of pointing at me and shouting, 'SHE'S MY LAWYER!' at any stranger who might be annoying her in my presence. It was as if I now possessed the powers of Gandalf, allowing Brenda every Get Out Of Jail card imaginable. 'YOU SHALL NOT PASS!' she would howl, then cackle with delight. Her days of getting her own way were now encrusted with jewels. She had a living, breathing lawyer on call, 24 hours a day, 365 days a year.

If I was going to love being a lawyer, it was going to be at Stephens Innocent. It was WONDERFUL. I was instantly given a broad litigation brief and as soon as I qualified, on 9 September 1994, I was off. My diary is packed with trial dates, deadlines for defences and hearings. I was handling copyright infringement, a fraught matrimonial case, helping on a criminal appeal that was making headlines, defending a household name in the Case of the Terrible Cheese, working pro bono on the biggest libel trial of the century helping out a young barrister by the name of Keir Starmer (you may have heard of him), and every other Wednesday I would volunteer at a law centre in Fitzrovia. It was all go.

With me now in a full-time job, my relationship with Brenda became sporadic. We would talk most days on the phone but face to face was now confined to the occasional weekend, the odd drop-in after a day in London and the usual high days and holidays. In my diaries every now and again, there's the marking of a terrible row with Brenda, noticeably when I am about to go back to London having been with her for any length of time, and it suddenly struck me that perhaps Brenda was upset. I had been to university, I'd gone away to America, I'd come back, I'd needed her again but now, I really didn't. She was, to put it bluntly, of no further use. We spend so long thinking about the damage parents do to children but we spend very little considering the damage children do to their parents. I was her only child, and I wasn't interested in her any more. No wonder she was upset. I want to be fair to her. Brenda was unable to cope when she felt upset. Lashing out was the only mechanism she had.

But for me, these were the days that were fulfilling and exciting but a small nagging What If was starting to creep through the back of my brain. It was that strange, elastic, indefinable urge to be creative and it wouldn't shut up. I kept my own counsel: if I allowed myself to think about my What If for any length of time, it spelled nothing but trouble, so I pushed it away.

I didn't tell Brenda about the doubts about my career that were beginning to swirl, instead I started going to a new club. It was called the Double Six and was run by an effervescent young man called Steve Furst. You'd book a table and turn up, be seated by waiters in tuxedos and given a menu from which you'd order board games. One night, over a session of Hungry Hippos, Steve told me about a new club he was starting, the Regency Rooms. It was going to be a nostalgic, tongue-in-cheek parody of the kitsch old easy-listening night clubs of the sixties and early seventies. He would be hosting as Lenny Beige, friend to the stars, and he wanted to know if I'd like to come and be part of it. I hadn't performed on stage in four years, put off by my last trawl around the block with the Oxford Revue in 1988. We'd had a particularly unpleasant Edinburgh: the young bucks of the Alternative Comedy scene had decided they hated everyone who went to Oxbridge and things got so bad, they started challenging people to fights. I remember one evening seeing a member of the Cambridge Footlights, a slight lad in specs, quietly folding his glasses into the top pocket of his jacket and putting his fists up as a much-loved comedy entertainer told him he was going to smash his face in but here I was, years later, thinking the Regency Rooms sounded quite the lark and so I said yes. I was to become the Bearded Lady, a hirsute woman in a bicycle helmet and thick specs, chained up on stage for three hours, only to be released to dance to the theme tune to *Hawaii Five-O*.

Colleagues from the office came to see me. Stars of stage and screen became regular audience members. I graduated to becoming Lorraine Beige, Lenny's sister-in-law, a rather monstrous, shuffling chanteuse singing 'Puppet on a String' to a brass band backing track. The entire thing was crackers. Just like that, I remembered what fun was.

By now, I was living in a tremendous flatshare, the sort you read about in authorised biographies but can't believe were actually real. The lead up to it had started the summer before, with another trip to Edinburgh: I was standing in the Pleasance Courtyard looking for Richard Herring who had vaguely offered me a bed to sleep in or a sofa to lie on, but he was nowhere to be seen. It was at this point I was approached by a skinny girl, dark hair scraped back into a ponytail. She had a baggy jumper on and tight black jeans. She was wearing DMs and had a fag on the go.

'Hello. We've met before.'

It was, of course, Sue Perkins. We had met before, about a year previously. I'd been standing with Ben Moor down at Putney Bridge enjoying a beer at the Boat Race. Someone had approached, in shambling manner, asking for a light before enquiring whether we'd seen Sally Phillips anywhere. That was Perkins. For a very brief moment, I'd mistaken her for a tramp.

Anyway, here we were, face to face again and with no Herring in sight, we meandered over to the bar and got absolutely shit-faced. It's hard to know who is going to be important on first meeting but Perks was to become my girlfriend. (Incredibly, I still, at this point, hadn't worked out I was a massive gay despite the one previous same-sex experience where I was overwhelmed by the woman who looked like Madonna – I mean she'd looked like Madonna, who in their right mind would have turned that down? Didn't mean I was a card-carrying gay, right?). She's also my dearest lifelong pal, someone who has stuck by me through thick and thin, been there at every important, catastrophic moment and is one of the very few people for whom I would take a bullet but back then, we were just getting drunk and making each other laugh.

I had been chucked out of my flatshare in Highbury Fields – turned out it really wasn't my room after all – and had found myself in posh, leafy Hampstead sharing with a proper lawyer who would go on to become the literary agent of the writer of the most successful book franchise of all time. Coming back from Edinburgh that summer, two things happened: I realised I couldn't afford to stay in the posh, leafy flat with the proper lawyer and Perks had moved into a soon to be demolished house a five-minute walk away. She was sharing with two pals from college: an up-and-coming actress called Nicola Walker and a woman destined to become one of the UK's greatest TV writers, Sarah Phelps.

Back then, all three of them were struggling and had no money and because I was still, at that point, a lawyer, I'd wander up there with a few bags of food and leave them in the kitchen. They were living in a house that belonged to the parents of a college friend. It was going to be knocked down and redeveloped into something stunning but for now, they needed people to live in it to stop squatters. The cooker was a two-ring camping stove, mushrooms were growing behind the toilet and whether there might be hot water that day was as random as the weather. They had nothing and seemed gloriously happy, and I have no doubt that watching them being prepared to slug it out until they got somewhere inspired me to jack in my sensible life.

With them living up the road, I started to spend more time with Perks and finally, after years of not being able to work out why I never fell in love with gentleman callers, she

Here we are with my Welsh grandmother, Emma.
I was convinced the Giles grandma was based
on her. It wasn't.

Bob tries yet again to take my eye out.

Tony and Brenda in the early eighties.

On holiday in Cornwall.

Mum, the teacher. She loved those clogs.

On a demo with Bob.

Bob in China.

Mum and me in Italy. I'm fifteen.

Poppy, the most excellent beagle.

Brenda, in her fifties, in her beloved France.

Brenda, in Italy, writing letters.

Tony and Brenda, now in her sixties, in the garden she adored.

Dad in the garden at Dallington.

persuaded me that I was in love with her instead. It coincided with my realisation that the posh flat down the hill was beyond my means and on a bright spring day, I moved in.

It's been an odd experience re-reading my diaries from 1987 onwards. They are filled with names of boys who I fancy, have snogged and in some cases, have had sex with. There are two relationships recorded that went beyond a hit and run fumble. I am happy and into them but it's also abundantly clear that a pattern emerges: I fancy a boy, I get the boy, the boy starts liking me back and at that point, I lose all interest. I had been indoctrinated from as early as I could remember that men would ruin my life. I was terrified of getting pregnant and even though I enjoyed sex with men, I think I was also afraid of it.

I would not tell my mother I was in a relationship with a woman for another seven years. I'm not sure why I was so reticent. She was a liberal-minded ex-hippy who had a loose relationship to sexual morality and yet there was a memory burned into me that stopped me short. When I was around seven or eight, I had been playing with a friend. It was a hot, sunny day and I was lying front down on the lawn, my top pulled up over my back. My friend, a girl, was spelling letters on my back. I had to guess the words. Brenda, seeing us, had rapped on the window and called me in. I found her lying in her bed, curtains drawn. She looked ashen. 'If you turn out to be a lesbian,' she told me, 'I'll kill myself.'

At that age, I had no real sense of what a lesbian was but I suppose it instilled in me two things: a marker that being gay was something terrible and that if I did turn out to be a lesbian, it would kill Brenda.

I really don't know where this came from – there was a story she would tell from her time in Nottingham about being pursued by a woman and it being unwelcome but my instinct leans more towards me being her only child and that if I ended up being something that society, certainly at that time, frowned upon then that would be a fresh shame for her to have to deal with. As a child, she would have seen what gay Uncle Leslie had done to his family. She didn't want that again, thanks very much, but she was also a woman who was painfully aware of what carrying the stigma of shame could do to a person. Quite simply, I think she didn't want me to be at a disadvantage.

Meanwhile, in the land of Brenda, she decided it was time to shake things up a bit. Her relationship with me was now on a par with a threadbare blanket and had withered to next to nothing. I was in work and in love. I had stopped giving her a second thought and it was at this point, when her sadness about me was at its zenith, that she chose, for the second time in her life, to have an affair.

I really cannot over emphasise how entirely happy she was with my father but as he sanguinely told me: 'One bloke was not enough.' It feels impossible to understand but my father was going to have to, yet again, look the other way, but that's what happened.

'He came on holiday with us.'

'I beg your pardon?'

'He came on holiday with us,' Tony repeated, 'and your mother used to tell me to go to the shops to pick up croissants. Or baguettes. Or brie. And I'd go because I was the only person who could drive and that's when they'd be at it.'

I thought my mother doing the previous lover in my child-hood bedroom wasn't going to be beaten but here we are in a villa in sunny France. Not only has she managed to persuade my father to have someone else in tow; she's dispatching him on errands so she can get her holiday banging in.

Brenda was in her early fifties at this point. Her lover was in his early twenties. Eyeballs on stalks, zoinks and away. What was going on here? Phyllis recalls Brenda being infatuated. 'She'd talk about him constantly, would mention him in every conversation. It was as if Tony didn't exist. She had no consid-eration for the consequences. I think she knew she could get away with it.'

Brenda was well used to 'getting away with it': it was her

superpower and speaks to the grip she had over people when she used her charisma as a weapon, but she was approaching menopause and was starting to feel the ivy of middle age curling up her.

'She was terrified of being old,' observed Phyllis. 'She started warning me about baggy eyes and scraggy necks. She was scared of becoming invisible.' Brenda was a woman who identified as a highly sexual creature. She needed to know she was attractive, that she still had what it takes. She needed attention.

I never met the other lover and I'm sure this was quite deliberate on my mother's part. Tom, my cousin, recalled meeting him: 'He was quite handsome, slim and rather shy. He didn't say much.' It's a small detail, but it stands out. She'd picked another quiet lad, one who would let her be the star of the show.

At the time, I remember being vaguely aware she was hanging out with a younger man, but I had no idea as to the extent of what was going on. It came as a huge shock when I finally did. It was a rather hot day in June and my father had turned up on my doorstep. He was agitated and upset.

'What's the matter?' I asked. 'Where's mum?'

He bundled me into my room and sat on the edge of the bed. 'I have just discovered your mother on her knees in front of (let's call him Jeremy) pulling down his pants.'

'Excuse me?'

'And do you know what she said to me?'

I was standing very, very still with my mouth open. I shook my head.

'Did she say, oh no, Tony, you've caught me about to give Jeremy a blow job in our bedroom? Did she say, this looks worse than it is? No. She looked at me and said, "What are you doing creeping round the house?"'

'What did you say?'

'I asked her what she was doing. She said she was analysing the difference between men and women's pelvises.'

I snorted at this, but I was raging. Never before, or since,

do I think I have been more angry. I left the room, rang her
and lost it. Perks remembered it as being the only time she
ever saw me completely out of control. I have never known a
fury like it. Every last scrap of resentment I had ever carried
about her was excised and when I put the phone down, I was
convinced I would never see Brenda again.

It was complicated. I was raging on behalf of my father but
I was also incredulous that he was prepared to put up with it.
I simply could not understand why he stayed with her. Tony
shrugs this off now. 'Marriages,' he told me, with not a scrap
of resentment, 'are ups and downs. We had patches where we
didn't get on so well, and patches when we got on brilliantly
but we always wanted to stay together. We were in a not-so-
well patch, but I knew we'd come out the other side. I just
went for nice walks. I was fine.'

I, on the other hand, was not.

It's difficult, when you love someone who is flawed and
complicated and selfish. Brenda was not built for monogamy.
Some people just aren't, but she was the only mother I had.
Somehow, like Dad, I was going to have to forgive her. It was,
as my senior partner had told me, none of my business.

When I asked Dad how her second affair came to an end,
his answer was simple: 'Her vagina dried up.'

Wednesday

CONGRATULATIONS ON SUNDAY TIMES *COUP.
HURRAY! HURRAY FOR EMMY!*[1]

Dear Emmy

*1st stop in a gorgeous old house, part of an estate. Two nights
here. Very restful – Swedish Gustavian style – white and grey
– very tasteful. We are both very tired today. Had good
evening in Paris but the Bastille area was hosting a very loud
band, the vibrations shook us up and down our fragile old
bodies. Everyone was there – including Sarkozy – very small,
pinched man – how did he get Napoleon tag? Celebrating
something to do with Mitterand. All the key left-wing royalty
were there – Daniel Cohn Bendit, Segolene Royal.*[2] *I
shouted out 'HURRAY FOR SOIXANTE HUIT!'*
  *Tony driving me mad over parking. Hit a rock in Verge,
DAY ONE.*[3]

Love Mum and Dad. Xx

★ ★ ★

1 I think this must be a reference to the hallowed bestsellers list. I've managed
to get on it twice – first with *The Tent, the Bucket and Me* and then again with
I Left My Tent in San Francisco. The first Tent had done super well but when
the second Tent managed to get itself on the list my editor at the time rang me
and said, 'I'm astonished.'

2 My mother's obsession with Sarkozy showing no sign of slipping here.
Daniel Cohn-Bendit is a French–German politician who was a student leader
during the fabled 1968 uprising and Ségolène Royal is a French politician for
the Socialist Party.

3 For such a short letter, it's rammed with incident. Well done, Brenda.

Dear Emmsie

The news that nearly 400,000 people left England this year to have a better life elsewhere came as no surprise.[1] Now that we're soon to have Hitchin to Paris direct in November when Eurostar leaves from St Pancras, two steps from Kings Cross, I am tempted to secure bolt-hole somewhere in Europe where you can buy REAL fruit and veg and meat that tastes of something.

Watching a film recently about a bread-line existence in India, my eyes popped with shock, not at the dead animals and corpses in the gutter – I'd seen them before – but at the fecundity of the fruit and veg market in a small Indian village miles from the nearest Marks and Spencer and the quantity, variety and quality of the fare on offer. When did I last see such jewels of delight in Waitrose? Never.[2]

We are eating food the Indians leave out for emaciated cats. Why don't we shout we want MORE AND BETTER? Because the English have forgotten what REAL food is like. Try counting the cardboard boxes that pretend to be food. Just think, Indians are desperate to come and live here! When they see those boxes, they will be on the first Eurostar back!

Mind you, the English have also spent their food money going to the dentists too often and the strychnine in whitening agents and their fancy toxic fillings have changed the chemicals

---

1 Brenda would have hated Brexit with every fibre of her being. I'd have paid money to see her heckle Nigel Farage.

2 This is harsh on Waitrose. Also: my mother never went food shopping, so this entire rant is pretty moot.

in their saliva and they can't taste anything.[3] But once they've got those flashing white smiles and no gaps between their teeth, they just dream about being in Hello! *magazine.*

Did you know that 1 in 7 women fantasise about flashing their teeth in a woman's magazine? Men are as bad. 1 in 5 pours so much Listerine down their throats they wouldn't taste Toilet Duck if you put it in a whiskey glass.[4]

Now while I'm on the subject of the English it is quite apparent that this lemming like exodus from the old country is a desperate need for REAL food, wooden teeth and a few friendly smiles. We've lost all that.

Northerners used to scare Southerners like myself with their enthusiastic hale fellow and well met social enthusiasm. Old fashioned friendliness. Well, that's gone. When we were in the Yorkshire moors some years ago now, we were the only people in the village pub for a week. We played cards in silence with a couple of beers in case we said anything which might have offended the landlord who looked permanently angry that we happened to keep coming back.

That was the last holiday we took in England. Not much point. The English aren't very good at tourism. IT'S TAKE THE MONEY AND GIVE 'EM A GRIMACE! Then shoot them if they start speaking in a foreign accent – that is RECEIVED PRONUNCIATION.

The South isn't much better. Down here MO is the order of the day – MEMBERS ONLY. And – all the other shit can KEEP OUT! MO and KO is practised widely in the South. You might like to know that they don't speak RP in the worst

3 It may astonish you, but my mother didn't have access to the internet. She wasn't reading this stuff on obscure and suspect Facebook pages or dabbling in the dark web. This is stuff she's decided to dream up.

4 No idea where she got these statistics from but if I had to guess it would be 'Random poll in *Cosmopolitan*'.

MO pockets. They speak PRINCE CHARLES which is an inability to get your words out, breathy intake, scrabbled vowels and consonants which are dropped in the huntin' fishin' shootin' style of George III – but he had very bad wind. The MO set must have a lot of indigestion.

England, sadly, has slithered into a grimacing. MO, KO, non RP speaking hiatus of 50's style upper class SNOOT. But it's the REAL people who are leaving England, the ones who don't aspire to MO and SNOOT but see a more egalitarian, funny, friendly welcome elsewhere. Who wants England now when the French call out 'Bon Appetite' to complete strangers tucking into a mixed salad, Italians pinch your bottom unasked,[5] the Irish keep you awash with black drink, merry tunes and superstition and the Spanish smear assorted delicacies on anything lying around to give you BOTULISM for free.

What is to be done? I used to love England. It was a going somewhere place and in the 60s and 70s we had our own films, our own really stimulating TV with wonderful cry your eyes out plays, laugh cleverly comedy and pop stars who had their own REAL voices. We laughed a lot, we had no money, we smiled at strangers and, best of all, they smiled back.

But then a terrible secret was let loose on the country. A secret that has been marinated in a the most loathsome bile. A rigor mortis secret.

I saw this secret once in Downing Street before it was set free to blight the light-heartedness, the warmth, the joy, the hope.

It had a close resemblance to a crow standing on very spindly legs clutching something that looked like a midwife's bag. It made a strangulated noise, a version of PRINCE CHARLES which even he wouldn't have been able to decipher.

---

5 If an Italian had pinched my mother's bottom unasked, she'd have gone Full Godzilla and killed him dead with sheer venom.

If you can picture a crocodile's mouth screaming 'GOAT my CIHR'[6] *over and over until a policeman had to come to its assistance, you will understand the intuitive feeling I had that this was a secret no one had heard about before and that it should be kept hidden in a dark place.*

But then the spindly legs moved and something unnatural reached into the midwife's bag and a strange object fell to the floor. At the time I could now know what it was. It had FILOFAX written across it.

Later I was told that what I had witnessed was a MARGARET THATCHER.[7]

I must have been one of the first to see it and to know what it was.

I think the first new Eurostar to Paris leaves on November 17th.

Maybe another 400,000 will be on it. Thank God we have a way out.

I knew you were feeling a bit down – hope this has cheered you up a bit.[8]

Lots of love Mumsy

PS Until now I have closed my mind to living in France because French women spend too much time in the kitchen and

6 I think she means 'GET my CAR' here but done in an over-the-top posh accent.

7 And there it is. We finally get to it.

8 This is another of those pain-in-the-chest moments for me. My mother was acutely aware of my own mental health and if I was in a down patch or things weren't going so well, she would go to great effort to try and lift my spirits. Later, as her life was coming to an end, she would tell me that I 'always knew what to say' meaning I was able to find the right words for the right moment when she might be on the verge of spiralling. It had got easier, dealing with her, during the last years of her life. My regret, of course, is that I was unable to find the right words earlier, when she had suffered so greatly.

French men are arrogant in a particularly backward Masonic way. But there is a Vend'este breathing through France. She is stubborn, sexually adventurous and disobedient. My favourite qualities. She is wonderful Cecile Sarkozy[9] and she has moved French women into a new feminist consciousness. And about time. I might have a small atelier in Paris of my own.

Kisses as ever xx

★ ★ ★

---

9 Actually Cécilia Attias, now the ex-wife of President Nicolas Sarkozy. A neat story – it was Sarkozy, in his capacity as mayor, who married Cécilia to her first husband and, four years later, she would leave that husband for him. In 2007, she ran off with her lover, Richard Attias, and married him a year later. Oh, the French!

Sixteen

It feels ridiculous to make references to a calling but it's the nearest I can get to explaining it. Creative people are compelled to make things, whether it be music, acting, painting, sculpture, writing – it doesn't matter – it's like someone lighting a beacon on a faraway peak and only you have a sense of urgency about it. I had rekindled the thing that had always given me joy, people who knew me kept telling me I should be writing and finally, one morning sitting on the tube on the Northern Line, the voice nagging away at the back of my brain became too loud to ignore.

It was early in the morning – I had a breakfast meeting to attend with a barrister. By my feet sat a boxy black case filled with files. I was sitting, hands in lap, deep in thought. A terrible thing had happened: I had stopped being happy and I had to do something about it. I glanced down the carriage, spotting all the other lawyers with their boxy black cases and was consumed with the realisation that this was going to be the next forty years of my life. I couldn't do it and so I stepped off at Chancery Lane, walked to my office and handed in my resignation.

'I'm going to write comedy,' I told Mark Stephens.

He thought I was playing a practical joke, but I wasn't. I meant it. I had no job to go to, no plan of any note. I just knew I had to get out and give it a go and put my What If to rest. To his credit, Mark was lovely – if I was ever going to be happy as a lawyer, it would have been working for him, but new pastures were calling, and I was about to jump out of a plane to try and find them.

My bigger problem, of course, was telling Brenda. There had been a thawing of the permafrost following her second affair and, six months on from my losing it at her down the phone, we had met, finally, on home turf and she dealt with it by mumbling something about not raking over old ground and would I like a canapé with a thing called tapenade on it because she'd had it in France and oh, my God, it's amazing. I thought about having it out with her again but really, what was the point? Dad had moved on and I never wanted to risk a row so on we rolled, as if nothing had ever happened. If you're thinking she got away with murder, well, yes, she did.

'Sorry.' She clamped her eyes shut. 'I'm not sure I understand what you're saying to me? You're giving up being a lawyer?' Opening her eyes, she stared at me.

'Yes, I've handed in my notice.'

'And you're not going somewhere else? To another firm?'

'No.'

'Do you want to be a barrister? Is that it? Because I always said you should do that.'

'Well, you didn't always say I should do that but, no. I am not going to be a barrister.'

She shook her head in disbelief. 'But what are you going to do?'

'I'm going to be a writer.'

There was then a long period of silence in which she sat, mouth open, looking at me as if I'd told her I'd murdered five people.

I'd never really believed Victorian illnesses existed, you know the ones – the murky, soft around the edges, indefinable afflictions that only seemed to affect women of a certain age – but the revelation that her daughter was no longer going to be a lawyer sent my mother into the sort of decline reserved for maiden aunts in gothic novels. The full-blown emotional eclipse was something to behold as she careered between disbelief, grief, fury, derision and back again. She simply couldn't understand it.

You can't blame her. Here she was, thinking her work was done – daughter into Oxford, law school, respectable firm, pathway to partnership assured. I'd be living in a house made of swans before she knew it, granny annex with a pool and a muscle-bound masseur to cater to her every whim; the sun would always be shining and no one would ever put weight on again but now here we all were, back at square bloody one.

It was around this time that Brenda lost interest in me. We'd been through the casual distancing I had set in place for my own well-being, but through it all, I'd still get regular phone calls and the odd letter. Now, I was to experience something akin to an Amish shunning. For the first time in Brenda's life, she gave up on me. I'd secured myself every chance in the world, chances she would have given an eye for, and here I was tossing them in the bin, and for what? A romantic notion that I might make my way in the world by scribbling a few things down? What a joke. All the effort she had poured in, all the encouragement, all the pride, disappeared down the sink. Now, when people asked her how I was, she'd snarl, 'Unemployed,' and move the conversation on. Instead, she shifted her attentions sideways to my cousins.

'She was the most funny, exciting, crazy member of the family,' Tom told me. 'She always let me be myself. Never made me feel embarrassed or ashamed. I loved how flamboyant and dramatic she was. She was like a second mum to me, really. When I moved to London, I'd see her once a week. We'd go to museums, to the cinema and get pissed. I was aware she and Phyllis didn't see eye to eye but I just have really fun memories of her. She was such a powerful woman. I never saw the temper. I dodged all the worst aspects of her personality and got all the best bits.'

This was something I rarely did with Brenda. I would see her at home or occasionally at our London flat but socialising with her, in the way she did with my cousins, was something that never happened. Brenda, at any given moment in her life, needed someone who would make her feel fun and adored.

Whether it was Michael, Tony, Daniel, Jeremy, Ben or Tom, Brenda had a deep desire to be the focus of attention. For all her strident protestations that all men were awful, she needed male applause and validation.

For ten months, I sat at home – the four of us were now living in a house in Childs Hill owned by an octogenarian called Rhoda Pepys who was, and still is, one of the most tremendous old ladies I've ever met. Every Friday, we would get a parcel from Fortnum & Mason, occasionally we'd be summoned for supper at her house in Hampstead. We'd stand in the hallway and she'd come down the stairs on a Stannah stairlift in a red turban, blowing a hunting horn. We'd be served cold avocado soup and other monstrosities and would find ourselves sitting next to other extraordinary pensioners some of whom thought nothing of getting frisky under the table.

My other flatmates were flourishing. I, on the other hand, was trying to work out whether what I'd done was going to be worth it. I'd been on a treadmill since my mid-teens and apart from the enforced break due to illness, it felt as if I hadn't stopped. My life was passing by in a blur but now, with no job, I was able to pause and work out whether I actually had any talent.

Now, when I'm giving talks at schools or colleges or to writing groups, I always start by saying, when you first try, you're shit. Everybody is shit. Nobody knows what they're doing. If I'd decided to become a concert pianist, I wouldn't sit down on day one and be able to play a Rachmaninov concerto, I'd be tinkering away at chopsticks. Writing, like painting or singing or playing an instrument, requires practise. You need to work out what it is you have to say and how to tell a story well. The latter can be learned from any number of books. Learn the basics and then it's up to you. It's the former, working out what you have to say, that's the trickier bit.

In those first months, I wasn't sure what to do. I wrote a short sitcom called *This Family Robinson*, an illustrated children's book called *Twitch Witch* and a novel based on the journey I took from San Francisco to New York when I was twenty-one.

Two of these things would be useless and would never see the light of day again. The latter would re-emerge over a decade later as the basis for my third book. Nothing is ever wasted. Everything you write will be useful at some point. The important bit is to write.

After ten months of writing and staring at the wall and watching my bank account dwindle to nothing, I decided it was time to get a job that actually paid money. I had wafted into the orbit of mighty agent Vivienne Clore, who I kept bumping into with Mel and Sue. I was personable and competent, and Vivienne asked if I'd like to be the tour manager for Bob Downe, an Australian stand up I loved. I leapt at the chance. I wrote in my diary 'What a difference leaving the law has made. I really do have a fantastic life, even if I am poor.'

I rang Brenda to tell her. 'Never heard of him,' she said, before quickly bringing the conversation to a close.

It was the next tour I was asked to manage, this time for comedian and impressionist Rory Bremner, that would prove the turning point in my mother's period of disinterest and despair. On being introduced to Rory, she stood beaming, tickled pink to be backstage like the very important person she was. She whispered, 'Thank goodness you gave up the law.'

The doldrums were over, it was show business here we come.

The never-ending conveyor belt of grafting had begun. I certainly wasn't idle and I was pushing here and poking there, trying to break through and get a career going. I ran myself ragged and at the beginning of 1998, after two months of feeling nothing but exhausted, a blood test confirms I've got the tail end of glandular fever again. I'm struggling and my encounters with my parents are described typically:

'Managed to do a little work this morning but everything went firmly out the window the minute the parents arrived. God bless them but they wear me out. I felt exhausted just having to listen to them. It was fucking grim and alas, I got very tetchy with them. Really short tempered. I wonder why I get that way with them. I'm not like it with anybody else.'

I recognise this feeling and it's one I regret. I recall a conversation with Brenda, many years later, where she told me to be 'nice to her because I won't be around much longer'. It's an impossible ask, of course, to constantly be the best you can be, especially when it comes to parents, but in an attempt to treat my mother as fairly as possible it is only right to add this disclaimer: it wasn't always her who was being difficult.

Shifting career was never going to be easy and I'd chosen to chip into one as hard as granite and by the summer of 1997, I was almost there but not quite: I'd appeared in the stage sketch show *The Big Squeeze*, with Mel, Sue and Geraldine McNulty, and it had done well. People were starting to notice me, and Vivienne offered to represent me.

I had never intended to return to performing, despite still putting in the odd appearance at the Regency Rooms. If I did things, I was doing them because I liked the people or fancied the lark so when I bumped into my old pal Ben Moor, who told me about a sketch show ITV were making, I thought why not and so I found myself in the office of an executive producer and an hour later, I had been cast in the surreal, science-fiction sketch comedy, *Planet Mirth*. If I tell you the ENTIRE budget for each episode was fifteen thousand pounds, you'll have a vague idea of what we were dealing with. We had to shoot nineteen episodes at breakneck speed and on the day our producer didn't have enough money to pay for a full crew, she handed me a kit bought from a toy shop and asked me to 'make Ben look like a werewolf'. Brenda would fondly remember it as 'the worst thing she'd ever seen' but I had proved to Vivienne I was employable. The work started rolling in.

A day's filming on the TV sitcom *Kiss Me Kate* led to my being cast in *The Sunday Format*, a new radio show written by John Morton. It would be my first experience of being in something that was properly excellent and from the moment it went out, I would not stop working in radio and TV as an actor and presenter for the next five years, an astonishingly lucky run. At one point, I found myself invited to Britney

Spears' twenty-first birthday party. I was in grave danger of actually becoming famous.

Brenda was in her cups. She was loving the attention by proxy. A shrine began to emerge in their hallway – great framed pictures of copies of Sony Awards we'd won, photos of me presenting *Soap Fever*, *Flatmates*, *The Real Holiday Show*, pictures of me on set in *People Like Us*, *This Morning With Richard Not Judy*, *The Smoking Room*, *Suburban Shootout*, on and on. A scrapbook of newspaper cuttings became my father's new life work; photos taken from the television of me at award ceremonies became Brenda's latest art installation. Everything was suddenly about successful, off-the-telly me but I'm afraid we've reached the part in the story where we're going to have to return to the delicate problem of my mother's dried-up vagina.

My parents had decided to take early retirement, a decision thrust upon them given the college they both worked at was being absorbed into another. Here they were with a sudden get out – the promise of decent redundancy pay, considerably more than if they stayed, and the prospect of endless, rolling holidays. They took it. Problem was, they were both still relatively young – Tony was fifty-five, Brenda fifty-two – and without anything to keep her occupied, Brenda was going to be in trouble. I think she regretted early retirement: she loved her job and adored feeding off the energy of the young people she surrounded herself with. That was all about to leave her and if there was one thing my mother was not equipped to deal with, it was boredom. Not only that but the menopause was about to hit her full on.

There were major changes in my life too: I'd bought my own flat, half an hour away, and after being badgered into handing them a set of keys, we entered the period in which they would think nothing of turning up whenever they damn well pleased. 'Coo-eeeee!' would come the call, as the front door opened, and in they would waltz, unannounced.

I'd also got myself a dog, something that was greeted with wails from Brenda, who hated the things. Then she met my puppy and that was the end of that little outburst. Poppy, the most excellent beagle, was to become the living thing my mother loved most.

'She's a person,' she would tell me. 'And she must have MEAT.' Every time I was away filming, Brenda would take her in and feed her up. 'This dog is starving,' she would tell me, pointing at Poppy's fat belly. She was like a grandmother secretly shovelling cake down the neck of a favoured child and whispering, 'Don't tell your mother.'

Poppy, for Brenda, was something to love who would love her back unconditionally, no strings attached. She was the new child she needed when her own child didn't have much time for her, but it went beyond that. Poppy arrived as the person Brenda thought she was seemed to be disappearing. She was putting on weight, something that had never happened before, her looks were starting to fade and the front door downstairs needed oiling if she ever wanted to open it. Any dreams she might have had of taking another lover in her twilight years were now out the window. Brenda had to face up to it. She was aging.

It was around this time Brenda's mental health began to deteriorate. It wasn't just the hot flushes, the night sweats or the difficulty sleeping, the worst of it was the impact on her mind. This was at a time when menopause care was, to put it mildly, appalling. The sex drive that had powered Brenda through life was fading, the anxiety that bubbled under the surface was brimming over. The person who was always the brightest light in any room was staring at the possibility she could be the only woman in a stadium and would now be unseen. Menopause has a serious impact on mental health and for someone already struggling, it was about to get worse. If menopause is a transition, Brenda wasn't ready for it. The mood swings she had managed to keep in check for the best part of twenty years returned with a vengeance but this time they came hand in hand with a revitalised paranoia, the likes of which were beyond all reason. She began keeping a book of imagined misdemeanours. 'That's going in the book!' she would say every time she decided my father had transgressed.

'I was once put in the book because I had gone shopping and not come back within forty minutes. She thought I was out having an affair. I wasn't. I was buying your mother conditioner.'

Nobody leading a remotely sensible life could read this and think this was anything other than bullying but my parents, married for forty-seven years, still managed to hold hands wherever they went and would stand kissing each other outside IKEA. On the days Brenda was stable, they would spend all of them laughing, but the days where Brenda was stable were becoming few and far between.

She had developed an intense hatred for a neighbour's daughter who was now using her parents' garage as a dog grooming parlour, something Brenda believed was not allowed – planning permission was contingent on the daughter living at the property – and so Brenda began keeping a book marked 'Diary of events'. In it are entries such as:

Repeat of Sunday incident. Car turns up. Mother comes out. No sign of daughter or car. Client goes back to car and waits. Is this a kennels incident?

And,

Mrs B energises customers to treat us with contempt. Gardening at front – friends arrived and grinned at us as if we were mad. Had to spend entire day checking how many dogs and clients.

It is filled with times when cars arrive, dogs dropped off or collected. She makes meticulous notes on when the daughter is staying there overnight and when she isn't. Every encounter is recorded, every slight. Every time a car was heard on the driveway, Brenda would run out to check on it. It became an obsession.

My mother had suffered postnatal depression at a time when it simply wasn't discussed. So too, she would now face the toll of menopause at a time where neither the physical effects of menopause nor the mental health complications that went with it were treated as anything other than a joke: hot flushes are funny, middle-aged women forget things, ha, ha, ha. What was really happening, to millions of women experiencing change, was a tsunami of anxiety and loss in confidence that they weren't equipped to deal with.

Women's mental health was, historically, treated in rough-shod fashion: if you showed the slightest sign of depression, anxiety or were remotely troublesome, off you'd be shoved to a lunatic asylum. Husbands wanting to be rid of their wives would think nothing of declaring them mad and there wouldn't be a damn thing the wives could do about it. Calling a woman mad was a means of ensuring compliance, being institution-alised often no more than a punishment for failing to align with feminine norms.

There might have been a time in Brenda's life, when she embraced the notion, as her favourite Romantic poets had, that melancholy was an indication of intellectual capacity: 'How to make madness beautiful', as Byron puts it in *Childe Harold*. Depression was, in the late eighteenth century, if you con-sidered yourself interesting or artistic, something to aspire to but the menopause, and with it the worsening of an already unstable mental condition, for Brenda, was not this. It was not an indulgence or a fanciful effort to be fashionable: it was heavy and frightening and real.

My mother's paranoia took me by surprise. There had been flashes of it all through her life – moaning about the Masons and the neighbours being up to something – but it was throw-away quibbles I hadn't taken seriously. I'd tell her she was being a 'bit silly', it was simply more eccentric Brenda, show off Brenda, drama queen Brenda and so now, when my mother needed proper help, she wasn't taken seriously because she never had been. The effects of menopausal paranoia screamed themselves into our daily lives: she was being plotted against, doctors were being paid to kill her, her phone was being tapped, the government had a file on her, the CIA were out to get her, her garden had been quietly bought by her neighbours who now had 'shares in her land', Tony was having affairs with every woman in Hitchin. Dallington, the house she loved, now became a millstone round her neck, the epicentre of all her worst impulses. People were trying to steal it from her, she would tell me, creeping, unseen forces, and was I in on it? She was in a state of constant stress, agitated and fearful and neither she, nor anyone else, did anything to ease her symptoms, nor find her a suitable therapy.

There's very little I can offer as explanation for this. It was exhausting. If we'd known what was wrong with her, it would have been a relief, if we'd known other families were also going through this, it would have been an enormous help but on both scores, we were in the dark. We thought this was a unique struggle, one we couldn't even whisper about: we weren't allowed to suggest she might have something wrong with her, we wouldn't have dared. If I had tried to take her to the doctor, she would never have forgiven me. The relationship we had, fractured as it was at this point, would have crumbled to nothing.

Having spoken to medical professionals since her death, I think there are clear front runners for what may have been wrong with her: paranoid schizophrenia, paranoid personality disorder, disruptive mood dysregulation, antisocial personality disorder, borderline personality disorder, ADHD . . . the possibilities stretch off into the distance and herein lies the problem. Brenda is no longer with us, or able to tell us precisely what was going on. Only she is capable of talking to a clinical psychologist and getting to the root of her problem but for my father and I, there is a resolution that lies just out of reach and I want to try and come as near to it as possible. Was she moulded by her pregnancy and her menopause? Or was she born with a condition she had no power to avoid?

'Whatever she had,' Phyllis said, 'Bob had it too. There was a viciousness to him, he could turn on a tuppence, be cruel and not be bothered in the slightest. He never said sorry, either. Just like Brenda.'

I feel for Phyllis, who I think often got the worst of her sister, with none of the good bits. Brenda was unguarded around her, not being her best self, failing to turn on the charm as she did for others.

'She stressed me out,' she told me, 'and there came a point where I didn't want to see her any more. I didn't want her in my life.'

Menopause and all that went with it – the weight gain, the fading looks, the loss of the sexuality that had powered through her – had stripped Brenda of everything she thought she was. No more was she the charismatic woman who lit up any room. 'I have become invisible,' she would tell me. 'I am abject.' What was left was a snarling, fearful, anxiety-ridden shadow of her former self.

So what was happening?

Did she find it hard to confide in people, friends or family? Yes.
Did she find it difficult to trust people? Yes.
Did she believe people were taking advantage of her? Yes.
Did she find it difficult to relax? Yes.
Did she perceive threats in everyday life, casual remarks or looks? Yes.
Did she constantly question people's motives? Be suspicious of friends, family, strangers? Yes.
Did she think people were trying to trick her? Yes.
Did she treat innocent remarks as personal attacks? Yes.
Did she respond with anger if she felt insulted? Yes.
Did she hold grudges? Hell, yes.
Did she think her partner was unfaithful? Yes.

It shocks me, even now, to look at that list. It's the checklist for Paranoid Personality Disorder. Where had this come from?

Was it the menopause alone or had the change just made an existing condition worse? Personality disorders can come from biological factors, they can be genetic, or they can be a result of the environment in which you grew up. Given her childhood, it's not hard to see where the seeds might have been sown. I don't have to imagine what it must have been like to be inside her head, because, during this time in her life, I saw the fallout of it, week in, week out. I would get phone calls, day and night, from my father, thrown out again because he had a mark on his head he couldn't explain, or because he'd failed to bring back a receipt from the supermarket. If she saw a neighbour in the lane, she'd ring me to tell me she was being spied on. There's a letter to BT in which she writes:

> *We would also ask whether any of our neighbours are using cordless telephones that could be used to listen to, intercept our calls or be used to make calls on our number. If this was the case, we would feel impelled to involve the Police, via the Fraud Squad, in bringing action against BT and other persons involved . . . if BT are . . . protecting any of our neighbours regarding our phone calls being hacked, BT would be a partner in a conspiracy to commit criminal offences*

It was relentless.

When we don't fully understand something, or find other people's behaviour difficult, it's easy to want to look the other way or wave something off until you don't have to deal with it any more. I think this was part of the problem: we were so worn down with her we didn't have the energy required to sort her out. Anything for a quiet day! But the quiet days were becoming few and far between and something was about to come along that was going to test us to the limits.

★ ★ ★

Cote d'Azur

Dear Emmy

Here we go again – on the road. But with trepidation now that Tony is 70 and has a smidgen of dementia.[1] Will he be okay on the French roads? We'll find out.

Lovely trip on Eurostar to Paris, very hot, stayed around park in Place de Vosges.[2] Later had smoked salmon salad – cost £12! We will be eating out of dustbins. Luckily, I brought plastic plates and picnic cutlery so we can at least eat something. The old £ now seems like a dead currency against the Euro. If we don't join, the Brits face years of holiday time on sewage strewn beaches. What a mess.[3]

If I ever won serious money, I'd buy my own TGV train.[4] I really love long journeys travelling 1st class on TGV. We had excellent window seats and our 1st class seats were like armchairs. Bliss watching miles of pure, unsullied countryside go by.

Very relaxed after our journey and we arrived at Aix en Provence Europcar rental not expecting any problems this time as we had paid for the car in England. But something about the French girl's hairstyle, one side much longer than the other and carefully fixed across her chin in a bizarre sort of beard

1 My father does not have dementia.

2 Place des Vosges is the oldest square in Paris. It's in the Marais.

3 Thank God she didn't have to endure Brexit. She'd have set fire to parliament and chased Nigel Farage wherever he went.

4 Not entirely clear what a TGV train would cost Brenda to buy, but the Queen's train cost £800,000 so we can assume that's the ballpark.

put me on edge.[5] *Tony left me to guard the luggage while he began the arrangements.*

I wasn't paying much attention as a very handsome young French man was standing at the other booth and I was having a carefully concealed admiring stare. When you are old you can never seem too interested! Can you imagine if you gave them a big come on grin. They'd probably have an involuntary fit of nausea. Ah well.

As I was dreaming away, I could see that Tony was very agitated. I left the luggage and approached the desk. The French girl was looking very sullen. It seemed that she had demanded an extra €25 a day for collision damage waiver. Tony was trying to tell her that Europcar in England had quoted €6 a day if we decided not to go for it. I thought we had paid for everything already, but this was an optional extra.

I had already paid £269 on my credit card so I was already annoyed with Tony for not telling me that more money was required. Of course, it just got worse. He hadn't insured us for theft and with the Europcar sticker prominent on the back window of the hire car, we would be obvious targets for the Mafia on the Cote d'Azur.[6] *The total extra cost would be another £100. I was livid.*

After 20 minutes of harsh words and much aggro French girl whose typical French facial winces and mew mouth eventually deteriorated into Merde[7] *at the end of every sentence, Tony just wanted to pay up and go.*

Out came my credit card. French girl wouldn't accept it without a driving license. I don't have one. More aggressive banter. French girl won't let us have the hire car because Tony

5 This made me laugh out loud.

6 OBVIOUS targets.

7 French for 'shit' AND WHO CAN BLAME HER?

*didn't have his own credit card. Now – whose fault was that?
I'll say no more.*

*Brenda now slips into lethal mode.[8] French girl says a lot
of very rude French things to French co-worker about old
English lady. English lady threatens to call a French gendarme,
plenty around if we don't have keys to the car in next five
minutes. Other customers watch drama being played out with
increasing horror. Brenda stands her ground. Much hard
staring and patrician ex PAT performance. Leave with keys.
Tony gets it in the neck. Great start!*

*Aix was next. We had decided to spend one night in Aix for
sentimental reasons. We were last there 13 years ago when it
was a charming provincial university town with lots of lovely
students drinking coffee in the famous Deux Garcons café[9]
and reading impressive academic tomes.*

*But now it has the TGV and a new peripherique[10] and a
vast hinterland half the size of London. Our hotel was outside the
city centre. We spent one and a half hours circling the new city in
35 degrees. Five people gave us the wrong instructions, we couldn't
find the hotel because we couldn't find the road. We were not
prepared for this. The last time we drove in Aix, it was a gentle
drift down the Cours Mirabeau to the car park. Now the Cours
Mirabeau was pedestrianised and every other street was one way.
By now we were blaming each other – whose fault was it coming
here – we were too old for this – we would never do it again.*

*In that heat I had a breakdown and started calling out the
window to no one in particular 'Fetch the police! Fetch the police!'*

*My calls were answered by a concerned Frenchman who
listened very patiently, asked for pen and paper, and drew us a*

8 Have you ever seen sharks in a feeding frenzy? That, but with added
sarcasm.

9 Café frequented by the likes of Cezanne, the painter, and Zola, the writer.

10 A ring road

*route out of the hell we found ourselves in. Saved. We found the
hotel.*

*The Madame was a shock. She was the spitting image of my
mother. She didn't speak English well so I used my en peu
French to ask her whether she was Irish/Jewish. Non.
Provencal. Mistral.*

'Oh, like the wind,' I replied.

Much wincing and mew mouth.

'Non, poet Mistral'

*Very bad mood after that. Lovely room. Lovely park. Aix en
Provence is not like Oxford Street. Don't let anyone you know
go there.*

*Next day we headed across country on very quiet roads to
the house. Let's hope the Holiday Gods stay in Aix!*

*The trees in this part of France are scrub oaks and in the
bright light they look lime green. We travelled for miles without
seeing another driver. Both in good mood now, very relaxed,
enjoying the sun, the perfume from the surrounding plants and
breathing really clean air. Maybe we should live here after all.*

*Stopped at small village for lunch. Some sort of Brocante
Fair[11] was on. Found a restaurant offering 2 courses for €16.
Terrible, but the cheapest we'd seen and we were starving.
Chicken and chips and tartes de pomme. Waitress comes to take
order. She couldn't understand Tony's French request for eau.*

*I butted in. 'Eau. Non gaz.' She still didn't understand. 'Une
bouteille de EAU. NON GAZ'*

Shook her head and walked off.

*Slowly we started to realise that this waitress was not up to
the job. She brought out three plates of lamb chops, but the
table of French customers had asked for chicken. Back went the
lamb chops.*

11 Vintage, crafty sort of affair.

When she next appeared people from four tables were all calling her. One table had waited 20 minutes for spoons while the tartes de pommes sat on the table. One woman fetched the puddings herself. Then another wrong order. Someone shouted at the waitress who became increasingly sullen. One French woman walked into the kitchen to complain. Laughter all around now. Our meal arrived but Tony didn't have his salad and there was no eau.

We tried to tell her – pas salade and sans eau. She just looked blank and puffed her cheeks out in a swollen wince. People around us took up the call. 'Eau! Eau!' We were all laughing now. The waitress started to cry. Noone cared. Stupid girl deserved to cry. Then I had to go into the kitchen to fetch our puddings and spoons. Whole area in uproar. One man refused to pay. Manager is sent for. Everyone shouting from tables. Hilarious. True French drama. France at its best – but – we never did get any water. Eau! Eau![12]

By 5pm we had arrived at our destination. When you book these houses you never really know what to expect but we knew that this house was set in its own park so we were really dreaming of something grand.

As we entered though the gated driveway, the park on either side we were not disappointed. The red tower could be seen through the trees. We knew we were going to enjoy being there.

The owner Marie, welcomed us in and took us to our room. The original house was 16th century and Marie's husband, an architect, had modernised the interior of the house apart from classic features like the staircase etc. The whole house had new cement floors which had been polished and they were marvellous. The surfaces reflected light and colour but the smooth surface was so pleasant to walk on.

---

12 This letter is giving me a stomach ulcer.

Our bedroom was striking in its design – a black 4 poster draped in grey silk, a wall size painting of green rocks, a very large Roman portrait of a young man framed in gold, black tables, silver lights, wonderful floral displays and silk quilts. Amazing and all for £65 a night including a sumptuous breakfast. And we had our own attached terrace. We couldn't believe our luck.

Marie was a lovely woman who gave us a very warm welcome and couldn't do enough for us. Sadly, her alsation dog, Daisy was dying. She died the next day but at least we were there to comfort Marie. She was relieved that we loved dogs. We told her all about Poppy and how much we loved her.

We had a wonderful three days there. At night we watched the stars, satellites, bats and giant moths in balmy evening heat.

So, we had a great time – lovely house – too hot, too dangerous, too expensive and lastly – too old. Our road trips are over. We'll never make it to Route 66 but we've had a good innings. Moscow next time.

Big hugs and cuddles.
Mum and Dad. Xxx

DAD Home made hamburger, chips and small salad, A snip at £19 !!![13]

* * *

---

13 I love, after all that, the only thing my father has to tell me is the price of his lunch.

Sweetheart

I have weeded front garden, sorted out trellis and moved the rose because it was smothered by an ant nest.[1]

Daddy cut hedge, had chat with lady in dressing gown next door and then I opened a Rose and felt like St Francis in the garden as a heavenly hose of birds flocked around oblivious of my presence.

Nut hatch
Thrush
Blackbirds feeding babies (gorgeous)
Collar dove
Rare pair I couldn't identify with yellow slashes on wings[2]
Crow (huge)
Magpie (very aggressive)
Wood pigeon

What a blissful garden this is.

Window boxes – I think they are a disaster! Sorry. Did my best.[3]

Have been reading Don't Panic.[4] *Most sensible section is*

1 TRANSLATION: I pointed at them and told Tony to do it.

2 I'm going to hazard a guess she means goldfinches.

3 She refers here to window boxes I had at my flat in London. They sat in front of two large sash windows looking out into the street. At their best, they flowed with trailing petunias, but their success was entirely down to whether I could remember to water them. Do I need to say more?

4 *Don't Panic* by Reid Wilson is a book about controlling anxiety attacks. She was easily given to panic, of course, and catastrophising can be a result of anxiety.

Existentialism – ie life is not easy – accept it. Don't wish to undermine seriousness of your problem but this methodology might be the best. Don't go to a Freudian – everything is sex! Forget that! If you want me to come with you anywhere, I will be only too glad. Trauma caused yours – VOMIT = death – it is as simple as that. Let me know if you are going to see someone.[5]

I can't speak on phone as I always worry[6] so I would just like to say that I am a bit worried about you as you seem so stressed out.[7] If this is just work, well, it's to be expected and you must make opportunities to relax. Your jobs are coming in now so financial worries won't be so great. Anyhow, remember that I can sort your mortgage out whenever you want – and you are an heiress to millions.[8] Never worry about money.

I just hope you aren't drinking that wine too quickly. Remember that I got kidney stones so a little now and then.

Daddy and I are getting quite old now and I expect we are a bit frustrating as we can't remember things well. It isn't nice being old, actually, it's quite horrid, so there.[9]

---

5 I have suffered from emetophobia since I was fourteen. Occasionally we would discuss doing something about it. It would take Brenda getting cancer for me to finally see someone. I saw two hypnotherapists. One was better than the other. I'm not entirely cured but I'm much better than I was.

6 She thought her phone was tapped. This is a rare admission in writing.

7 Reading this, I can't help but feel guilty. I went through a phase with Brenda where I'd just had enough of her. I was short tempered, dismissive, didn't want to spend any amount of time speaking to her. I can easily see how this would have been interpreted as stress. Yes, it was, but the cause of the stress was her.

8 I wish this was true. It isn't.

9 There's something about this sentence that makes my heart hurt. I suspect we'd had a falling out or I'd been short with her, and given she was never someone who was able to sit down and have a conversation about how she was really feeling, this is the closest she can come to asking me to be nice to her.

Two wood pigeons have just eaten 50% of the bread. Bullies! The blackbird is back trying to get a break to feed its babies. I might frighten the pigeon off but I can't as they are so sweet.

Bit drunk now. It's all I've got left.[10] *Thought about going to Krakow (is that how you spell it, probably not) but can't get any trains. No trains in Poland.*

Bought something you might find useful in Holland. Wish I could see those adverts.[11] *Aaargh! Small dangerous looking spider on armchair. Where has it gone – black and cream stripes. I bet it's exotic. Help!*

★ ★ ★

10 I love how she has just told me to go steady on the wine and then announces she's drunk. The 'It's all I've got left' is rather sad. That wasn't true, of course and this letter is a snapshot of Brenda feeling a little sorry for herself and not knowing how to reach out. She couldn't, for all her brilliant communication skills and ability to chat freely, ever tell us how she was really feeling. Brenda's greatest sadness was never being able to admit to weakness. If she had, she might be still alive.

11 I starred in a series of adverts that were only shown in Holland. They were about recycling and being responsible citizens. I played a rather prim and proper housewife, but the shoot was mostly memorable for the director taking his girlfriend into my dressing room one lunchtime and having sex with her in it while I stood outside with my arms folded waiting to get back in.

Seventeen

I was at BBC TV centre and had just finished recording a voice-over. As I was walking through reception and looking out into the iconic doughnut, the rotunda around which all manner of historic cultural moments had occurred, I had a call.

I looked at my phone. HOME, it said. Home, of course, did not mean my flat in Hendon. Poppy was a clever dog but not quite bright enough to teach herself how to use the landline. It was my parents' phone. It was an unusual time for them to be calling and my first instinct was that they'd had a row, again. I heaved a sigh and thought about not taking it but changed my mind and did. It was Dad.

'Where are you?' His tone was serious.

I told him.

'Can you sit down somewhere?'

I wasn't sure I had time for this. If he was going to tell me he was in a car park with a bag on the passenger seat for the tenth time this month, I wasn't sure I was interested. I was sick to the back teeth of being dragged into their arguments. It was making me feel ill and I needed it to stop.

'Just tell me.' I was irritated.

'Your mum's got cancer.'

Just like that, the world stopped.

I did sit down then, suddenly, on the long, curved banquette where I was used to waiting for auditions, or for production assistants to whisk me off to dressing rooms or studios. It was the seat where I had seen TV stars wandering to and from the lifts, where I'd lain one Comic Relief night, laughing like a drain with a hero of mine, pinching myself that this was my life now.

I had changed my life again and again and now, sitting listening to my father plod through the gravest nuts and bolts, I knew it was about to change again.

I didn't have to think twice. I leapt into a cab, got back to my flat, picked up Poppy and drove to Hitchin.

It was, in many ways, a perfect storm: a serious, life threatening illness was hitting at the peak of my mother's psychosis. The next three months would be hell. She had a lump in her left breast and it was cancerous. Now she had to make choices – have further investigations, consider surgery and, if it had gone into her lymph nodes, think about radiotherapy or chemo. Instead, we had a battle on our hands. Not only did my mother think she had been given cancer by a CIA operative in a bookshop in Cambridge, she also thought all suggestions of treatment were a plot between the doctors, Dad and I to kill her.

I was single at the time, having just broken up with a long-term partner and to say I was desperate was an understatement. Dad would manage to get Brenda to my flat and then it was down to me to try and get her to the Royal Marsden. At every single stage of the process, she refused to do what the doctors were offering, and it would take us two, sometimes three weeks, to persuade her each step was safe and in her best interests.

I wrote, *'We had a much-anticipated hospital appointment to keep this morning which had Brenda in bits. We're all in bits at the moment, if truth be told, but as everyone does in these situations, you just keep going. Today was a bad one. Brenda had a refusal at the water jump at the last moment and couldn't go through with it, despite all our pleas to the contrary. It induced much feelings of hopelessness and frustration.'*

But it wasn't all despair. That's the weird thing about cancer. It's an illness and it's a word and when you've got someone in the family with it you have bad days where everyone lies about staring at walls with plugs of snot creeping off their chins, but you also have moments where you almost forget it's happening at all. I had finally got Brenda to agree to the more exploratory biopsy she had fled weeks previously and I wanted to be there to see her before the procedure. It had involved a mad dash across London during rush hour, but I got there in time and arrived at the Diagnostic Unit to find her coming out of the toilet.

'There was much huggage,' I wrote. 'When you've got a nervous patient,' I continued, 'it's imperative to keep their minds distracted so I got out a piece of paper I'd taken from the National Portrait Gallery. The idea was that visitors could draw their own portraits. I handed it to Brenda with a pencil and said, "There you go, draw me a picture."'

What resulted was a bizarre domestic scene. There's a large window in the background, fancy curtains with a smart occasional table adorned with a voluminous pot plant. In front of it is a chair, French-looking and striped, with a naked woman with Princess Leia hair with one foot up on it. A dog is shitting to her left and on the floor lies a naked man tugging on his own cock. This was all done in the waiting room of the Royal Marsden. We were 'bent over double laughing' I wrote.

Despite the odd moments of light and the obligatory second breakfasts in nearby Carluccio's, this was the single most draining time of my life. The cancer *had* gone into her lymph nodes and time was of the essence. Finally, three months from initial diagnosis, we got her to agree to surgery.

She was afraid. That was at the heart of it. Of course she was. She'd watched her mother die in awful circumstances and was still haunted by the arm swollen by lymphedema her mother carried. As she sat in her hospital bed, she scribbled 'I do not want lymphedema' on her release form, which prompted a three-doctor crisis meeting at her bedside as they tried to explain they couldn't guarantee she wouldn't get it and asked whether she still wanted to continue. I stood, watching on, sick to my stomach, dreading her response, but thankfully, she relented. Dad and I had wanted her to have a mastectomy. I'd tried to persuade her to have a double mastectomy but there was no budging on that. She wanted the least amount to be removed and the smallest intervention. She agreed to one course of radiotherapy, turned down chemo (she didn't want to lose her hair) and decided to throw away the hormone drugs that would help stop the cancer returning.

In despair, I rang Mouse, now a qualified doctor specialising in cancer. He was my last defence. Brenda adored him. If anyone was going to talk her round it would be him.

'She was very manipulative,' he told me. 'I'd be very honest with her as to what her chances were and how she could increase them and crucially, what was likely to happen if she did nothing. She would beg me not to frighten her. "Don't scare me, Mouse," she would plead. It simply wasn't possible to persuade her to do something. She didn't want to know but she was so charming, she knew exactly how to turn it on. She'd accept a little bit of treatment to keep the doctors onside. As for her agreeing to see a psychiatrist, not a chance. Not for a second would she have complied with a psychiatrist.'

Herein lay our problem. Brenda desperately needed help for her mental health – her paranoia was threatening to be the death of her but there was no help to be had. So, we waved her off into surgery and Dad fell into me crying and we drove straight to the Greek restaurant where Tony used to wait for mum when she was at college.

'[We] spent four days in a state of hyper-suspension, dragging ourselves between our own beds and the bedside of Brenda. It was grey faces and weeping in corridors all round.' I wrote, but then added, *'Even when everything seems just about as bad as it can be, we still find things to laugh about. On Friday night, when Brenda was cracked to the tits on morphine, we'd been taking it in turns to hold her hand. She turned to Dad and said, "Can you scratch my eyelid please. I hope I haven't been bitten by an insect."*

"Well, they do have tsetse flies at the Marsden," Tony replied.

At which point Brenda, slumped into her pillow, grimaced and in all seriousness said, "That's all I need. Malaria."'

It was such a strange, difficult time. Life ground to a halt. I went to see a hypnotherapist to help me with my emetophobia so I could sit with her on the cancer ward. Because she was so unstable, the hospital allowed Dad and I to be with her all day and we would arrive just after breakfast and sit with her till supper time. Friends of mine came to see her. When Perks arrived, she sat up properly for the first time and smiled.

She would be in hospital, drain in her armpit, for eight days. On the day we took her home, we sang songs in the car all the way. 'I don't think I have ever been more happy', I wrote, 'to see that little face sitting back on the sofa, in front of the fire, ordering everyone about. She's doing just great.'

The feeling would be short lived and, having discovered the spread of cancer was worse than they had first feared, we had a call telling us Brenda would need another operation. She was shattered by the news – we all were – but she still refused to have a mastectomy. She would only allow another slightly bigger scrape away and the removal of more lymph nodes. That would be it.

She returned to hospital the day after Mothering Sunday on which we had danced together in the sun to 'Automatic' by the Pointer Sisters, gone for a walk and had a minor drama regarding a half-dead pigeon. The following day we sat on a ward at the Marsden, my mother in a bed next to a much younger woman. She'd had a double elective mastectomy and Brenda was staring at her new breasts, reconstructed at the same time.

'Are they made of silicon,' she had asked.

'No. They're made from my belly. I got new breasts *and* a flat stomach.'

I had thought in that moment, with Brenda cooing as to what a brilliant idea that was, to suggest she might have a double mastectomy too but there was really no point. She wanted the minimum of treatment and within days, post-operation, she was 'back to bossing everyone and everything sideways and back again'.

She had a longer stay this time round. All the lymph nodes in one armpit had been removed and it was a steady wait for the fluid draining out from it to turn clear. We played Pass the Pigs and Scrabble. I helped her wash her hair. She was, as she always was, charming to every nurse and stranger. She chatted easily to the women around her. She was, in every sense, someone I had forgotten.

I'm not sure I can overstate how terrible the ten years before her diagnosis had been. When she lost all interest in sex, she lost all sense of herself. She had been a powerful, sexually motivated woman for all of her adult life. Now she didn't know who she was or what her purpose was. She'd been a teacher, a lover, a bright and intoxicating star, but postmenopause she was the lump that sat on the sofa staring out the window feeling furious.

Women now, thankfully, are starting to feel more clued up when it comes to menopause, there are calls for GPs to be more on top of it, and more women are sharing their experiences. It doesn't pass me by that Brenda, with her lack of a female support group, was unable to share any of what she was going through with anyone. At this point in her life what Brenda needed most was female friends but she really didn't have any. When you don't like yourself, it's near impossible to expect anyone else to and that had been my biggest problem. We accepted all the bullshit because she was fun, but Brenda had stopped being fun and I had, unfairly, stopped liking her. Yet now, something was shifting. We were laughing again, even during the bleakest of moments. I was spending more time with her. I was starting to remember.

On the one day I wasn't able to be with her, I got a call telling me she'd been told she could go home. She'd been given the all-clear and would require no further surgery. I cried with relief, of course, but cancer is a long, tedious climb. We were only over the first hump. The harder bit was yet to come. I wrote: 'when others need you a bit more than you need anything, even food, you have to put thoughts of yourself to one side and cover them with a heavy, indistinguishable sack' and 'because my family is a symbiotic lump, if one of us is down, we're all down'.

This was entirely true. Our moods were dictated by whatever mood Brenda was feeling, whatever state she might be in. For as long as I could remember, Tony and I were satellites circling Planet Brenda. Everything she felt, we felt too, but in the few weeks of recovery, post-surgery, a lightness began to creep back in through the cracks.

I didn't have time to think about that yet, though. Brenda was starting the course of radiotherapy we'd finally managed to get her to agree to. She'd had a tiny tattoo so they could line up the machine, something that allowed her to tell anyone and everyone she'd 'got a tattoo' and had taken to suggesting we might all 'live together again'. We practically were all living together again, of course, mostly at my flat where they would arrive, bursting through the door with bags in hand shouting they'd 'brought milk'.

There were no rows during this stretch. Brenda wanted me to 'make her laugh every day', so that's what I did. I'd leave chocolate buttons out as a trap so I could catch her eating them. I'd drive her to the Marsden in my Eunos Roadster with the top down. We watched World Cup matches together (previously unimaginable) and commentated on *Deal or No Deal* daily. I wrote: 'Having my parents living with me has been an illuminating experience. Who knew they used so much toilet paper?', but the mood was light and filled with hope. Brenda was coming to the end of her treatment and we were all getting on again.

I went off to Edinburgh to be in a stage production of *Midnight Cowboy*. It would be the only time in my life when my genitals would be reviewed in a national paper and when I came back, Brenda was a new woman. 'I'm thinking about becoming a plasterer,' she told me. 'I think it's high time I learned a trade.' Brenda, to my great joy, was back.

I took her to set during filming the second series of *Suburban Shootout* (she brought apples from the garden for Amelia Bullmore and gave Anna Chancellor a ham sandwich made by Tony). I took her to Richard and Judy (the real ones), where, after the show, she shook Judy's hand and said, 'Thank you, Julie.' I took her to *Loose Women* which she mistakenly thought was called 'Laid Back Sisters' and she did a photoshoot for my first book, *How To Bring Up Your Parents*. 'Did I do OK?' she asked me in the car, as we drove home. Yes. She did brilliantly. The end of 2006 into 2007, then, was a giddy time. Brenda was happy and making us laugh again. I wrote about a morning back in Hitchin where my mother shouts at me in my bed from her bed and tells me to 'ring the landline and tell Tony I want another coffee', there are recollections of conversations in which she is chiding Tony for constantly interrupting her. 'How can I have a conversation?' she wails, 'when all he does is interrupt?' Tony sticks up for himself, pointing out there's no way of knowing when any given sentence coming out of my mother's mouth is going to end and that he has to jump in during the moments she might be stopping to take a breath. Brenda concludes the only solution to this problem is for her to 'buy a whistle. I'll speak and when I'm finished, I'll blow it and that's your cue to pipe up.'

I had also begun the process of changing the focus of my career again. I'd had a book published and needed to think of an idea for the next. I had been going home every Sunday and after one jolly lunch, I had pulled a photo album out to remind myself of our first holiday abroad. We started to discuss the disasters that followed us wherever we went. We were helpless with laughter. Would anyone else, I wondered, be remotely interested in another family's shitty attempts to go on holiday? I pitched it to the publisher and just like that, *The Tent, the Bucket and Me* came into being.

This was the book that will always mean the most to me. Each week, I would return home and interview them – Tony had an extraordinary memory for times, dates, road routes and details, while Brenda had an uncanny recall for every single argument she'd ever had, word for word. I would sit and watch them re-enacting minor bickering and heartfelt fury with French girls who refused to sell them rotisserie chickens. It was wonderful. It stirred the pot, lit the kindling, got us all going again. When it became a success, Brenda was agog.

'It's mad isn't it?' she would say, '*Sunday Times* bestseller all because we were fucking useless.'

It was our book, not mine, and her astonishment at becoming a legend in her own lifetime was a joy to behold. Wherever I took her with me, people were beside themselves to meet her. 'I love your parents,' strangers would tell me. Yes, and I had remembered I did too. Get to the back of the queue.

It was the perfect book at the perfect time for my family. We had crawled out of a traumatic year, crushed and listless. I'd picked myself up and decided to concentrate on the one thing I had given everything up for – writing. Being in front of a camera was all very well but writing was the thing I was best at, it was the thing that gave me purpose, it was who I was. It had taken me ten years from leaving my job as a lawyer to work that out, but I'd got there in the end. Everything worthwhile takes time. Never give up.

Things were on the up, then. We were getting on better than we ever had before but now, it was my turn to get ill.

Inevitably, the stress of the previous year had taken its toll. I was exhausted, weighed down with the burden of trying to keep my mother on an even keel and Perks, now living in Cornwall, told me to come and stay. I needed the break. It was there, one evening, as I was eating a delicious Portuguese stew she had cooked, that I thought I had a mouth ulcer. I love spicy food, spicier the better, but that night, every mouthful was like eating fire. I went to the bathroom to have a look and was shocked to see a spider's web of white lines on the inside of my cheeks, the underside of my tongue was similarly marked. Something was badly wrong with me.

On my return home, I went to the GP who told me I had oral thrush and prescribed me some thick, disgusting ointment I was to apply twice a day for a week, but it wasn't and the medicine did nothing. I was told to go and see my dentist who, on looking into my mouth, became very serious indeed. He gave me the name of a private dentist off Harley Street who I was to 'go and see immediately'. I asked him why. He wouldn't tell me but by now, the secret was out. They all thought I had cancer. I had absolutely no intention of telling Brenda.

After having a biopsy, I found myself on the South Bank, walking towards the offices of the TV production company, Talkback. I was supposed to be auditioning for *Peep Show*. Overwhelmed with everything and feeling desperately alone, I keeled sideways into some railings, put my forehead onto the back of my hands and sobbed. I then pulled myself together and went to the audition. I didn't get the part.

The news, however, was good. I did not have cancer. What I did have was oral lichen planus. I'd been in agony from the moment I'd first become aware of it: the sensation being like a badly burned tongue smothered in ulcers. Anything acidic, spicy, salty, alcoholic was intolerable. I could eat scrambled egg and mash and that was pretty much it. But I didn't have cancer so I was ecstatic. Even so it came as something of a shock to discover there was no cure for it.

'I can give you a steroid inhaler and some corticosteroid lozenges to help with the pain. That's it,' my doctor told me.

'But how long will I be in pain for?' I asked.

He looked at me, leaned forward in his chair, knitted his fingers together and cleared his throat. 'If you're lucky, eighteen months, if you're not – thirteen years.'

Excuse me? No cure? Thirteen years? What? I went home that day, in the back of a cab, paper sack full of drugs that might help a bit but not much, and stared out the window.

'But what causes it?' Brenda asked.

'Stress or trauma, he said.'

There was a long pause.

'This isn't my fault is it?' she asked.

But I said nothing. When I got to my flat, I went straight to bed and lay there looking at the ceiling. If it hadn't had been for Poppy, I don't think I would have got up again.

Thank God for dogs.

Dear Emmy

Hope you've recovered now. Keep soaking your feet until they've hardened up.

House is charming and nearby medieval villages are wonderful. Air is so clean and pure and I keep taking gulps of it.

Only had two fights with Frenchmen so far. One wouldn't move his car so we could park and the other wouldn't let me use his posh bar toilet. Big row.

Apart from that we are resting and relaxing. Go to Finn and Lone in Cabris on Saturday but we are leaving here on Friday, staying overnight in a hotel to split the journey for Tony's sake. He's an old man now.

All our love
Mum and Dad xxx[1]

* * *

---

1 You have to hand it to her – in four short paragraphs she's given me marathon advice, managed to crowbar in arguing and has put down my father. These were her three favourite hobbies: unsolicited advice on topics about which she knew nothing, having a right old bust-up with strangers and telling anyone who would listen that my father was in a decrepit state.

My dear love (CONFIDENTIAL)[1]

Don't worry about money. In the short term, you're a bit stuck but in the long term you're a multi-millionaire![2] *Should anything happen, follow instructions:*[3]

> *1. Read everything carefully in 3 boxes on my desk. They include business card of developer, current house prices for terraced housing built by developer, land prices, newspaper clippings about developments in Hitchin etc. John Prescott has just instructed local councils to build 50 houses per hectare in urban areas. That allows for 25 on our site. House at bottom of garden keen to come in with us. Negotiate for at least £7million, sell everything.*[4]

> *2. Insurances are in the big blue box.*

1 Brenda thinks I might plaster this letter up on a streetlight or tree trunk but the CONFIDENTIAL here goes to the heart of her paranoia. She really did think nefarious powers were at work and that any slip within the Ring of Trust would lead to certain ruination.

2 Could not be further from the truth.

3 Whenever the pezzers went away, I would get a call with very strict instructions as to what to do if they died unexpectedly. Every time I would roll my eyes with utter disdain, but I have found myself now doing it to Georgie whenever I have to go to London. 'IF I DIE,' I wail, etc., etc., to fade. The acorn, it turns out, does not fall far from the tree.

4 Re-reading this, I heaved a heavy sigh. When my mother was at her worst, she never stopped going on about the value of 'the land'. She was like Gollum but she never wanted to put the house on the market or test out her wildly inaccurate theories about how much it was all worth. She was living in Cloud Cuckoo Land. My dad did sell, eventually, and it went for precisely what you'd expect a three-bedroom cottage with a tiny kitchen, rubbish bathroom, a washing machine in an outdoor shed and no central heating to go for.

3. *Photographs of contents of house also in box to give you some idea of worth. Nearly everything's valuable.* [5]

I'll try to bring you back a Russian watch! If it works!

Love you so, so much.
Mum xxxxxxxxxx

★ ★ ★

---

5 Nothing was valuable. Nothing.

Eighteen

My mother had started picking her nose.

She wasn't quite at the end of her treatment, but a sore had developed at the back of her nostril. It had scabbed over and every time she picked it, she'd have a nosebleed. We couldn't stop her doing it. Years later, a doctor would tell her, in the only instance I am aware of a medical professional trying to address her mental health, it was a form of self-harm. Again, and again, she would pick it off, again and again we would stand her over a sink, blood pouring out of her.

They were at my flat, staying over as they liked to do when a treatment was early in the morning. I'd fed them and the mood was calm. Brenda had wandered off to the sitting room while I dealt with some emails. Suddenly, all hell broke loose. My father, who has multiple skills but one weak spot – blood – cried out and ran into the hallway. The nosebleed my mother was now experiencing, having picked her nose yet again, was the like of which I have never seen. My flat looked like a murder scene. I helped her to the bathroom where she stood gripping the edges of the sink.

'Help me,' she whispered. 'Please, help me.'

I think about that moment often. She wasn't asking me to help her stop her nosebleed. We'd done that many times before. She was, I think, asking me to help her stop self-harming but I could tell her to stop picking that bloody scab until I was blue in the face – she was never going to, because hurting herself gave her comfort.

A few days after she died, I was clearing out her things and, going through a drawer, I found a tiny plastic bag filled with hard, grey flakes. I stood, staring at it, trying to work out what they were, and then I suddenly realised. They were scabs from her nipple. When her cancer came back, a huge scab had formed. She was obsessed with it and when bits came off, she would stroke them – dead bits of her, as precious as jewels. To discover she had kept them, like treasure, was revolting and disturbing.

Excoriation disorder is a mental illness related to obsessive compulsive disorder, it's a recurrent skin picking that results in lesions. She didn't pick at her skin to create lesions, what she did was not let things heal. She didn't want to be better. I was reminded of a conversation we had with her when she was on the mend after her first bout of cancer. She was sitting looking a little glum. I'd asked her if she was all right. Her response, 'Nobody's interested in me, now I'm better.' What she really meant, I think, was that she had enjoyed being the centre of attention again. She had been reminded of what her life was like premenopause. Nothing else had mattered during those terrible months, except her.

It had got to the point where Brenda had stopped letting us sit with her when she saw the doctor. She no longer wanted us to know what they or she were saying. Perhaps they *were* trying to address her mental health and she didn't want us to know about it? God knows if I'd been in a room where it was brought up by a medical professional I'd have shouted, 'Yes! Yes! Please do something about it!', but I never was. It must have been screamingly obvious, yet Brenda made no allusion to it other than the brief mention of being advised she was self-harming. She had told me in a hushed tone, not with any degree of alarm or embarrassment because the doctor's reve-lation, it was clear to me, had thrilled her. All I could do was tell her he was right. She was hurting herself.

As to why she did it, I don't know. Perhaps it was her way of dealing with having cancer? A release for her now low self-esteem, stress, an outlet for her anxiety? She didn't try to hide it, if anything, she flaunted it. Perhaps she was crying out for her distress to be acknowledged, to be finally taken seriously. It was too late for that, sadly. Besides, she didn't take it seriously herself, how were we expected to?

The upside to all this, now I was living with a debilitating auto-immune disease, was that Brenda, who always bucked her ideas up when I was ill, began to calm down. Her cancer had saved our family and now my oral lichen planus would provide the even keel. We loved her and she loved us, and we'd stick together through thick and thin.

With her happier and calmer, it might have been a perfect time to address her mental health but it was like we'd all come back from a war, battle fatigued and beaten. After years of dealing with uncontrollable outbursts and a deficiency of all reason, I don't think we had the energy or the inclination to pick up another flag and mount the harder barricade. We all just wanted a rest and so, yet again, the matter was not pursued.

It's dangerous, the gratefulness for quiet days, and if I could go back, I wouldn't have been so defeatist. I had one conversation with my father, where I'd asked him if he should speak to their GP on his own. 'Can you imagine if she found out?' he'd replied. It would have been a betrayal and, he knew she'd never let him forget it, so on we rolled in the rickety boat we'd found ourselves in.

Brenda, now the worst of the menopause was behind her, was a woman reborn. She had lost lots of weight – thanks, not to the cancer, but to gallstones – and had stopped drinking alcohol. She was less paranoid, was getting on with Tony and my own relationship with her was back on track. Like many who have stared down the barrel of a serious illness, she was now consumed with an urge to get out and see the world. The travelling spree, which would mark the next few years of her life, began. The letters came pouring in but the choices she had made about her cancer treatment were about to catch up with her.

It's 2012 and I've been asked, at short notice, if I'd like to be on *Celebrity MasterChef*. I'd been doing bits and pieces, the odd sitcom episode, the occasional drama, a couple of podcasts, but the years since Brenda's diagnosis had been consumed with writing books and I'd penned nine of the things. I had just finished one and was about to start on another. Fancying a break, I said yes to the show, but the main reason I agreed to do it was because I needed a distraction: at a routine check-up, a doctor had discovered a small lump in my mother's breast. The cancer was back.

It's a terrible thing, to sit next to someone you love and have to listen to the end of their life being mapped out. There were things the doctors could do to give her more time, but this was it. She was now on a cast-iron trajectory to the end. Given the horror show we'd experienced first time round, I was terrified we were going to have a re-run of all the previous difficulties but, to my complete astonishment, they never materialised. Brenda was a different woman. She was over the worst of the menopause and had had six years of travelling and reconnecting with Tony. I sat, amazed, as she agreed to chemotherapy, the treatment she had previously refused. Surgery was not an option.

For the woman who had floated through life as a rare beauty, I was worried that losing her hair might catapult Brenda back to the bad days of her deepest depression, but as it began to fall out, she was nothing but sanguine. It was startling how calm she was. When I asked her if she'd get herself a wig, her eyes lit up. A wig! She'd forgotten about wigs! So, arm in arm, off we went to Selfridges to find one.

It was always difficult with Brenda to know what was bravado and what was genuine mischief, but here she was, mooching through the long wigs, the shoulder-length wigs, the short wigs and the downright outrageous wigs, with the air of a bride picking out the perfect diamond. Here was someone who was neither embarrassed nor depressed. She was simply interested in being her fabulous self.

'Shall I go blonde?' she trilled, fingering a voluptuous Dolly Parton offering.

She tried it on, pulling it over her already balding scalp, tipped her head sideways and put a finger to her lips. 'I'm worried, of course, that I may be mistaken for a children's entertainer. Or a woman selling knock off shellfish. Or someone on the run from the police.'

'Yes,' I added, 'you don't want to be arrested.'

'Or do I?' she mused, turning her face from side to side. She was sitting in front of a large, illuminated mirror. She looked tired, her skin thinned by the treatment, but her eyes were dancing. 'How have I never been arrested?' She shook her head in disbelief then turned to look at me. 'Do you think I've still got time?'

I smiled but didn't reply. It was a question I was determined not to think about, a conversation we were yet to have. The question of how much time Brenda had was never entertained. It was something I pushed away, becoming angry, even, if we ever skirted near it. She would ring me, asking me to be nice to her, because she wouldn't be here for long and I would be short with her, dismissing it as nonsense. I wish I hadn't, but the thought of Brenda having an end point felt like an impossible affront.

As her condition worsened, she wrote to her Danish friend, Lone:

I'm not well at all, I'm afraid. The drugs I've been taking haven't worked well so now I've got to have the nasty ones. Cancer is like a Grimms' Fairy Tale – when you're fit and well and unsuspecting it strikes without you knowing. The medical profession put on a brave face, but they know they can't beat it. We carry on as normally as possible. Every day counts now.

I am so grateful to Lone for sharing her letters with me. My mother was an enthusiastic correspondent, and I can only wonder how many she sent during her lifetime. Her letters to Lone, her neighbour of just over two years, are full of news of me, adventures she's thinking of having, adventures she's actually having, all sprinkled with a liberal dash of annoyance at any passing political enemy, but this letter stopped me short. At no other point is there a record of her complaining about her lot or expressing any regret or acknowledging her own mortality and this was the weird thing: the worse she got, the happier she became.

'She wasn't even on painkillers,' Tony told me. 'Not until the very end. And she would have been in terrible pain. No doubt. Especially from the lesions. The one on her chest ate her breast away. It was horrific. Not a word of complaint. And this was a woman who would lose her shit if I spilled coffee on the dining table or dropped a lump of coal.'

'The only time Brenda was ever nice to me,' remembered Phyllis, 'was when she had cancer.'

We were about a year from the end on the day we went shopping for wigs. She had been in a buoyant mood, happy to be out with me on our own, feeling special. We got her two: a grey bob that was the nearest to what her hair had looked like before she started losing it and a shoulder-length blonde va-va-voom number because, to hell with it, why not? I can still hear her laughing in the car as I drove her home. She pulled out the blonde one and put it on, wound down the window and shouted, 'Cooeeeeee!', at every hunk we passed. She thought it was hilarious.

'I must get cancer more often.' She flicked her fingers in a coquettish wave at a builder in a fluorescent tabard and a hard hat. He waved back at her, delighting her even more.

At first, she seemed to be responding pretty well to treatment. The large cankerous, wart-like scab that had totally enveloped her nipple fell off, (this was what I found in the small plastic bag after her death) but the progress was short lived. Lymphedema, the condition she so dreaded, had taken hold and small bloodied lesions were breaking out on her chest and neck.

There was a six-month lag between my winning *MasterChef* and it being broadcast and I was under strict instructions to keep it secret. I had refused to tell Brenda whether I had won, which infuriated her, so she tried every trick in the book to get me to give in. 'I may not be alive by the time they show the final,' she would say. 'Is that what you want? For me to go to my grave not knowing.'

'If you're on your deathbed,' I would reply, 'and I've had it confirmed by a medical professional that you are within moments of ceasing to exist then I may be prepared to divulge the result, yes. But even then, I might not tell you because I am contractually obliged not to and even in your last moments, you'd find a way to tell every person within hearing distance. You're worse than a fog-horn when it comes to showing off.'

'Yes,' she acknowledged, solemnly. 'That is true.'

But she did make it and got to enjoy the surprise. 'Well, you've made it now,' she told me. (ASIDE: I hadn't, as per usual.)

Now we knew Brenda's health was going one way, we quickly settled into a routine. I would call every day and go to see her every Sunday. On treatment days, she would come and stay at my flat. I'd cook for them and make sure I had a box of the tiny pastries she loved from the local bagel shop. My beagle, Poppy, would be something for her to fuss over, and we still went for walks while we could but as the lymphedema worsened and the cancer spread, she began to retreat from life. This, for me, was the worst part: watching the woman who never stopped, slowly running out of batteries.

There was one more thing that would provide my mother with great comfort. I'd been single for a while – I'd had two long relationships with women then decided I wasn't gay at all only to realise I was gay, don't be ridiculous. I'd finally confessed all to Brenda one Sunday morning, weeping as I told her. She didn't say much other than to ask me, with deadly seriousness, whether this was going to harm my career. Despite this coming as no surprise to her whatsoever, she still told me at the time not to tell Tony. She'd tell him in her own time. I can't hold this against her. Here was a woman who had spent her entire life hiding serious mental health issues. In her mind, being gay was firmly in the same bag and she was worried my life would be difficult, but she embraced me, she embraced my partners and she embraced Ben and Tom (who also turned out to be gay) and that will do for me. We got there in the end.

Everyone has a final stop when it comes to finding the person you're meant to be with and, as luck would have it, I found myself with singer Alison Moyet, sitting on a sofa at a do. I'd known her for a while and, that evening, she leaned in and said, 'I'm going to introduce you to my manager. I think you'd get on.'

She was right. We started dating and eighteen months later, Georgie drove to my parents' house, without me knowing, and told Brenda she was thinking of asking me to marry her. She'd wanted Brenda to feel involved.

'Brenda nodded as I was telling her and then she leaned back, pursed her lips and said, "Of course, you know it's possible she'll say no . . ." Her eyes were nothing but mischief.'

This still makes me laugh.

Days later, Georgie surprised me and announced we were off to Venice. She'd timed it perfectly – it was her birthday and I thought that was why we were going. One evening, she handed me a small silver key ring. There were three dates on it.

'What's the significance of those dates?' she asked me.

I stared down. 'That's when we first met, that's our first kiss and . . .'. I stared at the last one, a panic setting in.

'I don't know what that one is.' I looked up at her, shitting myself.

'That,' said Georgie, 'is the day I asked you to marry me.'

And that, for anyone thinking about proposing, is how you do it. The end.

Brenda was delighted but it went beyond the usual maternal joy at the announcement of an engagement. With her health steadily deteriorating, Brenda didn't have to worry about me any more. Georgie was a keeper, something she would prove in spades on the day my mother died. Brenda wouldn't make it to our wedding – that would take place the summer after her death – but she left knowing I was going to be well looked-after and loved. The final missing piece was in place.

Thinking back, I was rarely told the full extent of what was going on. Talking to Dad for this book I was shocked to learn of what would turn out to be my mother's last appointment at the Marsden.

'We thought we were going in to discuss whether Mum was having another round of chemotherapy, but the consultant told us there was nothing more to be done. He told her to go home and be with her family. It was shocking but even then, she wasn't upset. I think she just accepted she was going to go the same way as her mother before her. She was entirely at peace with it.'

I have no recollection of ever being told this. Perhaps it was one last act of maternal protection. What was the point in telling me? Except there was a point. I was still working: I was writing a novel and the comedy *The Kennedys* for BBC1. We were set to film the pilot that June. If I'd known her death was imminent, I'd have made different choices. In the six months prior to her death, she had deteriorated physically. She was now unable to leave the house except in a wheelchair and her right arm was bloated beyond belief, but seeing her each Sunday, she didn't strike me as being close to the end. That's the thing about a slow deterioration: when you watch it creeping, you don't quite notice how fast it's going but then we see what we want to see and hear what we want to hear. I think the answer here is that I was in deep denial.

She was having trouble breathing one Sunday, noticeably so, and having called the doctor, we were told to take her to the local A&E. Her lungs were full of fluid and a kind surgeon, who Brenda would see on repeat until the end, drained them for her there and then. A scan was called for and we knew the cancer was in her lungs. I'm still glad we never told her.

In the weeks leading up to her last day, she handed out money from her savings. She was saying goodbye, getting her affairs in order. There was an awful day where she had asked Tony to take her to the bank so she could get out a thousand pounds she'd intended to gift. It was to be the last kick in the teeth from the remnants of her paranoia. Brenda didn't trust banks and so she had Dad withdraw the money in cash and insisted, as she sat in the wheelchair behind him, that he count it out again before they left. As they did, they were mugged, instantly, by a man and woman. I have never wished ill on anyone but for the people who robbed my dying mother, I think I'll make an exception. *I hope you rot in hell.*

It finished her off, that incident, and she went into a terminal decline. No longer was she interested in reading, listening to the radio or watching films. All the things she had enjoyed or kept her going were meaningless. Dad would get her out of bed and help her downstairs and she would sit, staring out the window, nothing to say. 'She knew,' Tony told me. 'She knew how close it was. I think she wanted to go. She'd had enough.'

Whenever I hear or read arguments for euthanasia, I remember my mother's last fortnight. I wouldn't have put my dog through it, let alone someone to whom I owed everything. She was in pain, she was uncomfortable, she could barely breathe and her quality of life was for shit. My mother was done with life but on she had to go, grinding out the last weeks, days and hours in terrible circumstances, sipping on morphine from a tiny bottle so she couldn't overdose on it. If I ever find myself in the same position as my poor, dear mother – give me a gallon of the stuff via a funnel, knock me out, wave me goodbye as I trip off into the darkness. Put me out of my misery, please. I'll thank you for it.

If I had had the means to end her life, I would have. Making her carry on was a cruelty I will never forget. Instead, Brenda had to crawl on, unable to leave bed, unable to get up and pee, struggling to eat, bleeding constantly, full to the brim with constant nausea, rotting away before our very eyes. What an undignified, sad end to such a vital life.

So, we arrive at the point where we began. Brenda, finally, had breathed her last and in those first, terrible moments, I felt nothing but relief.

The grief was yet to come.

Tony has been insufferable with this bloody coat. He keeps dressing up in it.[1] I'm fed up and bored stiff. The weather has been so dreadful we haven't been able to go anywhere. My cold cough is at last starting to get better.

I'm seriously thinking of getting an evening job because I am so bored. There is absolutely nothing to do in Hitchin except join the Tory ladies club.[2] I've also seriously thought of doing another degree in Art History – well, it would be something to do.

How are you? I hope you've been keeping warm and looking after yourself. One of our students got pleurisy because she didn't keep herself warm. How did the exam go? Do you need a doctor's letter? Let me know. Don't forget to sell your shares – do it as soon as possible – with all these City scandals the banks could collapse.[3]

Oh, I'm in a pessimistic mood! Try to ring on Sunday if you've got time.

Take care, eat well and don't work too hard.

Lots of love
Brenda and Tony xxxx

* * *

1 Tony, in an idle moment, had popped into a Sue Ryder shop where he had discovered, for the price of £5, a very posh Chester Barrie coat. He was beside himself and swanned round the house in it, wearing it to the dinner table, wearing it whenever anyone came to the door, wearing it while he made toast. You name it, if he was standing, sitting or lying, he was wearing it.

2 For the avoidance of doubt, my mother was the exact opposite of a Tory.

3 This is a puzzle because I have never owned shares.

Nineteen

We had a challenge on our hands. Brenda didn't want a church service. She didn't want a priest anywhere near her body, she didn't want anyone from any faith presiding over her coffin and she also didn't want to be cremated 'in case she was still alive'. So, bar hiking her up a mountain and leaving her for the birds, it fell to me to work out what to do with her.

You know when someone dies, and you send a card or a text or an email and you ask the bereaved person if you can do anything to help? Don't wait to be told. What you want, when your brain is wading through the treacle of despair, is people who just turn up and do stuff. Thank you, Miranda, for turning up with the box of food. Thank you, Perks and Mo, for turning up for me to cry on, and a million thanks to Tracey, Mel and Emma, who turned up and made a ton of sandwiches.

Grief is a heavy weight. On bad days, you can't get it a millimetre off the ground but on some days, you have people who can help you lift it. In the ten days leading up to my mother's funeral, people helped me carry my grief and I will forever be grateful. I felt like a shattered hull, stuck on rocks: the crying was uncontrollable – not melodramatic wailing – but like a cup being constantly overfilled. I wasn't crying, I was dripping.

There were practical arrangements to be made. We had to choose a coffin, book the undertakers, make sure there was a hole dug. We had to choose an outfit for her to see out eternity in, pick things she'd want to be buried with. All of it was accompanied by a never-ending conveyor belt of water-filled eyes and wet cheeks. I could now have a perfectly reasonable conversation while crying. It became my superpower. I stopped apologising. This was who I was now.

It threw me a little, not being allowed to have any member of anything official preside over her grand exit but then Brenda, who had been unique in life, would be unique in death too. She always did hate people in positions of authority and so we would hold a short ceremony at the house, with Brenda's coffin in the sitting room, everyone around her. Here she was, queen of the party again. I would say a few words, the undertakers would carry her into a hearse, and I would walk everyone from the house to the cemetery. It was a beautiful sunny day. We'd pop her in the ground and walk back, eat sandwiches and lie on the grass getting pissed.

My grandfather, Bob, well into his nineties, was still alive and here he was, graveside, holding himself up on two sticks. The plot where Brenda would finally put all this to an end was under a fat beech tree, out of the midday sun. She would have approved. As the undertakers laid her coffin on planks and stood back, Perks stood forward and read a Gerard Manley Hopkins poem I'd had to guess might be the one my mother wanted. Alison Moyet then sang a folk song acapella and everyone clapped along. There was a jolly mood. Phyllis shouted out suddenly, 'She was horrible to me!' and then Bob hobbled forward and made an impromptu speech about the horror of burying your children. He finished off by veering sideways towards the hole and had to be grabbed to stop him falling in.

What Brenda would have made of all this, I'm not sure, but I like to think she was sitting somewhere up in that tree looking down, totting up the famous names that had gathered to send her off and cackling that her own death almost precipitated that of her father. The undertaker, having lowered her into the ground, stood staring up at the sky and muttered, 'This is the weirdest funeral I've ever been to.' Yes, it was, and quite right too. I can only dream of such a send-off. It was a glorious shambles.

The days that followed were bewildering. Dad wasn't quite ready to be on his own yet and I was happy to stick around, sitting in the blue wicker love seat she would spend all day in, staring out at the garden or lying on the lawn, teasing the moss out with my fingers. Time slowed down and days bled into each other as we all worked out quite what we were supposed to do. The engine had been removed from the family – how did we get about now?

Brenda had been dead for three weeks, and I was in a council house in St Albans, staring at my new Brenda, Katherine Parkinson. She was head-to-head with Dan Skinner, who was playing Tony; beside me sat the real one, headphones on. They were playing a scene from the first episode, where my father has grabbed my mother and I and absconded to the bathroom in order to reveal in hushed tones that he and Emma have inadvertently witnessed an affair. It was one of the scenes based on true events, a word-for-word recreation of a moment in my father's distant past that had actually happened. The scene was almost at its end. The monitor huddle was in the room next door. We were surrounded by director, producer, make-up artists and crew. Suddenly, my father looked as if he was going to sneeze, and I put a hand on him and made a sign telling him to try and remain quiet until the director called cut, but he couldn't. It wasn't a sneeze. He was breaking down. Emma Strain, my wonderful producer, quickly cleared the room and we sat, holding hands as he cried it out.

Sometimes, you just have to pick yourself up and carry on as best you can and, to this day, I'm still not sure if having to film a pilot all about my mother immediately after she had died helped or hindered. I was consumed with sadness that she would never meet Katherine, would never hang out on set. She would have been adored. She would never see the final series, never see the lovely messages, never get to enjoy being in that rare breed of people who are so fabulous, they're immortalised. If you fancy seeing *The Kennedys*, you can buy a DVD from Germany.

I was just glad to be busy, I think. It's not possible, when you're grieving, to spend all your time being miserable. Even in the thick of it, I would catch myself laughing at a small memory, an act of outrageousness I'd forgotten. Friends would ring and remind me of their favourite Brenda moments: the time she was found staring into the road looking for loose change so she could buy a paper, the time she told a pal of mine to 'stop taking cocaine' even though she had never taken cocaine in her life, the time she got Nicola Walker's nickname horribly, horribly wrong – everyone that had ever met her seemed to have a story about her.

These are the gifts people leave behind, the stories that carry forward and if I'm grateful for anything, it's that I had a mother who nobody will ever forget, but the days after her death drifted into weeks and weeks drifted into months and months became years and I did forget. Instead, the memories that shouted the loudest were the dark ones, the angry shapes, the scent of her cancer on a spring day. When Dad rang to tell me he was finally selling my childhood home, the first thing I said to him was, 'Brenda will haunt the fuck out of it for the rest of eternity.' I'd always imagined I would live there one day but going back was no longer what I wanted to do. That house was nothing without Brenda. It was time, I realised, for the final goodbye.

On the day of moving, I found myself the last person left, finishing off the cleaning and getting ready to hand over the keys, and my thoughts were consumed with Brenda. The house had been cleared of furniture but there was one item Dad had asked them to leave. It was the blue wicker love seat Brenda always sat in. I moved it back into the sun lounge where she liked to look out over the garden and sat for a while, remembering scenes from our lives: Dad in the bush, lying on my belly with a glass of Pimm's, the French cricket game that ended in disaster, drying out the tent ready for another summer adventure, the hoe being brought down on my father's head, hammocks, apples, giant poppies, running from may-bugs, secret snogs behind the rose bush. Fun, terror, laughter, crying: all of it swirling itself into a time capsule to be buried forever the moment we left.

I'm glad she died in that house. It was the culmination of everything she had strived for. It had allowed her to be the queen of her own court, the generous hostess, the dictator of her own land. It had also driven her mad, became the focus of her paranoia, but in her final days, it had been her comfort. Dallington was as much a member of her family as we had been. She'd loved it and now we were leaving her there forever.

It was a grey day, the kind where damp hangs in the air and cold gnaws your bones. The garden, which would be in such fulsome bloom in spring and summer, was pared back and lacklustre, in winter mode, as if it too was mourning the woman who had adored it so intensely. I walked slowly down towards the orchard, filming as I went, wanting to remember every nook and bend, every tree and gnarl before I left, knowing I would never return. I didn't need to, of course. Every inch of that garden is etched into my heart: the cistus that dropped white petals, the old iron mangle, the Victorian plough, the nettle bed we never could get rid of, the borage, the shrub that bent over on itself, the mysterious appearance of the marijuana plant, the wildflowers that grew in a certain patch of grass if you let them. I could shut my eyes and be there whenever I chose, standing on the crooked stones of the pathway, staring up at the sky through the apple trees, lying on my back on the soft moss lawn.

I stood, that day, looking up at the house. It had felt so huge when we moved in but, in reality, it was a small, cramped three-bedroom cottage with a tiny galley kitchen and no central heating. It was freezing cold all year round. We used to joke we were going outside to warm up. Leaping into thick socks on winter mornings, double duvets pulled over my nose, hot water bottles tucked into bed for me to find, sitting round the fire, fetching in the coal – our entire life there was consumed with keeping warm. Still, to this day, I struggle with central heating. It was like being brought up in 1880. It was a small property that felt like a mansion. It was Brenda to a tee.

I took my phone again and walked through the rooms, now empty. I stood for a long while in the room my mother had died in, remembering every second of it. 'Be nice to them,' I asked of her.

It was cathartic, I suppose. As I stood in the empty sitting room, the scene of so many triumphs and disasters, Dallington stopped feeling like our house. It was a space waiting for the next family to arrive. In a matter of months, it would be gutted and rebuilt, unrecognisable from the house I grew up in. There's no point feeling sad. Histories never stand still and memories can't be erased. I can sit here now and see my mother in her blue wicker love seat, staring out over the garden. I hope they kept it.

After closing the door for the final time, I got into my car, drove to the cemetery and left some flowers on my mother's grave. It's a good job the wind was up or I'm sure I would have heard her howling. A monotonous drizzle had set in, but a weight had lifted from my shoulders. The era of Brenda was now truly over but there was going to be one more twirl around the carousel.

I was about to receive a gift from my grandmother, the one I never met.

THIS IS A RED LETTER DAY! KEEP THIS LETTER TO
SHOW YOUR CHILDREN IN THE YEARS TO COME. THE
REVOLUTION HAS BEGUN.

THE QUEEN MOTHER HAS CALLED THATCHER TO
TASK (AND AN OLD BAT) SHE HAS RAISED THE
MONARCHY! FLAG OF PROTEST AGAINST THIS
UNCARING, CALLOUS GOVERNMENT. LET US NOT
FORGET THAT OUR DEAR OLD QUEEN MUM (BLESS HER
LEGS) WATCHED OVER THE BIRTH OF THE WELFARE
STATE AND TENDED IT WITH CARE – OPENING ALL
THOSE HOSPITALS AND SHAKING ALL THOSE YOUNG
DOCTORS HANDS.

WELL – QUEEN MUM HAS WRITTEN A SHORT SHARP
AFFRONT TO THATCHER AND HER GOVERNMENT
BECAUSE THATCHER WAS FOOLISH ENOUGH TO CLOSE
A HOSPITAL IN WALES WHICH YOUR OWN DEAR Q MUM
ONLY OPENED WITH OWN DEAR HAND LAST YEAR.

THERE HAS BEEN AN OUTCRY – THE TORIES ARE
BAYING IN TRUE E WAUGH FASHION. THEY WANT OUR
DEAR Q. MUM'S BLOOD. LABOUR (WEAK AS EVER BUT
TO THE POINT) SAID 'THANK GOD THE QUEEN MUM IS
CHALLENGING CRUELLA D'EVILLE WE WILL SUPPORT
HER'

I am personally going to write a thank you letter to Q
Mum and I'm going to pledge my loyalty to the monarchy.
BRING BACK KING CHARLES AND THE CAVALIERS!
DOWN WITH CROMWELL AND HIS TOO TWICKY WAYS! I
WANT TO WEAR A WIG!

I think it's bloody marvellous – an eighty-year-old ex-queen
boxing Thatcher's ears. Bloody wonderful.

Terry Jones has also joined the attack – read his own Modest Proposal.[1] *I really think your reviews should contain a political assault on Thatcher and a revered reference to Q. Mum.*

I hope I get a reply. I shall frame it if I do.[2]

All my love
Your mum and MONARCHIST.
XXXX

★ ★ ★

---

1 'A Modest Proposal' was an essay written by Jonathan Swift in the early eighteenth century, a satirical attack on the English ruling classes. I wish I knew what Brenda was referring to here. Sadly, I do not. Although much of the work of the Pythons was dedicated to taking swipes at the English class system, so maybe she meant that.

2 She didn't.

Twenty

Brexit had happened.

Like many Remainers, I was depressed and despairing. 'It's just so embarrassing,' people kept saying to me. 'It's like going to a dinner party, eating all the food then doing a shit on the table.'

The morning after the referendum result, I was due at a script meeting at the BBC. I walked around Regent's Park, stunned and weepy. My Polish neighbour had knocked on my door – some post had gone to his house by mistake – and he'd stared up at me and asked if I'd voted for it.

'No, no,' I assured him.

His face was a picture of disbelief and shock, 'I make a contribution. I pay taxes. Why do people want me to go home?'

I couldn't answer him. Europeans were our friends, neighbours, colleagues, lovers, partners but in one sudden blow to the head, the nation decided they could all fuck off home now, thanks.

There would be many pain-in-the-arse inconveniences we would now have to deal with – forty years of integrated systems torn apart in a fit of pique – but the single thing I was most upset to be losing was my right as a European Citizen to Freedom of Movement. It infuriated me, in fact.

'Haven't you got an Irish grandmother?' a friend asked me, one morning, sitting over coffee in the BBC canteen.

'Yes,' I replied, 'but she's dead. And so's my mother.'

'You can still apply. If you have a grandparent who is Irish, you can apply.'

I went home and thought long and hard about it. I had

never met Elizabeth – it was a great family sadness I had not – yet here I was, fifty years on from her death, with a hand reaching back towards her. She had been cast adrift from her Irish family, partly because she had married a communist with no love of God, partly because her brothers and sisters were dispersed, but there was a sense that in reconnecting to her and the family I had never known it would be a pathway back. She'd been embarrassed about being Irish, now here I was desperate to be, but it went beyond papering over the inconvenience of Brexit: it was a nod to my mother, something she'd have loved.

I didn't know where to start. There would be certificates to locate, birth, marriages, deaths. I did some digging on the internet and found a lone reference to my grandmother in the 1911 census. She was two. Hang on a minute, I thought, and then worked out she had been thirty-one not twenty-one when she married my nineteen-year-old grandfather. Where had my mother got it from had been a constant refrain. Now, I was starting to find out.

I was given the name of a researcher who worked on *Who Do You Think You Are?* We struck a bargain, and the search was on. She had her work cut out. My great-grandmother had not only entered my grandmother's name incorrectly on her birth certificate, she'd got her own husband's name the wrong way round. My researcher, coming up against a brick wall, passed me over to some colleagues in Ireland. The mighty ladies of Timeline Research Ireland would now take up the hunt.

Good GRIEF it was complicated. A casual mistake made over a hundred years ago was now creating the most enormous snafu. I'd get another email, throwing up another administrative ball-ache caused by my great-grandmother's lackadaisical approach to accuracy. I imagined myself in her shoes, turning up, babe in arms, exhausted, lower regions in tatters, flapping like a windsock.

'She's my seventh child, put down whatever name you want.'
'But hang on Bridget, what's your husband's name again?'

'Pffft. Does it matter?'

YES BRIDGET, IT DOES.

The tangled morass bequeathed to me by my great-grandmother would require Sherlock Holmes-level unravelling. Thankfully, the mighty ladies of Timeline Research Ireland were up to the task – and if you're on a similar odyssey, I can't recommend them enough. The search would require the trawling of obscure parish records, the finding of a registrar, sworn affidavits and considerable expense, and all because the lady got her own bloody husband's name the wrong way round. Bridget, I hope you were blind drunk. I hope you were crawling on your hands and knees enjoying your first knees-up after the successful conclusion of another pregnancy. I hope you had the finest day imaginable and slept it off in a bush before going home.

Months later, having made an application to have my grand-mother's birth certificate corrected, I finally received a thick A4 envelope, filled with embossed, official-looking papers. They would be the lifeline pulling me back to a shore I never wanted to leave. Eight months after that, I would receive another package through the post and as I stared down at my burgundy Member of the European Union Irish passport, I felt an overwhelming gratitude towards my mother and the grandmother I had never met.

It does all boil down to who you think you are, doesn't it? I was raised by a Welshman and a firebrand whose own mother's experience had taught her to hate the English. We joined the EEC when I was six. I've been a European citizen ever since. That's who I am. That's what I want to be and now, thanks to my grandmother, it's what I am again. There will be many millions of people like me who would also like to still be the person they think they are, and I hope, in the absence of parental connections, that one day you will be again. We can't stay out of the Single Market forever. Never give up.

I had hoped to have found Irish relatives still alive but, at time of writing, there are Record Offices in Ireland closed due to COVID. The hunt, for now, is on pause but there is some good news: I have cousins in Canada. May, the elder sister of my grandmother, emigrated there with her two children, one of whom, Pauline, was a favourite cousin of Brenda. I was often told I looked like her. May passed away in 1995 at the ripe old age of ninety-three and Pauline died in 2015, a year after Brenda. Her sister, Madeleine, after a battle with cancer, died in 2001. They had children and I have, today in Canada, four living cousins.

I have every intention of going to visit.

In the process of my search, I discovered things about my family I would never have known and came to understand my mother better than I ever did in life. We are all complicated, secretive, worried creatures. My greatest sadness is that I didn't fully understand her while she was living and then one day, I found myself with Phyllis in my kitchen.

'I went to see a psychic,' she told me. 'Brenda came through.'

'Are you joking?'

'No, Bob, Paul and Brenda. I had all three of them.'

'What did she say?'

'The psychic told me she was overbearing and then she apologised for being horrible to me. Paul told me Bob was getting on his nerves.'

I thought long and hard about pursuing this avenue of enquiry. I am very aware that the art of the medium is primarily one of entertainment, a form of therapy for people who are in pain and have unanswered questions, but I thought to hell with it, why not? If nothing else, I'll come away with a story. Given much of my mother's history can be found with a cursory search, I booked the appointment in a different name. I would also be wearing a mask.

I really wasn't expecting anything to happen, I was certainly not expecting to come away upset. For me, this would just be the crossing of a 't', the dotting of an 'i' with my author's hat on, but when the medium looked at me and said, 'There's something wrong with a birth certificate,' I leaned forward.

'What's wrong with a birth certificate?' I was very careful not to give a single thing away.

'Your mother says the names are wrong on the birth certificate.'

OK. *Now* she had my attention.

'And she's worried about your father's leg. It still hurts.'

At this point, I found myself gripping my elbows and staring. Tony had broken his leg six months after Mum died. He'd torn his cruciate ligament and his knee still gives him a bit of trouble.

'I'm getting a sense I'm talking to two people,' the medium frowned. 'It's like she's two different people.'

If you're muttering, 'What the fuck?' at this point, well, yes. So was I.

'She wants you to know she regrets how she treated your dad. She was overly dominant, didn't appreciate him but he was so kind to her. She wants him to know she loved him. She thinks the new house he's in suits him down to the ground. She's glad he's got nice neighbours. She can't believe what they've done to the old house. She's had a wander round.'

I bet she has but then came the moment that gave me the greatest pause.

'I'm getting the sense she was misunderstood in her lifetime. There was unhappiness when she was a child. It was never dealt with. If she'd had counselling, early on, she'd have had a very different life.'

I want to make it very clear here that at no point did I give a single thing away. There were other things the medium told me – how Brenda liked the new bird feeders I'd put in the garden, there was a message from a friend's father about a test she was waiting on, a hello from a childhood friend, an assurance from a dead colleague that he was keeping an eye on me, but it was the suggestion that Brenda may have been desperately unhappy in childhood that felt like a key finding the right lock. It left me heartbroken.

Perhaps we had misunderstood Brenda all along. Perhaps

my thinking she had a borderline personality disorder or depression wasn't right at all. She had tried to kill herself aged eleven. A happy child doesn't do that. Brenda was impulsive, had unpredictable mood swings, was quick to anger and easily given to negative emotions. She found it difficult to trust people and had an almost pathological need to seduce. There was an emptiness inside her that she needed to constantly refill. Sex validated her. When she was unable to have more affairs, she went into a terrible decline. Brenda's bouts of what I thought of as depression were perhaps, not that at all. She wasn't given to days of not being able to function, she didn't take to her bed or stop eating. What she had were short, sharp temper tantrums, screaming being her way of coping. Occasionally, she would be violent towards my father and me but, in those moments, she was never trying to hurt us physically, it was a lashing out she couldn't stop. If Brenda ever did real damage, it was more often to things: my homework, her mother's treas-ured trinkets, a wooden sailboat my father had made for her. What she did, in those moments when she was out of control, was destroy things to make others feel as upset as she was.

She had been taught to keep secrets, to never reveal her inner pain, to never complain. What she did talk about, however, was her absent father and how much she hated him, how she blamed him for her mother's demise and for inflicting upon the family a sense of shame she could never quite shake off. Bob was a notoriously difficult man, and it is in him I think Brenda's edges were forged. He abandoned her and she never forgave him for it. There's a solid, heavy chain that connects our childhoods to the adults we become and, in that moment, sitting in the medium's front room, I was overwhelmed with a sense that, whether by dumb luck or a genuine message from beyond the grave, I had something that felt like a very sad answer.

Suddenly, her keen feelings of abandonment and shame, her issues with her father, her inability to trust came into sharp focus. Everything about Brenda started to make more sense.

For a woman who was never backwards in making sure everyone around her knew what mood she was in, she was also adept at giving very little away but here I was, sitting on a stranger's sofa, experiencing a clarity that had, up until this point eluded me.

I left the medium's house not in a state of shock or disbelief but with a sense of calm. It didn't really matter whether it had been real or not. By whatever means, I had finally, after all these years, experienced a breakthrough in how to look back at my mother's life but there's a little more to add to the story, a final twist.

A family member called to say they had had a diagnosis of Attention Deficit Hyperactivity Disorder and following it, Phyllis and I found ourselves wondering whether Bob had also had it. ADHD can be genetic but the more interesting point was this: the children of a parent with ADHD, according to the *Diagnostic and Statistical Manual of Mental Disorders*, Fifth Edition, can commonly develop conduct disorders.

There's a chance Brenda may have had ADHD herself, but I'm not convinced. I don't think she satisfies the diagnosis criteria. She struggled to control her emotions, yes, but having trouble focusing or concentrating was never part of who she was. It's difficult. I'm not a clinical psychologist. I have long accepted that I may never know, beyond all doubt, precisely what was wrong with my mother but I'm no longer sure it matters: she's not here and can't be cured or medicated or given the therapy she needed, but I wrote this book to find answers and, in the absence of a definitive diagnosis, I feel comfortable in reaching a best guess – that my mother had a conduct disorder from childhood and it was never dealt with. Like so many millions of others, she would have suffered with mental health issues alone and unaided at a time when to speak of such things meant certain ruin.

My mother was an ambitious woman from a poor background who was determined to make the best of herself. Her mental health was something she thought would hold her back.

I have long made my peace with who she was and find myself left with nothing but understanding and empathy. If my mother had had the help that is offered so openly now, her life might have been calmer and happier.

A year after Mum was buried, we gathered round her grave to see the stone that was now in place.

We hadn't had to think long about what the engraving was going to say.

A BRILLIANT WOMAN

Yes. She was.

Writing this book has been a cathartic exercise for me, one I hadn't fully appreciated I needed. It's so hard, when someone has loomed large in your life, to understand what to do with the hole that's left but I think, finally, I have a release.

'She likes to sit in your garden,' the medium told me. 'And she visits you. An unusual bird, uncommon. Black head but with white flecks on the wings.'

As I'm writing this, there's a greater spotted woodpecker sitting on the trellis outside my window.

I'm going to leave the last word to my mother. This is the earliest letter I have from her. I had gone on holiday with a friend's family to Cornwall. I received this on the second day. Advice to live by.

Thanks, Mum.

1. *Keep putting suncream on you or you'll burn badly*
2. *Put clean pants on every day*
3. *Wash your face*
4. *Don't come home with any cuts or bruises so watch those rocks*
5. *Pick your nose*
6. *Keep away from boys*

* * *

About a month after I finished the final draft of this book, I found myself still thinking about Brenda and what might have been wrong with her. Even though I had reached a moment of clarity, there were still small niggling doubts I wasn't able to shift. I chatted to my editor and we discussed the possibility of sending the manuscript to a psychiatrist for an expert read, someone who could cast a clinical eye over Brenda's letters, her life and my thoughts and make sure I hadn't got anything catastrophically wrong. Perhaps, I wondered, it would provide a final insight, a scientific end line that would provide a moment of true closure.

In due course, I received the following letter from Rafa Euba, a consultant psychiatrist. I found it so fascinating I asked his permission to reproduce it here. Thankfully, he said yes. We are all complicated creatures with corners we struggle to understand. Sometimes, we go to the ends of the earth to keep our worst or more frightening impulses hidden. Brenda was no different in that. Having read Mr Euba's letter, I was reminded of a fleeting moment. We were discussing a family friend who had gone on antidepressants. 'I could never take them,' Brenda told me. 'I need to feel everything.'

This was true. She lived, she loved, she hated. Her life was rammed with every feeling imaginable except, perhaps, regret. It was a life filled with extremes, blazed through like a shooting star. Nothing we could ever have done would have stopped her true path.

I am satisfied, having read his assessment, that our handling of Brenda's illness, the mitigating of her worst outbursts and the survival of our collective experience was far from perfect but, in the circumstances, was the best we could have hoped for. It's a comfort, of sorts.

Here is Mr Euba's letter. I hope you find it as illuminating as I did.

Dear Emma,

Thank you for asking me to evaluate Brenda's fascinating life from a psychological perspective.

Reading the book, I reflected on the fact that in day-to-day clinical practice psychiatrists rarely have the opportunity to get to know their patients in great depth. The histories we elicit tend to be very heavily biased towards the recent past and, for obvious reasons, we never obtain a very detailed, structured and very readable story of their lives. But in this case, I do have such a story, Brenda's story, and its richness and complexities have forced me to approach her psychological difficulties in a way that, I hope, has done her justice, avoiding the over-simplifications that would come with a single, cold and rigid psychiatric diagnosis.

It is debatable in fact whether I should attempt to provide a diagnosis at all, given that I never met Brenda (which is a shame) and that diagnoses are medical concepts designed to formulate a treatment plan and a prognosis, neither of which are relevant now. And yet, when confronted with a list of psychological symptoms, my training inevitably compels me to think in diagnostic terms.

There is of course an obvious difference between Brenda and the patients we see in clinic, which is the simple fact that she was never seen by a psychiatrist. I realise that this was because she would not agree to be assessed, but it also means that the situation, dire as it was for long periods of time, never reached the point of being utterly intolerable, at least for Brenda.

Almost all psychiatric out-patients attend clinics voluntarily because they want their suffering to be alleviated with *interventions such as psychotherapy and drugs. Brenda, and others like her, probably felt that a mental health diagnosis would have wounded her self-image and sense of autonomy, and that the pain of this wound would have outweighed the benefits of the remedies offered by the doctor. I sympathise with this feeling, even if I don't agree with it. The brain is where we reside, so no-one wants to hear that theirs is faulty. We know now that a mental health disorder shouldn't define an individual and that mental health professionals are able to offer some effective treatments that improve quality of life, but Brenda wouldn't have shared this view.*

The fact that her periods of distress were short-lived (even if they happened very frequently during certain stages in her life) would have made her less likely to accept help. On the other hand, the suffering associated with the paranoia she had in later life probably had a duller quality than the explosions of anger and acute dysphoria caused by the fragility of her mood. Most older paranoid patients are very reluctant to agree to be seen by a doctor and sometimes one has the impression that their paranoia is fulfilling a psychological function, by occupying a void that would otherwise be even less bearable than the psychosis itself. You've recognised an element of this yourself when you say that 'there was an emptiness inside her that she needed to constantly refill'.

It seems that at least on one occasion a doctor was made aware of Brenda's problems; you've indicated that when she was sixty-one she was seen by a consultant (an oncologist, perhaps?) and explained how Brenda reacted to this: 'she'd been given cancer by a CIA operative in a book shop in Cambridge. She thought her phones were bugged. She refused treatment because she thought it was a plot between Dad and the doctors to have her killed. She thought her neighbours had secretly bought her garden.' Even if that doctor wasn't a psychiatrist,

I presume he or she did come up with a diagnosis of paranoid psychosis, which may have been communicated to the GP.[1] In any case, it is clear that Brenda never allowed anyone to address her mental health problems.

It is also clear that Brenda struggled with her mental health since childhood and throughout her entire life. As a child, she was impulsive and had frequent and very severe temper tantrums. The episode when she jumped from the upstairs window, aged twelve, was an early manifestation of poor impulse and emotional regulation. This, of course, needs to be understood in the context of a very unhappy childhood, after her father abandoned the family.

I believe Bob contributed to Brenda's problems in two different ways: first, by abandoning and shaming the family and depriving Brenda of the paternal care she needed. This would have had an important psychological impact on Brenda, but it is not in itself enough to explain her chronic difficulties. Phyllis, her sister, was also abandoned and yet she had enough psychological resilience to endure this trauma. The difference, I suspect, is that Brenda inherited more of Bob's personality and genes than Phyllis did. I am referring here to certain aspects of Bob's personality only, such as his expansiveness, disinhibition, and his brittle affect. You have described Bob as having 'a brashness that bled into unpleasantness. He was a pest who would think nothing of sexualising everything.' On one occasion, he even pulled a knife on Brenda and threatened to kill her. It is interesting, incidentally, that Bob's mother, Violet, was a bigamist, but we don't have enough information about her to speculate whether she may also have had this type of personality herself.

---

1 Sadly, there is no evidence this was ever done. It may have been, but Brenda didn't communicate to us that her GP had been in touch or asked to see her to discuss her mental health.

Many of Brenda's personality traits suggest what ICD-10 called an 'Emotionally Unstable Personality Disorder' (ICD-10 F60.3; this category has disappeared from the newer ICD-11, but remains very much in clinical use.[2] The Explosive and Borderline disorders you've mentioned as diagnostic possibilities fall within this category):

> *Personality disorder characterized by a definite tendency to act impulsively and without consideration of the consequences; the mood is unpredictable and capricious. There is a liability to outbursts of emotion and an incapacity to control the behavioural explosions. There is a tendency to quarrelsome behaviour and to conflicts with others, especially when impulsive acts are thwarted or censored. Two types may be distinguished: the impulsive type, characterized predominantly by emotional instability and lack of impulse control, and the borderline type, characterized in addition by disturbances in self-image, aims, and internal preferences, by chronic feelings of emptiness, by intense and unstable interpersonal relationships, and by a tendency to self-destructive behaviour, including suicide gestures and attempts.*

Brenda was able to keep her marriage and her job, which suggests her disorder was – in relative terms – not particularly severe, although it is obvious that the tolerance of others towards her misbehaviour, as well as her intelligence and charm, played a part in this.

After her retirement, the picture changed very significantly. Brenda developed a 'Late Onset Schizophrenia', also known as 'Late Paraphrenia' (included into the Delusional Disorder category in ICD-10: F22.0), characterised by well-defined

---

2 International Classification of Diseases. ICD-10. See https://icd.who.int/browse10/2010/en

persecutory delusions, often in the absence of hallucinations. This type of Schizophrenia tends to affect women more often than men (unlike the earlier onset variety) and sufferers often have a history of personality difficulties before they develop their psychotic symptoms later in life. The persecutory delusions in Late Onset Schizophrenia often involve neighbours, who are able to harm and interfere with the sufferer in a variety of very strange ways, like in Brenda's case. Neighbours feature much less frequently in the delusions of early onset schizophrenics.

I think it is better to regard these two diagnoses as different manifestations of the same basic psychopathology, even if they are supposed to be completely separate entities. The fact that one (abnormal personality) predisposes the sufferer to the other (Late Onset Schizophrenia) is consistent with this approach.

There are paranoid highlights in her letters, which were presumably written before she became frankly psychotic. The episode with the 'East German' in the train to Berlin, and more clearly in Gaeta, Italy, with its NATO base, have a strong persecutory flavour. The Renoir letter is interesting: was she playing with the idea, or did she actually develop the belief that she descended from Renoir? It points perhaps towards a poorly defined ego, a feature in some emotionally unstable personalities.

I agree with your view that the fact that Brenda found her comfortable life in her home in Hitchin stressful, after she retired and before she developed cancer, implies mental instability.

As an aside, you're also right in noticing that your mother's use of capital letters seems to be associated with paranoia. It is indeed a very typical paranoid mark.

I believe it is better to look at Brenda's personality as a whole, accepting that the good bits in it were closely related to the bad ones. Her personality, while in my view clearly pathological (impulsive, unstable, disinhibited, explosive, aggressive, argumentative), also clearly had very positive components (she was funny, creative, warm, charming). In my opinion, each one of these traits represented a different aspect of her core personality dimensions. In other words, what made Brenda problematic also made her charismatic. And like a shaken can of pop, what made her fizzy also made her explosive.

Brenda had at least one episode of sustained depression following the delivery of her baby. This is not surprising, given the general fragility of her mood. The vast majority of chronic psychiatric histories include at least one episode of depression, whatever the underlying primary diagnosis may be.

I don't think I can escape the need to mention the behavioural dimension in Brenda's illness. She was allowed to get away with many things, although I quite understand the reasons behind this. Confronting her would have been a Herculean and even dangerous task, and she was able to use her charm to compensate to some extent for her misbehaviour. I believe humans, whether mentally ill or not, have a tendency to do exactly as they please if they can, and Brenda was no exception. The problem was that, in her case, doing as she pleased often involved grossly maladaptive behaviour. She was indeed an 'evil genius'.

I know you have spoken to a variety of doctors about your mother and they gave a number of different diagnoses, which I'm sure must have been confusing. The different personality disorder diagnoses in fact overlap considerably not only between themselves, but also with a possible Bipolar Affective Disorder (which you also highlighted as a possibility) and even schizophrenia, even more so when a clinical presentation changes over time, like in Brenda's case. Pragmatically, an illness such as Brenda's would probably have been treated with certain antipsychotic medications that also have mood-stabilising *properties. Unfortunately, patients often put on weight on these tablets, so she would have been very unlikely to accept them, even if she had somehow been persuaded to see a psychiatrist.*

To summarise, I believe Brenda was born with a genetic loading that predisposed her to develop a psychological disorder, then her very difficult upbringing made matters worse, a pattern of unstable and abnormal emotions and behaviour was firmly set, and finally the ageing process destabilised her further, both in terms of bringing with it a loss of her looks and self-image, but mainly because an already fragile and now ageing brain lost the ability to process input in a way that was not paranoid, sensitive or suspicious.

Evaluating Brenda's psychological problems has been, as I've said, a rare experience and one that I have found intellectually stimulating. Your mother must have been a remarkably fascinating individual and I'm sorry not to have had the chance to meet her.

Kind regards,

Rafa Euba

(Dr Rafael Euba MRCPsych, Consultant Psychiatrist)

AUTHOR'S NOTES AND
ACKNOWLEDGEMENTS

I have only led one life and there are a few stories in this book I have told before, either in books, articles or podcasts. I took the view they bore repeating, not least because it would be fanciful to expect anyone reading this book to have read anything else I've produced but mostly because the story of Brenda would be incomplete without them. If you have read all my other books and articles and listened to every podcast I've been on and remember those stories, first, thank you for liking me so much and second, I hope you have enjoyed the retelling here.

When the suitcases arrived, I found some other letters from Brenda tucked away in various boxes and I've included a couple of those for no other reason than that they are amazing. There were seventy-five letters in total. I could have merrily included them all but the book would have been the size of a plinth. I hope I've included the best and most entertaining. Apologies to Brenda if I made the wrong choices.

I did try and find out if Bob married Kathleen but after an extensive search there is no evidence that their marriage was ever official. For once, I didn't have another bigamist in the family.

If you're wondering what a carbolic smoke ball is, it's from the legal case *Carlill v Carbolic Smoke Ball Company*. It's the first case you learn in contract when you're at law school and involved a flu remedy and a promise from the manufacturer that if it did not work, the buyer could claim an award of £100; a huge amount of money in 1893. The company was held to be bound by its advertisement, which was judged to be an offer and that by using the smoke ball, the buyer was accepting that offer and creating a contract. A spot of trivia: the defence counsel in the lower court was H. H. Asquith, who went on to become prime minister, and the plaintiff in the action, Mrs Louisa Carlill, lived until she was ninety-six and died of old age and . . . flu.

Another lady who lived to a grand old age was my old English teacher, Mrs Graebe. I only recently discovered she lived to ninety-three and died in November 2020. She changed my life forever and I hope that wherever she is now roaming, she has a good novel in one hand.

I couldn't have written this book without the help of two people: my lovely Dad, Tony, and my extraordinary aunt, Phyllis. They have both been supportive and encouraging from the off, and I think I speak for all of us when I say working on this book together has been a form of therapy. Thank you both.

To my cousins, Ben and Tom, dear God, the sights we have seen. Thank you for the endless laughter and for being the nearest things to brothers I will ever have. I adore the bones of you.

For everyone who happily chatted to me for this book – Linda, Angi, Daniel, Val and Mouse – your memories were invaluable. Thank you for the time you gave.

Huge thanks to Aruna Vasudevan, my copy editor, for making sure everything was shipshape and to Izzy Everington for ensuring all things were above board.

To my editor, Myf, your continuous faith in me is quite something. Other than Mrs Graebe, I think you're the only other person who has so consistently believed in me. Don't think that's gone unnoticed. I'd walk to the moon for you.

Sheila, my unflappable agent, the woman with the coolest head in the business, who puts up with every stupid thing I do, Brenda would have been in quiet awe of you, and I don't think there can be any higher praise. Thank you for everything you do for me. Don't ever chuck me.

And lastly, to Georgie, the woman who saved my life and makes everything all right, when I sang you that song, I meant every word of it. I thank all the gods you decided to pick me.